First published 2015

Survival Books Limited
Office 169, 3 Edgar Buildings
George Street, Bath BA1 2FJ, United Kingdom
☎ +44 (0)1225-462135, ✉ info@survivalbooks.net
💻 survivalbooks.net and londons-secrets.com

British Library Cataloguing in Publication Data
A CIP record for this book is available
from the British Library.

ISBN: 978-1-909282-76-6

Printed and bound in China by D'Print Pte Ltd.

Acknowledgements

The authors would like to thank all those who helped with research and provided information for this book. Special thanks are also due to Robbi Atilgan for editing; Peter Read for editing and proof-reading; David Woodworth for final proof checking; John Marshall for DTP, photo selection and cover design; and the authors' partners for the constant supply of tea, coffee, food and wine (and for continuing with the pretence that writing is a real job).

Last, but not least, a special thank you to the many photographers – the unsung heroes – whose beautiful images bring London's foodie scene to life.

The Authors

David Hampshire's career has taken him around the world and he lived and worked in many countries before taking up writing full-time in the '80s. He's the author, co-author or editor of some 25 titles, including *Living and Working in London*, *London's Secret Places*, *London's Secrets: Museums & Galleries*, *London's Secrets: Parks & Gardens*, *London's Secrets: Peaceful Places* and *A Year in London*. David was born in Surrey but lived and worked in London for many years and still considers himself a Londoner. He now divides his time between London and Bath.

Graeme Chesters is an experienced journalist, copywriter, non-fiction and travel writer. He knows London well, having lived in the northwest, centre and southeast of the city, and is the author of a number of London books, including *London's Hidden Secrets*, *London's Secret Walks*, *London's Secrets: Bizarre & Curious* and *London's Secrets: Pubs & Bars*. Graeme is also a wine writer (and enthusiastic drinker!) and has written two wine books. He lives in Bexley in southeast London with his wife Louise.

Readers' Guide

♦ **Contact details:** These include the address, telephone number and website (where applicable). You can enter the postcode to display a map of the location on Google and other map sites or enter the postcode into your satnav. The nearest tube or railway station (as applicable) is also listed.

♦ **Opening hours:** These can change at short notice, therefore you should confirm times by telephone or check the website before travelling. Unless indicated otherwise, the first time shown is am and the second is pm (days not listed mean it's closed), e.g. 8-7 indicates a venue is open from 8am to 7pm. Most restaurants and gastropubs open for lunch and dinner on at least six days a week, although some are closed at weekends.

♦ **Cafés/Restaurants:** There's often little difference between cafés and restaurants (except in price), and many self-styled cafés are in fact full service restaurants. The criteria we have applied to 'real' cafés is that they must open in the mornings and serve coffee/tea and snacks all day. They don't usually open in the evenings.

♦ **Prices:** The table below provides a rough restaurant price guide, based on two courses but excluding drinks. Most gastropubs fall into the inexpensive or moderate price ranges, while cafés are usually firmly in the 'inexpensive' price bracket for a two-course meal.

PRICE GUIDE		
£	Inexpensive	less than £20 per head
££	Moderate	£20 to £40 per head
£££	Expensive	£40 to £60 per head
££££	Splurge	over £60 per head

♦ **Bookings:** Many places listed in this book can be visited spontaneously and are open on most days, although most restaurants and gastropubs (and some cafés) require a lunch or dinner booking, possibly weeks or months in advance for the most popular places. Note that some restaurants don't accept bookings and you just have to turn up and join the queue.

Contents

Introduction

Writing this book has been a labour of love – a love of food (and drink) and of the people who grow, produce, cook and sell it. Not just any food, however, but food created by artisans and specialists who are passionate about their produce and cuisine; people dubbed 'food heroes' by TV chef and restaurateur Rick Stein.

London for Foodies, Gourmets & Gluttons is much more than simply a directory of cafés, markets, restaurants and food shops. It features many of the city's best artisan producers and purveyors, plus a wealth of classes where you can learn how to prepare and cook food like the experts, appreciate fine wines and brew coffee like a barista. And when you're too tired to cook or just want to treat yourself, we'll show you great places where you can enjoy everything from tea and cake to a tasty street snack; a pie and a pint to a glass of wine and tapas; a quick working lunch to a full-blown gastronomic extravaganza.

Researching *London for Foodies, Gourmets & Gluttons* has been a voyage of discovery, a culinary adventure and a sheer pleasure. In seeking out the city's best foodie hotspots we have left no stone unturned. Our epicurean journey has taken us to trendy cafés, cosy tearooms and amazing street food vendors; stunning food halls and bustling markets; innovative restaurants and atmospheric gastropubs; the best wine, beer and spirit merchants; and fascinating classes that teach almost every foodie skill, from butchering a pig to tempering chocolate and enjoying fine wine.

Like most Londoners, we were well aware that the quality and variety of food and drink on offer in the capital had improved beyond all recognition in recent decades, but we were still amazed at just how much the city's gastronomic landscape had changed. The days are long gone since London's culinary scene – and British food in general – was the subject of international contempt and ridicule. The city has seen a foodie revolution in the last 20 years and now offers a choice and quality that's the equal of any city in the world, including ingredients from asafoetida to za'atar, from almost every country on the planet.

In London, the world really is your oyster… it's also your bagel, bammy, chaat, dim sum, enchilada, falafel, injera, kimchi, lahmacun, pierogi, raclette, ravioli, satay or tapa! All have been introduced by immigrants and been eagerly devoured by a grateful population keen for gastronomic adventure. It's London's incredible ethnic diversity that makes it such an exciting place to eat (and cook and shop), as much as its creative chefs and Michelin-starred restaurants.

So whether you wish to revitalise your jaded palate, increase your culinary repertoire, expand your foodie knowledge or experience the ultimate in fine dining – or maybe you're just hungry – you're bound to find inspiration in **London for Foodies, Gourmets & Gluttons**.

Bon appétit!

David Hampshire &
Graeme Chesters

December 2014

Natural Kitchen

1.
Artisan & Specialist Food Shops

'The odds of going to the store for a loaf of bread and coming out with only a loaf of bread are around three billion to one.'

(Erma Bombeck, American humorist)

Food with heart and soul!

Artisan is the new buzzword among foodies: artisan food is food prepared, usually by hand, in a traditional way and on a small scale. The antithesis of fast food and TV dinners, this is food produced by non-industrialised methods, often handed down through generations, using processes (such as fermentation and maturation) that allow flavours to develop slowly and naturally.

Artisan producers respect and understand their raw materials – they know their sources, farmers and growers – and are sensitive to the impact of their production on consumers and the environment. The result is food created by craftsmen with love, integrity and attention to detail, focusing on quality not quantity – food with soul!

When it comes to food shopping Londoners have never had it so good; the city has an abundance of artisan food shops, delicatessens, food halls (see chapter 5) and markets (chapter 7), ethnic food stores and specialist supermarkets. From this edible bounty, we have highlighted some of the city's best purveyors of artisan foods, be it the best of British fare – superb cheeses, tempting breads, top-quality meat and fish, the freshest fruit and vegetables – or exotic produce from all corners of the globe, such as aromatic spices, sensuous chocolate and luxury oils.

> Artisan doesn't mean organic, although it can be; in fact, there isn't a universally-accepted meaning of the term 'artisan food', which has no legal definition.

Ultimately, artisan food is all about taste: the proof of the pudding really **is** in the eating! Food crafted in small batches with care cannot help but taste better than its processed counterpart. It's also better for you, as it's free from preservatives and artificial colouring and unnecessary additives such as excessive salt, sugar and fats – all the stuff that processed food is laced with to make it more appealing (and addictive), cheaper and give it a longer shelf life.

The only downside to artisan food is that it invariably costs more, but in terms of value for money it's well worth it.

Alexeeva & Jones
A world of divine chocolate

Alexeeva & Jones is a *'salon du chocolat'*; a boutique where you can choose from an exclusive selection of hand-made chocolates from over 20 of the world's best artisan chocolatiers. It's owned and run by husband-and-wife team Natalia Alexeeva and Gareth Jones, and sells luxurious chocolates from renowned producers such as Amedei (Italy), Friis-Holm (Denmark), Menakao (Madagascar), Pacari (Ecuador) and Valrhona (France).

You may think £14 is a lot to pay for a choccy bar but one bite and you'll understand, especially if you accompany it with a glass of champagne. There's also a tasting club for incurable chocoholics.

Alexeeva & Jones, 297 Westbourne Grove, W11 2QA (020-7229 1199; alexeevajones.com; Ladbroke Grove tube; Tue-Wed 10-6, Thu-Sat 10-7, Sun 12-6).

Allen & Co
Prime cuts from Mayfair's master butchers

Allen & Co is a traditional butcher with a history stretching back some 120 years. David House and Justin Preston acquired the shop in 2006 and have revitalised the business, which supplies many of London's top chefs and flagship hotels. The owners work closely with the best producers to ensure that their produce comes from the best-quality sources and is fully traceable back to the farm.

Allen also offers butchery classes, which are an enjoyable way to learn the basic skills on seasonal cuts.

Allen & Co, 117 Mount St, W1K 3LA (020-7499 5831; allensofmayfair.co.uk; Bond St/Green Pk tube; Mon-Fri 7-7, Sat 7-5, Sun 10-2).

Artisan du Chocolat

Indulge yourself at Heston's favourite chocolate shop

Artisan du Chocolat is a *'chocolateria'* founded in 2000 by Irish-born pastry chef Gerard Coleman. After training in Belgium, Coleman began selling his chocolates from a Saturday stall at Borough Market, where he was discovered by top chefs Heston Blumenthal and Gordon Ramsay, before opening his first shop in 2002.

Artisan takes its chocolate very seriously, so much so that it produces its own chocolate from ground beans, rather than buying in *couverture* (high-quality processed chocolate) from a larger concern. Coleman's creations include sea salted caramels, incredible Os (wafer-thin chocolate shells with liquid fillings) and a wide range of bars – milk as well as plain – plus drinking chocolate and more.

The focal point of the shop is an illuminated ceiling dome, decorated with a panoramic scene from a cocoa plantation, while a flat-screen TV plays video footage of the chocolate production process. Special events include chocolate and cocktail tastings, featuring alcoholic drinks made by distilling spirits such as vodka or rum with cacao.

Artisan has another branch in Chelsea (89 Lower Sloane Street) and a concession in Selfridges – plus the Borough market stall where it all began.

Artisan du Chocolat, 81 Westbourne Grove, W2 4UL (0845-270 6996; artisanduchocolat.com; Bayswater tube; Mon-Sat 10-7, Sun 12-5).

Belle Epoque Patisserie
Perfect pastries and a taste of Provence

Belle Epoque is a traditional French patisserie, bakery and chocolatier that's widely recognised as one of the best pastry-makers in London. Secreted away on Newington Green, the shop was opened in 2002 and offers bespoke cakes, pastel-hued macarons, mouth-watering viennoiseries, fluffy quiches, traditional French bread and much more, accompanied by deliciously strong espresso.

There's a lovely tearoom behind the front shop, decorated in Provençal style, while on sunny days you can enjoy the secluded garden.

Belle Epoque Patisserie, 37 Newington Green, N16 9PR (020-7249 2222; belleepoque.co.uk; Canonbury rail; Tue-Fri 8-6, Sat 9-6, Sun 9-5).

Biscuiteers
Oh crumbs, what a choice!

Founded in 2007 by passionate biscuit makers Harriet Hastings and Stevie Congdon, Biscuiteers' USP is, of course, biscuits – but not any old biscuits. They're famous for their personalised, handmade luxury biscuits, which they sell at their delightful 'biscuit boutique & icing café' in Notting Hill. Other tasty offerings include cakes, traditional sweets, hand-iced cupcakes, macarons and customised chocolates, which can be decorated with flowers and letters to spell out a message.

The shop also offers icing classes, where you too can learn how to become a biscuiteer.

Biscuiteers, 194 Kensington Park Rd, W11 2ES (020-7727 8096; biscuiteers.com; Ladbroke Grove tube; Mon 10-5, Tue-Sat 10-6, Sun 11-5).

Bumblebee
Buzzing with natural goodness

Bumblebee (they keep bees in the garden behind the shop) has been a north London institution for 25 years, during which time it has spread along Brecknock Road where it now occupies three shops: a grocer (the original store), greengrocer and bakery. It offers a comprehensive range of vegetarian and organic foods, household goods and natural remedies.

Bumblebee's ethos is quality foods at reasonable prices, and it stocks many locally produced goods. Services include a vegetable box scheme – free local delivery of seasonal fruit and veg – and hot takeaway food at lunchtime.

Bumblebee, 33 Brecknock Rd, N7 0DD (020-7607 1936; bumblebeenaturalfoods.co.uk; Caledonian Rd tube; Mon-Sat 9-6.30).

La Cave à Fromage
A grand fromage among cheese shops

Founded in 2007 by Eric Charriaux and Amnon Paldi, La Cave à Fromage offers the very best of (primarily) French and British artisan cheeses. The pair founded their business in 1999 and now supply top restaurants around the UK, including Le Manoir aux Quat' Saisons. La Cave doesn't just sell cheese but also matures it, so that you buy it when it's perfectly ripe.

If you want to try before you buy, the shop hosts regular tasting events, and you can also order online. There's a second branch in Notting Hill (148-150 Portobello Road).

La Cave à Fromage, 24-25 Cromwell Pl, SW7 2LD (020-7581 1804; la-cave.co.uk; S Kensington tube; Mon-Thu 10-7; Fri-Sat 10-9, Sun 11-6).

Covent Garden Fishmongers

Fish so fresh you don't need to cook it!

This top-notch fishmonger started life in 1982, when Philip Diamond had a stall in Covent Garden's Jubilee Market. He moved west to set up shop in Chiswick and has been one of London's best fishmongers for over 20 years. Covent Garden are proud of the range and quality of their fish, which is from sustainable stock and line-caught whenever possible; it's fresh enough to eat raw, and ingredients such as nori seaweed and soy sauce are available so that you can make your own sushi.

Staff are happy to fillet your purchase and advise you how to prepare it.

Covent Garden Fishmongers, 37 Turnham Green Ter, W4 1RG (020-8995 9273; coventgardenfishmongers.co.uk; Turnham Grn tube; Tue-Wed, Fri-Sat 8-5.30, Thu 8-5).

Damas Gate

Eat your way around the Middle East

Founded in 1989, Damas Gate is one of the oldest Middle-Eastern food wholesalers in the UK, as well as being the first to sell halal products. DG's bustling supermarket on Uxbridge Road typifies their dedication to the quality and provenance of their food, and their understanding of customers' needs.

It's an Aladdin's cave of edible goodies with aisles overflowing with olives, nuts and dates, pickles and pulses, herbs and spices, and flatbreads and pastries; fridges full of sheep's cheese and yogurt, ready-to-eat falafels and kebabs, mounds of fresh fruit and veg, and a halal butcher's counter too.

Damas Gate, 81-85 Uxbridge Rd, W12 8NR (020-8743 5116; damasgate.uk.com; Shepherd's Bush Market tube; daily 9-10).

Daylesford Organic
The undisputed king of organic food

Pimlico was Daylesford's first London base and now hosts a farm shop and café. This large, well-designed shop, with its clean white spaces and grey marble, offers three floors of top quality organic food to eat in or take home. What's more it's located near Mozart Square, a pretty pedestrianised space where there's a farmers' market selling more organic bounty on Saturdays.

Daylesford has other London outlets in Notting Hill (208-212 Westbourne Grove, W11) and Selfridges Food Hall (see page 126).

A pioneer of organic farming, Daylesford has been established for over 30 years and is one of the most respected food producers in the UK. All their produce travels directly from farm to fork: meat and poultry from their pastures, fruit and vegetables from their market garden, bread from their bakery, and cheese, milk and yoghurt from their creamery.

Daylesford grows over 300 varieties of organic fruit, vegetables, salad leaves and herbs on their 20-acre farm in Gloucestershire, including many unusual and heritage varieties. They also offer a range of award-winning, ready-to-cook meals, soups, jams and chutneys, made from their own produce whenever possible.

Daylesford Organic, 44B Pimlico Rd, SW1W 8LP (020-7881 8060; daylesford.com; Sloane Sq tube; Mon-Sat 8-8, Sun 10-4).

The East India Company

Best of British from the world's greatest trading company

The East India Company was granted its first charter in 1600 by Elizabeth I, permitting it to explore (and plunder!) the riches of the Orient, which led to it becoming the greatest trading company the world has ever known. The company was dissolved in 1874 but the name was revived in 2010 by Sanjiv Mehta, who plans to turn it into a global player once again.

The Conduit Street store offers gourmet food, luxuries and edible gifts, mostly made in Britain, but influenced by tastes, cultures and traditions from around the globe. They include tea, coffee, biscuits, preserves, chutneys, sauces, mustards, oils, specialty sugars, chocolate, cordials, fine wines and more.

Tea was (and remains) a key ingredient of the East India Company's trade, and the tea library allows you to choose from a huge range of green, black, herbal and flavoured teas; there's also a bespoke coffee 'station' where you can mix your own brew from some 60 core blends.

The store is modelled on the house of a Georgian gentleman officer and is packed with a wealth of striking design features, combining Georgian elegance with exotic flourishes, in shades of black, gold and red.

The East India Company, 7-8 Conduit St, W1S 2XF (020-3205 3395; theeastindiacompany.com; Oxford Circus tube; Mon-Sat 10-7, Sun 12-6).

Euphorium Bakery
Flour, yeast and a pinch of magic

The first Euphorium Bakery opened in 1999 in Upper Street, Islington, and has since expanded to 31 outlets. Euphorium are justly famous for their delicious artisan bread, cakes and savouries baked fresh daily (the bakery is still located at its flagship Upper Street store) using seasonal and British-sourced ingredients.

The award-winning range features rustic breads such as campagne and black olive, savoury treats such as sausage rolls and quiche, and sweet sensations, including Bramley apple tart and the irresistible-sounding Chocolate Lovers' Cake. There's also an expanding range of non-baked goods, including preserves, juices and pâté.

Euphorium Bakery, 202 Upper St, N1 1RQ (020-7704 6905; euphoriumbakery.com; Highbury & Islington tube; Mon-Fri 7-10, Sat-Sun 8-10).

FarmW5
An organic taste of the countryside

The folks behind FarmW5 have a passion for organic food, working in partnership with over 50 small UK growers and producers. All produce on sale at the Ealing shop is certified organic or slow food (see slowfood.com). FarmW5 claim that everything they sell is 'simply the best' (no false modesty here!), including meat and poultry from organic farms in Somerset and Cornwall; fish from sustainable stocks landed in Looe and Brixham; mushrooms from Winchester; and honey from just round the corner in Ealing.

There's a coffee and juice bar too.

FarmW5, 19 The Green, W5 5DA (020-8566 1965; farmw5.co.uk; Ealing Broadway rail; Mon-Fri 8-7.30, Sat 9-7, Sun 11-5).

La Fromagerie
A feast of fromage and more

La Fromagerie's lovely little gourmet shop is widely recognised as one of London's (and the UK's) best cheese shops and is a favourite of chefs, gourmets and foodies. Patricia and Danny Michelson opened their first ship in Highbury in 1992, and the Moxon Street outlet followed ten years later; both feature special cellars with on-site *affinage* (the process of ageing and maturing cheese) and signature walk-in cheese rooms.

La Fromagerie specialises in farmhouse cheeses, both regional British and European, sourced directly from artisan producers and carefully matured to peak condition. There's also a floor dedicated to other well-sourced produce, including seasonal fruit and vegetables, freshly-baked breads, extra virgin olive oils and vinegars, and other essential dry store ingredients and condiments. The on-site kitchen produces preserves and chutneys, biscuits and cakes, along with a daily changing menu of food to take away or enjoy in the café, a welcome respite from London's busy streets. Usefully, the shop is next door to the acclaimed butcher, Ginger Pig (see page 22).

La Fromagerie has an excellent website with advice on creating the perfect cheese plate – and choosing wines to go with it.

La Fromagerie, 2-6 Moxon St, W1U 4EW (020-7935 034; lafromagerie.co.uk; Baker St tube; Mon-Fri 8-7.30, Sat 9-7, Sun 10-6).

R. Garcia & Sons

Spain on a plate

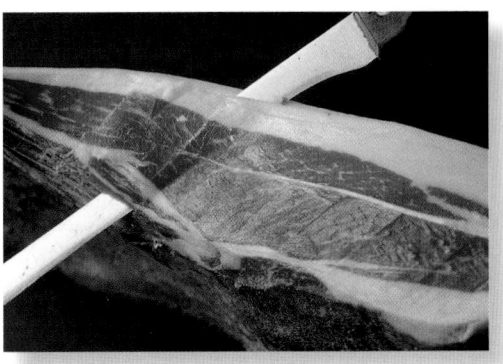

Established in 1958 amid the bustle of Portobello Road, Garcia's is London's largest and best Spanish grocer and delicatessen. It's worth visiting just for its excellent charcuterie counter, offering a mouth-watering selection of top-quality Spanish cured hams and sausages, including jamón ibérico and serrano ham, *morcilla* (a type of Spanish black pudding), spicy chorizo sausage, salted pork ribs and tasty salamis.

There's a comprehensive selection of Spanish cheeses, including Minorcan mahón, tetilla from Galicia and the ever-popular manchego, plus an abundance of olives, olive oil, sherry vinegar, preserves, paella rice, almonds, pistachios, dried beans, tins of snails and jars of *boquerones* (anchovies), herbs and spices, sweets (try the turrón) and much more. Not forgetting a splendid selection of Spanish wine, sherry, cava and brandy. Garcia's has all the ingredients you need to produce authentic tapas or a full-blown Spanish feast, plus free advice on tap from the friendly staff.

You can whet your appetite at Café Garcia or at one of the local Spanish eateries. Try an authentic cortado coffee, hot chocolate and churros, or a few tapas with a glass of fino. ¡Buen provecho!

R. Garcia & Sons, 248-250 Portobello Rd, W11 1LL (020-7221 6119; rgarciaandsons.com; Ladbroke Grove tube; Mon 10-6, Tue-Thur 9-6, Fri-Sat 9-7, Sun 10-7).

The Gazzano's

A taste of Italian sunshine in the City

This fourth-generation Italian deli is something of an institution on Farringdon Road, which draws Italians from miles around. Gazzano's stocks a wide range of Italian specialities, including mountains of fresh and dried pasta, sausages, salamis and hams, Parmigiano-Reggiano, rustic breads (ciabatta, focaccia, etc.), truffles, capers, pesto, tapenade, marinated artichokes, sun kissed tomatoes, balsamic vinegar, delicious olives and olive oil, wines, liquors, and much more – all of Italy is here and at reasonable prices.

At the rear is an espresso and panini bar.

The Gazzano's, 167-169 Farringdon Rd, EC1R 3AL (020-7837 1586; Farringdon tube; Tue-Fri 7.30-5.30, Sat 9-5.30, Sun 10-2).

Gelupo

Just one cornetto, give it to me...

Since opening in 2010, Gelupo has been widely acclaimed as the best gelateria in London, producing a superb range of gelati and sorbetti. Jacob Kenedy – the chef/patron of sister restaurant Bocca di Lupo (see page 194) – develops, tests and tastes all the wonderful flavours, which include ricotta, chocolate and black pepper, and vanilla and saffron.

What makes Gelupo's gelato stand out as authentically Italian is the low fat content and slow churning methods, creating a dense, creamy texture that really lets the flavours sing. Gelupo is also a deli, but most people come just for the gelato.

Gelupo, 7 Archer St, W1D 7AU (020-7287 5555; gelupo.com; Piccadilly Circus tube; Mon-Thu 12-10.30, Fri-Sat 12-11.30, Sun 12-10).

Ginger Pig
Everything but the oink!

Ginger Pig began over 20 years ago with a near-derelict farmhouse and three Tamworth pigs, and now farms over 3,000 acres of its own pasture and moorland in North Yorkshire as well as working with a network of like-minded farmers. At the heart of the business is good animal husbandry and welfare; happy pigs taste better!

Ginger Pig has six London outlets (Borough Market, Clapham, Hackney, Marylebone, Shepherds Bush and Waterloo) – we have chosen to feature the Hackney branch – and is one of the few places in this book that warrants two entries (the other is for butchery lessons – see page 105). It's London's most celebrated butcher and where many of the city's top chefs and restaurants buy their meat, choosing from a mind-boggling range of products, including beef, lamb, chicken and duck, as well as pork.

The Hackney outlet is small but perfectly formed, situated in Victoria Park village, home to cafés, restaurants, pubs and a fishmonger. In addition to the usual butchery counter there's a selection of cured meats, cold cuts, chutneys and dry goods, plus Ginger Pig's celebrated sausage rolls and pies.

Ginger Pig, 99 Lauriston Rd, E9 7HJ (020-8986 6911; thegingerpig.co.uk; Homerton rail/Bethnal Grn tube; Mon-Wed 9-5.30, Thu-Fri 9-6.30, Sat 9-6, Sun 10-3).

A. Gold

Patriotism and nostalgia on every shelf. Rule Britannia!

A Gold looks like an old-fashioned grocer and styles itself as 'a village shop in the City' – somewhere you can buy a cup of slow-brewed Monmouth coffee, a bag of traditional sweets or a homemade scotch egg. Located in busy Spitalfields (next door to Verde & Co – see page 43), it's the only deli in London to offer entirely British produce, championing small independent producers from across the UK. Founded in 2000 by Ian and Safia Thomas – the name comes from Amelia Gold, one of the building's former residents – it was taken over by Philip Cundall and Paulo Garcia in 2010 and has since gone from strength to strength.

This Aladdin's cave of a shop offers a wealth of nostalgic treats, such as bacon and toffee from Cumbria, Campbell's tea and Camp coffee, sugar mice and hand-made fudge, Stinking Bishop cheese, English mead, Dorset knobs (a type of biscuit), Cornish gingerbread, London honey, Henderson's relish, lemon curd, cream soda, sloe gin, gooseberry wine, brandy snaps and much, much more. Or you can buy a hamper and indulge your every whim.

Gold's takeaway food service includes excellent coffee, imaginative sandwiches, traditional pies and their famous scotch eggs.

A. Gold, 42 Brushfield St, E1 6AG (020-7247 2487; agoldshop.com; Liverpool St tube/rail; Mon-Fri 10-4, Sat-Sun 11-5).

Hampstead Butcher & Providore

Putting the ham into Hampstead

Established in 2010 by entrepreneur Philip Matthews, with a team led by renowned chef Guy Bossom, the Hampstead Butcher & Providore was an immediate success. This foodie gem is Hampstead's premier butcher, delicatessen, charcuterie, cheese and wine shop, offering an extensive range of meat and poultry, sausages and hams, pates, marinades and savoury snacks, many of which are made on the premises. HB&P also stocks an extensive range of larder essentials, including bread, cakes, chocolates and fine foods from artisan suppliers.

It's a sociable venue, with regular tastings, dinners, events and even butchery classes.

The Hampstead Butcher & Providore, 56 Rosslyn Hill, NW3 1ND (020-7794 9210; hampsteadbutcher.com; Hampstead tube; Mon-Sat 9-7, Sun 9-6).

Steve Hatt
Catch of the day!

This fourth-generation fishmonger has been providing north Londoners with fresh fish since 1895 and the shop's enduring popularity is confirmed by the queues outside. The wet fish window display allows you to check out what's available: wild and farmed fish and seafood, plus less familiar fishy treats such as crayfish and sea urchins. A typical day's catch might include wild Scottish halibut, bluefin tuna, sea trout, plaice, lemon sole, gilt head bream, lobster and scallops.

Having chosen your fish supper, you can have it skinned, boned and filleted on request, and also buy a range of accompaniments including samphire and French sauces.

Steve Hatt, 88-90 Essex Rd, N1 8LU (020-7226 3963; Essex Rd rail; Tue-Fri 8-5, Sat 7-5).

Hive Honey Shop

Honey for tea... and breakfast, lunch and dinner!

Beekeepers for three generations since 1922, James Hamill and his family have owned and run the Hive Honey Shop in Clapham for over 20 years. The family maintain their own beehives at sites around the country, thus allowing them to offer a wide variety of single-floral honeys, including sweet chestnut, heather, linden blossom and hawthorn, plus dozens of specialist honeys such as rum and raisin and vanilla infused honey.

They also make delicious treats such as chocolate-coated honeycomb, honey bonbons, honey sticks (tubes filled with honey and fruit juice), chocolate insects and glorious honey fudge.

The business is a pioneer in the creation of hand-made health and medicinal lotions, potions, ointments and cosmetics – using natural ingredients harvested from beehives – which include fresh royal jelly, propolis capsules, luxurious moisturiser, and honey and lemon lozenges. Other products include honey mustard, chutney, cakes, sweets, mead, honey cider, pollen grains and beeswax candles.

The centrepiece of the shop is a five-foot high, glass-fronted beehive, home to a colony of 20,000 Buckfast Abbey bees, allowing visitors a peek into the fascinating world of the honey bee.

Hive Honey Shop, 93 Northcote Rd, SW11 6PL (020-7924 6233; thehivehoneyshop.co.uk; Clapham Jct rail; Mon-Tue, Thu-Sat 10-5, closed 1-2, Wed 10-2).

Indian Spice Shop
The place to spice up your cooking

In business for more than 15 years, the Indian Spice Shop prides itself on its vast range of exotic herbs and spices, fruit and vegetables and other Indian foodie essentials. Plus it offers great service and reasonable prices, all within a few hundred yards of Euston station.

Don't be deterred by the slightly shabby exterior; this delightful, unpretentious shop offers an unrivalled variety of spices, chutneys, pickles and pastes, while outside is a tempting display of exotic produce, from mangos to passion fruit, chikoo to karela, fresh curry leaves to bunches of coriander.

Indian Spice Shop, 115-119 Drummond St, NW1 2HL (020-7916 1831; indianspiceshop.co.uk; Euston tube/rail; Mon-Sat 9.30-9, Sun 10-9).

Italian Farmers
A true taste of Italy

Italian Farmers is a ray of epicurian sunshine in Stroud Green. Boasting a rustic welcome, the store is an outpost of *Campagna Amica*, a movement run by a farmers' trade union that promotes eco-friendly food produced by small farmers in Italy.

Here you can delight in lush San Marzano tomatoes; authentic cheeses, from buffalo mozzarella to gorgonzola and nutty pecorino romano; and top-quality meats, including wild boar sausages, Parma ham and porchetta. All around, the shelves are laden with tempting sauces and spreads, olive oils, pastas, jams, biscuits, bread, rice, olives, truffles, pickled vegetables and more. Tasting sessions take place three evenings a week. *Bellissimo!*

Italian Farmers, 186 Stroud Green Rd, N4 3RN (020-3719 6525; Crouch Hill tube; Mon-Thu 8.30-8.30, Fri-8.30-10.30, Sat 9-10.30, Sun 10-8.30).

Japan Centre Food Shop
Make your own sushi

If you love Japanese food then this one is for you. Recently relocated, the Japan Centre's spacious new premises are divided into distinct sections with neat rows of products, making it easy to find what you want. The front half of the store is given over to the Umai Sushi Factory: metres of chill cabinets stuffed with fresh sushi and sashimi, pickles, salads and rice bowls for the microwave. There's also a hot food counter serving Chinese-style dim sum, as well as Japanese *gyoza* (dumplings), tempura, noodles and bento boxes.

At the rear is everything you need to cook authentic Japanese cuisine, from *wakame* (edible seaweed) and *dashi* (broth) to *kimchi* (cabbage pickle) and tofu. As you'd expect there's a good seafood counter featuring oysters, razor clams, prawns, cod roe, sea bass, black cod and more, and an in-house bakery selling red bean biscuits, jasmine tea-scented muffins, curry breads and cartoon buns. Fruit and veg is limited (the choice is better in nearby Chinatown), as is the meat section, but there's a huge choice of store-cupboard items such as rice crackers, ramen and udon noodles. There's a good selection of saké too.

You can order online via the website, which also contains recipes.

Japan Centre Food Shop, 19 Shaftesbury Ave, W1D 7ED (020-3405 1246; japancentre.com; Piccadilly Circus tube; Mon-Sat 10-9.30, Sun 11-8).

Leila's Shop
A bijou gem of a grocer

Leila's (owned by Leila McAlister) is a bijou gem in Shoreditch; a combination of old-fashioned grocer and modern café. Farm-fresh fruit & veg is displayed outside in woven baskets, wooden crates and glazed bowls, while the rustic interior is piled with seasonal produce, breads, cheeses, butter, eggs, olive oil, almonds, juices, chutneys, jams, gourmet coffee, leaf tea and much more.

After you've restocked your larder, you can pop into the café next door for delicious coffee and cake or a simple but tasty lunch.

Leila's Shop, 15-17 Calvert Ave, E2 7JN (020-7729 9789; Bethnal Grn tube; Wed-Sat 10-6, Sun 10-5).

C. Lidgate
Feed the man meat...

Danny Lidgate is the fifth generation of his family to run this 160-year-old butcher's business. He and his father David source their organic and grass-fed beef, lamb and pork from selected free-range and organic farms and estates. Their organic chicken comes direct from small farms in the West Country and East Anglia, and they also sell wild game such as red leg partridge and grouse.

Other specialities include homemade sausages, cured hams, award-winning pies in ceramic dishes, and a range of perfectly matured cheeses. Not surprisingly, their client list contains some famous names, including Oliver Peyton.

C. Lidgate, 110 Holland Park Ave, W11 4UA (020-7727 8243; lidgates.com; Holland Pk tube; Mon-Fri 7.30-7, Sat 6.30-6.30).

Lina Stores
Pasta worth crossing London for

This family-run Italian deli with its classic '50s green ceramic frontage is a landmark in Soho, where it has been trading since 1944. Although spruced up in recent years, Lina Stores has lost none of its rustic charm. Its centrepiece is the huge marble and green-tiled deli counter, surrounded by mouth-watering hams hanging from the rafters and shelves over-flowing with tempting produce.

This iconic treasure house stocks all the essentials for *la dolce vita*, such as homemade pesto, sauces (heavenly passata), breads, marinated artichokes, truffles, oils and olives. There's a splendid selection of cheeses, including taleggio, fresh buffalo mozzarella and *pecorino brigante* (sheep's cheese), and those famous meats: Parma ham, homemade Italian sausage and salamis such as *lardo* (salami cured with rosemary) and *finocchiona* (salami with fennel). Lina's is perhaps best known for its fresh pasta, especially ravioli and tortelloni, which customers travel miles to buy (Jane Grigson was a famous customer). Classic fillings of spinach and ricotta or pumpkin jostle with specials such as porcini, artichoke and truffle oil, or pea and mint.

Cakes and desserts are baked on site, including the Italian classic *Torta caprese* (chocolate and almond cake), panettone and mascarpone muffins, plus a selection of regional Italian wines. *Buon appetito!*

Lina Stores, 18 Brewer St, W1F 0SH (020-7437 6482; linastores.co.uk; Piccadilly Circus tube; Mon-Tue 8.30-7.30, Wed-Fri 8.30-8.30, Sat 10-7.30, Sun 11-5).

Loon Fung
A Chinatown classic

There are many food shops in Chinatown, but Loon Fung is worth a second look; opened over 40 years ago, it was one of the first Chinese supermarkets in the UK. It offers an exhaustive range of products at reasonable prices, including everything you need to dish up an authentic Chinese banquet: meat and fish from the in-house butcher and fishmonger, plus a wide variety of exotic fruit and veg.

Loon Fung stocks well-known brands such as Amoy and Yeos, but also sells exclusive products such as their famous Wing Wing air-dried sausages. There are other outlets in Alperton, Silvertown and Tottenham.

Loon Fung, 42-44 Gerrard St, W1D 5QG (020-7437 7332; loonfung.com; Leicester Sq tube; daily 10-8).

MacFarlane's
Somewhere to avoid if you're on a diet!

This delightful deli in Clapham – established over 12 years ago – specialises in fine cheese. In fact, it claims to stock one of the finest ranges of cheeses in London. and you'll be spoilt for choice with the variety of high quality pasteurised and unpasteurised cow, sheep and goat milk cheeses, sourced directly from producers and trusted suppliers throughout Europe.

MacFarlane's also stocks cured meats and charcuterie, farm-produced hams, artisan pâtés, organic Scottish smoked salmon, delicious dips and antipasti (including hummus and pesto), Italian olive oil, Belgian chocolates and its famous homemade sausage rolls.

MacFarlane's, 48 Abbeville Rd, SW4 9NF (020-8673 5373; macfarlanesdeli.co.uk; Clapham S tube; Mon-Fri 10-7, Sat 9-6, Sun 10-5).

Melrose & Morgan

Grocer par excellence

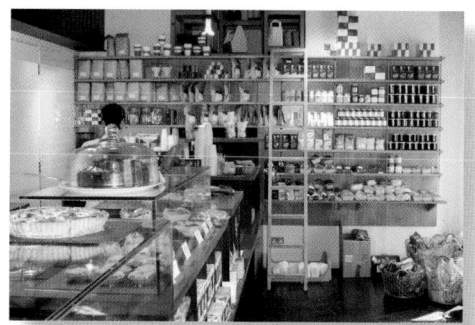

Melrose & Morgan in chic Primrose Hill calls itself a 'grocery shop', although it certainly isn't your average corner shop but rather an outstanding gourmet delicatessen and café. This grocer-cum-kitchen supplies artisan products and ingredients, as well as freshly-prepared meals, for those who care about the quality of their food and its preparation, and can afford to pay for the very best. Some two-thirds of M&M's food is made in-house in small batches and what they don't make themselves is carefully sourced from local artisans and independent retailers.

The Primrose Hill shop (their first outlet – there's a second in Hampstead) opened in 2004 and has a café where you can enjoy breakfast, lunch or tea, or pick up something for supper. As well as its freshly-cooked range of pies, soups, pastries,

cakes and tarts, M&M sells a wealth of first-class produce, including organic and free-range meat and poultry, cheese and everyday supplies such as milk, bread and juices. There are also hand-made chocolates, wines and oils, plus fresh fruit and vegetables.

It's a lot more expensive than Tesco, but that would be like comparing chalk and cheese when it comes to flavour and quality. You can order online too.

Melrose & Morgan, 42 Gloucester Ave, NW1 8JD (020-7722 0011; melroseandmorgan.com; Chalk Farm tube; Mon-Fri 8-7, Sat 8-6, Sun 9-5).

Mr Christian's
Great tastes conceived by a TV chef

A foodie institution, Mr Christian's delicatessen in Notting Hill was founded in 1974 by Tim Dawson and Glynn Christian. Glynn was one of the original TV chefs, on BBC1's *Pebble Mill at One* and later *BBC Breakfast Time*, and the shop soon had a devoted customer base. Gregg Scott later took over the business and in 2003 it became part of the Jeroboams wine merchants group (jeroboams.co.uk). However, it remains a thriving foodie business that's true to its founder's vision.

There's a great choice of quality products on offer, including unique cheeses and charcuterie, smoked fish, organic ice cream and own-label jams, pickles and honey, as well as home-cooked lunch dishes – such as roast butternut squash and goats' cheese risotto cakes – salads and sandwiches.

Mr Christian's is particularly famous for its breads (it sells over 50 types) and pastries, including homemade sausage rolls, savoury pastries, sweet treats and freshly-made patisserie.

The deli also stocks a range of top-quality basics such as French butter, crème fraîche, sea salt, herbs and spices, organic milk and free-range eggs, mustards, chutneys, marinades, oils, vinegars, dips, organic teas, coffee, chocolates and much more.

Mr Christian's, 11 Elgin Cres, W11 2JA (020-7229 0501; mrchristians.co.uk; Ladbroke Grove tube; Mon-Sat 7.30-6, Sun 8-3).

Moxon's
A taste of the sea in Kensington

Fishmonger Robin Moxon is regarded as one of the best fishmongers in London, with four outlets: Clapham, East Dulwich, Islington and South Kensington – the one featured here. They sell ethically-caught fish sourced daily from London's Billingsgate Market (see page 171) and suppliers around the UK, including Newlyn in Cornwall, Brixham and Plymouth in Devon, Peterhead and Loch Duart in Scotland, Scalloway in the Shetland Islands and Newhaven in Sussex.

Moxon's sells an exhaustive range of fish and shellfish, with the emphasis on freshness and seasonality. Depending on the time of year, you can buy Cornish bream, Dover sole, halibut, herring, monkfish, mullet, plaice, rock salmon, smoked mackerel, tuna, turbot, plus wild smoked salmon and sea bass, while the choice of shellfish encompasses clams, crab, lobster, mussels, oysters, scallops and more.

The friendly staff are happy to offer advice and prepare fish to suit your needs, and you can browse their library of cookbooks for inspiration. The shop stocks a range of fish-friendly accompaniments such as samphire and various store-cupboard goods.

Moxon's also has a fish bar in Clapham (moxonsfishbar.com) serving seriously good fish and chips.

Moxon's, 17 Bute St, SW7 3EY (020-7591 0050; moxonsfreshfish.com; S Kensington tube; Tue-Fri 8.30-7.30, Sat 8.30-5.30).

The Natural Kitchen
Food emporium au naturel

The Natural Kitchen in Marylebone (with other outlets in Baker Street, Fetter Lane and Trinity Square) is a high-class food emporium, founded in 2007 and now operating as a deli with a café/juice bar upstairs. It sells artisan, organic and wild food – ethical foods, sustainably sourced – supplied by the likes of River Cottage, Paxton & Whitfield (cheese), and Vintage Roots (alcoholic and non-alcoholic organic tipples).

The Natural Kitchen's speciality is high quality, free-range meat and poultry, sourced (where possible) directly from small traditional farms, such as Monkshill Farm in Kent which supplies salt marsh lamb, 'Kentish Ranger' free-range chickens, and pork from Oxford sandy and black pigs. Butchers Andy and John (chefandbutcher.

co.uk) are happy to proffer expert advice on choosing and cooking their quality meats.

If you're short on time or cooking skills, a tasty range of ready-to-cook meats is available such as chicken Kiev, veal and basil meatballs, and salt marsh lamb koftas, while the 'Food to Go' counters offer a large choice of seasonal salads, quiches, soups, pies and sandwiches, plus a range of drinks.

The Natural Kitchen, 77-78 Marylebone High St, W1U 5JX (020-3012 2123; thenaturalkitchen.com; Baker St tube; Mon-Fri 7-8, Sat-Sun 8-7).

Neal's Yard Dairy
The best of British artisanal cheese

Neal's Yard Dairy opened in 1979 selling fresh cheese and other dairy produce, and now supplies shops and restaurants around the world. It buys from some 70 British and Irish cheesemakers and sells the produce in its stores in Borough Market, Bermondsey and Neal's Yard (Covent Garden). The business maintains close contact with its cheesemakers, visiting them regularly, and it's this attention to detail that has made Neal's Yard a byword for top-quality cheese.

Many of the cheeses are either matured on the farm or in the dairy's maturing rooms in Bermondsey, located in brick railway arches under the main line from London Bridge to Dover. The insulation provided by the venerable Victorian brickwork helps maintain excellent conditions for the cheeses – humid and cool – which are meticulously cared for until they reach peak condition. Neal's Yard also has its own creamery on Dorstone Hill (overlooking the Wye Valley in Herefordshire), where it makes Greek-style and strained Greek yoghurt, goat's curd and some splendid goat's milk cheeses.

Neal's Yard runs various cheese classes at its Bermondsey warehouse, where the experienced team guide you through a tasting of traditional and modern artisan cheeses, with liquid accompaniments.

Neal's Yard Dairy, 17 Shorts Gdns, WC2H 9AT (020-7240 5700; nealsyarddairy.co.uk; Covent Gdn tube; Mon-Sat 10-7).

Oliver's Wholefoods Store
Health food store for foodies

Oliver's is an award-winning neighbourhood store sourcing the best organic produce from small, local producers. It was established in 1989 by ex-chef Sara Novakovic, previously employed at the Institute for Advanced Nutrition. Sara believes strongly in the close link between good health and natural foods, and much of the produce sold at Oliver's is organic, including fresh fruit and veg, fish, meat, cheese, juices, local honey, bread, dried goods and wine.

The store also caters for special diets, selling wheat- and gluten-free foods, along with natural and homeopathic remedies, nutritional supplements and bodycare products. There's even an in-store nutritionist!

Oliver's Wholefoods Store, 5 Station Approach, TW9 3QB (020-8948 3990; oliverswholefoods. co.uk; Kew Gdns tube; Mon to Sat 9-8, Sun 10-8).

Paxton & Whitfield
Iconic Georgian cheese store

The origins of this iconic cheese store date back to 1742 when Stephen Cullum set up a cheese stall in Aldwych market. However, (ironically) its name comes from Harry Paxton and Charles Whitfield, two partners who came on board in 1797, by which time the business was established in Jermyn Street where London's gentlemen bought their garments and victuals (as they still do today).

Today the name is synonymous with the best of British and French cheeses, the latter sourced from its partner, Paris-based Fromagerie Androuet. A Paxton & Whitfield Stilton still graces the most discerning Christmas tables…

Paxton & Whitfield, 93 Jermyn St, SW1Y 6JE (020-7930 0259; paxtonandwhitfield.co.uk; Piccadilly Circus tube; Mon-Sat 9.30-6, Sun 11-5).

Persepolis

Full of Eastern promise

Co-owned by the indomitable Sally Butcher, Persepolis in Peckham is much more than a food shop – it's an Aladdin's cave of all things Persian, from samovars to shisha pipes. But don't let the handicrafts distract you; this charming shop is a serious foodie haven. It's packed to the rafters with exotic foods, including fresh dates, preserved limes, dried lemons, exotic herbs and spices (such as sumak and za'atar), pomegranate molasses, rosewater, stuffed vine leaves, sour cherries, baklava and much more. There's also a café serving excellent mezze dishes.

Sally is the author of half a dozen celebrated cookbooks (see the excellent website for information).

Persepolis, 28-30 Peckham High St, SE15 5DT (020-7639 8007; foratasteofpersia.co.uk; Peckham Rye rail; daily 10.35-9).

Poilâne

Classic French bread from a Parisian bakery

Opened in 2000, this was the first London outlet for this Parisian boulangerie famous for its sourdough bread (there's now a second store at 39 Cadogan Gardens in Chelsea). Poilâne bakes its bread on-site in an exact copy of a Roman wood-fired bread oven, using only the best stone-ground flour, sea salt and rising agents.

Poilâne produces only a small range of breads to ensure their quality, including its signature round loaf and a number of flavoured breads, such as rye and raisin. Don't miss the 'punitions' – butter cookies that are a treat, not a punishment. *Magnifique!*

Poilâne, 46 Elizabeth St, SW1W 9PA (020-7808 4910; poilane.com; Sloane Sq tube; Mon-Fri 7-7, Sat 7-3.30).

Prestat
Roald Dahl's favourite chocolate factory

Prestat is England's oldest chocolatier, founded in 1902 by French émigré Monsieur Antoine Dufour, which numbers Her Majesty the Queen and the late Roald Dahl among its customers. This bijou boutique, appropriately located in genteel Princes Arcade off Piccadilly, is packed with chocolate marvels, including vanilla ganache, marzipan, dark chocolate-dipped apricots, hot chocolate flakes and their world-famous truffles.

Prestat's chocolate bars allegedly contain up to three times more antioxidants than standard dark chocolate due to the gentle processing methods – so they really are good for you!

Prestat, 14 Princes Arcade, SW1Y 6DS (020-7494 3772; prestat.co.uk; Piccadilly Circus tube; Mon-Fri 9.30-6, Sat 10-5, Sun 11-4.30).

Quality Chop House Shop
Chop licking good

Located next door to the Quality Chop House restaurant, the QCH Butchers and Food Shop follows the latest trend of restaurants opening their own food shops. The handsome shop is traditional yet stylish, with 'antique' floorboards, old-fashioned black and white tiles, and pristine wooden cabinets.

As well as the meat, which is delivered straight from the farm and prepared on site, there's a wide selection of other products, from British cheeses and charcuterie to QCH produce, conserves and preserves, smoked fish, terrines and parfaits, pies and sweet treats, plus staples such as milk, eggs, butter and bread.

Quality Chop House Shop, 92-94 Farringdon Rd, EC1R 3EA (020-3490 6228; thequalitychophouse. com/shop; Farringdon tube; Mon-Thu 11-7, Fri 10-8, Sat 9-6, Sun 11-5).

Scandinavian Kitchen
A smorgasbord of Scandi treats

The Scandinavian Kitchen was established in 2006 by Bronte (a Dane) and Jonas (a Swede) who, having failed to find authentic Scandinavian food in London, decided to sell it themselves. It's a unique treasure trove of over 600 Scandi treats from Sweden, Norway, Denmark and Finland – from meatballs and dill-cured salmon to cinnamon rolls and lingonberry jam. Plus, you can sample the daily smorgasbord in their café.

Scandinavian food is simple, natural and honest, made with the staple produce of the land – they call it *husmanskost* (farmer's fare). It's also delicious… except, perhaps, the fermented herring, which is definitely an acquired taste.

Scandinavian Kitchen, 61 Great Titchfield St, W1W 7PP (020-7580 7161; scandikitchen.co.uk; Oxford Circus tube; Mon-Fri 8-7, Sat 10-6, Sun 10-4).

F. C. Soper
A legend among London fishmongers

Established in 1897, Soper supply south Londoners with an unparalleled range of fresh fish and seafood. They pride themselves on good old-fashioned customer service and top-quality stock, with most fish sourced from Cornwall, Devon and Norfolk, and bought direct from day boats before it even reaches the quayside. Line-caught fish, such as Cornish sea bass, is a speciality and the majority of produce is from sustainable fisheries.

The large open-plan shop boasts vibrant displays of fresh wet fish, with dedicated sections for shellfish and smoked fish, while the website features praise from top chef Angela Hartnett and food critic Jay Rayner.

F. C. Soper, 141 Evelina Rd, SE15 3HB (020-7639 9729; fcsoper.com; Nunhead rail; Tue-Fri 8.30-5.30, Sat 8-5.30, Sun 9-2).

The Spice Shop
The ultimate spice rack

The Spice Shop has been a fixture on the Notting Hill shopping scene since the '90s. It began life as a market stall on Portobello Road to supplement owner Birgit Erath's income while she was studying at university and moved into the shop in 1995, since when Birgit's fame as a spice trader has spread far and wide. Today it offers a range of more than 2,500 products and is the only one of its kind in the UK, frequented by famous chefs and TV cooks who draw upon Birgit's knowledge as a source of inspiration and recipe ideas.

As well as all the staples, the Spice Shop stocks an astounding variety of the more exotic and esoteric spices from lemon myrtle to medieval ginger. There are sections devoted to fresh herbs, chillies, paprika, flavoured salts and peppercorns, plus Birgit's own herb and spice mixes. You can also order online and have spices delivered anywhere in the world.

As well as running the shop, Birgit teaches at local bookshop Books for Cooks, advises major food corporations, and has even found time to co-author a book (*Barbecue*) about 'fire-powered' barbecue food.

The Spice Shop, 1 Blenheim Cres, W11 2EE (020-7221 4448; thespiceshop.co.uk; Ladbroke Grove tube; Tue-Sat 9.30-6, Sun 11-4).

Tavola

A taste of la dolce vita

Tavola is an outstanding Italian deli in west London – run by former top chef and television celebrity Alastair Little and his wife Sharon – which defines the zeitgeist of the London food culture. Out front there's a colourful display of fruit and veg such as artichokes, aubergines, fennel, lemons, peppers and plum tomatoes, while inside the shelves overflow with balsamic vinegar and virgin olive oil, jars of French fish soup, haricot beans, olives, risotto rice and Italian pearled spelt (*farro*), truffle paste, pasta in every shape and size, Valrhona chocolate and wonderful Italian breads.

The centre of the shop is given over to cooked foods: scarlet peppers stuffed with white mozzarella, squelchy braised fennel, chicken liver pâté and braised rabbit. Little also produces some of the best pasta sauces in London, such as pesto alla Genovese, a rabbit sauce for pappardelle

and a rich beef ragu. And to complete an authentically Italian table, there's a display of exquisitely painted Italian pottery, superior cookware and crisp linen napkins.

Tavola has no coffee or sandwich service, nowhere to sit, no website and no mail order service – it's simply an old-fashioned deli with fantastic food.

Tavola, 155 Westbourne Grove, W11 2RS (020-7229 0571; Notting Hill Gate tube; Mon-Fri 10-7.30, Sat 10-6).

Turkish Food Centre
A supermarket full of Turkish delights!

If you like Eastern Mediterranean food you'll love the Turkish Food Centre. The first outlet in Dalston opened in 1980 and there are now 14 stores across London, from Waltham Cross to Croydon. They're called supermarkets, but these foodie oases have little in common with Tesco or Waitrose. And while they major on food from Turkey, Greece and Cyprus, they also sell products from other Mediterranean countries plus Denmark, Holland and even Africa.

Every store has its own bakery, where traditional Turkish sourdough and flatbread and both savoury and sweet pastries (such as baklava), are baked hourly, seven days a week. All meat and poultry is purchased daily from selected suppliers to ensure the highest quality is maintained. The fruit and vegetable department is a riot of colour with a plethora of sunshine produce such as

okra, prickly pears, fresh figs and apricots, Swiss chard and herbs, while the deli counters stock mezze dishes and olives in huge vats.

The grocery section offers a full range of Turkish and European brands, including pulses, spices, nuts and snacks, plus Turkish delight, apple tea, rosewater and other traditional products. If you want to find fault, Turkish wine is an acquired taste, but the juices are delicious.

Turkish Food Centre, 89 Ridley Rd, E8 2NP (020-7254 6754; tfcsupermarkets.com; Dalston Kingsland rail; daily 8-10 or 9 in winter).

Verde & Company
Time warp tuck shop

This traditional grocery shop in Spitalfields is a 19th-century treasure trove stocked with 21st-century edible luxuries. The building is owned by writer Jeanette Winterson – who is keen to maintain the area's traditional Georgian atmosphere – while the old-fashioned grocery is the inspiration of chef-proprietor Harvey Cabaniss. The shop retains all the charm of yesteryear, enhanced with a lovely display of antique china, Staffordshire figures, toy theatres and 19th-century clocks, but sells food that's bang up to date with the latest foodie culture: fresh, natural and artisan. It's an up-market foodie Mecca with an emphasis on Italian food.

V&C is packed to the rafters with Harvey's favourite deli treats such as Belgian Pierre Marcolini chocolates, fresh pasta, homemade preserves, fine olive oils and balsamic vinegars. It also offers a selection of homemade cakes and pastries and a range of delicious salads and sandwiches, such as bresaola with sun-blush tomatoes; chorizo with Gorgonzola and sweet chilli; goat's cheese with grilled aubergine; and suckling pig with piquillo peppers. Food is available to take away (delivery available) and there are some seats for the lucky few.

Verde & Company, 40 Brushfield St, E1 6AG (020-7247 1924; verdeandco.co.uk; Shoreditch High St tube; Mon-Thu 9-5.30, Fri 9-6, Sat-Sun 10-6).

Bar Italia

2.
Cafés, Coffee Shops & Tearooms

'It is inhumane, in my opinion, to force people with a genuine medical need for coffee to wait in line behind people who apparently view it as some kind of recreational activity.'

(Dave Barry, American comedian)

Café culture revival

London's flourishing independent café and tearoom scene has enjoyed a renaissance in the last decade, which has done much to cement the city's newfound position as one of the world's leading foodie destinations. Residents and visitors can now enjoy artisan coffee from a plethora of independent roasteries, and specialist teas from around the world, including one of the city's favourite treats: traditional afternoon tea. And most cafés also serve delicious – often homemade – food.

> In London's new café society, it's goodbye cocktails and hello coffee/tea and cake!

Coffee sales have soared in recent years at big chains such as Costa Coffee and Starbucks, as have the number of outlets, but there's also been equally impressive growth among independent coffee shops. Britain's love affair with coffee has gone (quite literally) from strength to strength; not so many years ago it was difficult to find a London café serving anything but insipid filter coffee, but now fresh, bean-powered brews are everywhere, thanks in no small part to a legion of expat baristas from Down Under.

The British are famous for their love of a good cuppa (tea) – which, as every Brit knows, cures all ills – although nowadays it may be a delicate white, energising green, aromatic and complex Oolong, or a mysterious aged Puer, rather than builder's brew. The right tea has become a vital component of the foodie's brunch or the quintessentially English pastime of afternoon tea.

There's much more to London's café scene than food and drink; the staff, clientele, décor, location and atmosphere all play their part. This chapter celebrates some of the best cafés, coffee shops and tearooms in London, chosen for the excellence of their refreshments but also because each offers something special that makes it stand out from the crowd, be it a handsome building, a calming ambience or a lovely (often alfresco) space to retreat to.

Allpress Espresso

Beans meanz Allpress!

A popular artisan roastery café in buzzy Shoreditch, Allpress serves perfect coffee and tasty grub. It was established in New Zealand in 1986 by Kiwi Michael Allpress, who invests much time tracking down small farms, estates and co-ops that specialise in high-grade beans and are managed sustainably with high standards of agricultural practice.

In 2000, Allpress expanded into Australia, teaming up with Sydney chef Tony Papas to oversee the new café's homemade food. The London branch opened in 2010, when Papas brought over a skilled team of staff from Auckland and Sydney, since when it has greatly expanded awareness of how coffee should taste among both coffee drinkers and café owners, many of whom buy their coffee from Allpress. The food menu is simple – a selection of breakfast plates and sandwiches – but it's the coffee that takes centre stage.

The roaster can be seen in action during the week, while the freshly-roasted blends and single origin coffees can be purchased for home use. You can also attend a class on how to make the perfect espresso.

Allpress Espresso, 58 Redchurch St, E2 7DP (020-7749 1780; uk.allpressespresso.com; Shoreditch High St; Mon-Fri 8-5, Sat-Sun 9-5).

The Attendant
A café flushed with success

One of London's most unusual cafés, the Attendant occupies a former gentlemen's public convenience (loo), built around 1890 and mothballed in the '60s. After two years of planning and restoration, it opened in 2013 as a tiny café, reached via steps descending below a splendid wrought iron canopy. The attendant's office has been converted into a kitchen and the original porcelain urinals revamped into a coffee bench, with green seating to match the original Victorian floor tiles.

It isn't, however, just a novelty attraction; the Attendant was runner up as 'Best Coffee Shop in London 2013' (londonlifestyleawards.com) and serves great (Caravan) coffee, gourmet sandwiches, salads and delicious cakes.

The Attendant, 27A Foley St, W1W 6DY (020-7637 3794; colourtesting.co.uk/attendant; Goodge St tube; Mon-Fri 8-6, Sat 10-5).

Bar Italia
Soho's 24-hour coffee stop

Treat yourself to a coffee at Bar Italia, a family-run business founded in 1949 by Lou and Caterina Polledri and passed on through three generations; first to their son Nino, who took over the reins in the '70s, and then to his children – Antonio, Luigi and Veronica – who now run it alongside their Little Italy restaurant next door

A Soho institution, Bar Italia serves excellent, if pricey, Italian coffee and delicious pastries and cakes – and service is always with a smile. Open around the clock, an outside table is a great place for people watching on a sunny afternoon.

Bar Italia, 22 Frith St, W1D 4RP (020-7437 4520; baritaliasoho.co.uk; Tottenham Court Rd tube; daily 24 hrs).

Bea's of Bloomsbury
Enjoy afternoon tea with Bea

This old-fashioned sounding tearoom opened only in 2008 but soon established itself as one of London's best. Located in a former bank, Bea's is a cosy place with shabby-chic décor and an open-plan pastry kitchen, where you can watch the staff conjuring up brownies, cookies, cupcakes, loaf cakes, marshmallows, meringues, etc.

The Bloomsbury shop caters for Bea's three outlets (the others are in St Paul's and Farringdon – takeaway only). Most famous for its heavenly cakes and pastries, Bea's also serves up superb savoury food, including homemade frittatas, filled focaccia loaves, marinated chicken thighs, spinach and ricotta rolls and much more.

Although you can have lunch or just a snack, Bea's is famous for its afternoon tea, where you can tuck into freshly-baked scones with Cornish clotted cream and jam, fruity marshmallows, assorted brownies, mini savoury brioche buns and baguettes, all washed down with a selection of loose leaf teas from the Jing Tea Company – plus an optional glass of champagne. Note that bookings are necessary for full afternoon tea (weekdays 2.30-7, Sat-Sun 12-7). Gluten-free afternoon tea is available too.

Bea's of Bloomsbury, 44 Theobalds Rd, WC1X 8NW (020-7242 8330; beasofbloomsbury.com/pages/bloomsbury-1; Chancery Ln tube; Mon-Fri 7.30-7, Sat-Sun 12-7).

Blend
Tea, coffee and martinis!

Blend is a new kid on the block in Haringey, opened in 2013 and hailed as one of the best café/bars in north London. The relaxing space has a great atmosphere and stylish Scandinavian design, including lovely reclaimed parquet flooring.

Blend styles itself a café, wine and cocktail bar – serving martinis all day! – along with superb Climpson & Sons coffee, delicious homemade cakes and pastries (try the cherry Danish), and imaginative sandwiches. It's an excellent venue for brunch with a menu offering everything from granola to a veggie tomato curry. It mutates into a bistro in the evenings.

Blend, 587 Green Lanes, N8 0RG (020-8341 2939; localblend.co.uk; Turnpike Ln tube; Mon-Fri 9-5, Sat-Sun 10-5).

Books for Cooks
London's tastiest bookshop

Books for Cooks is a mecca for cooks, chefs, foodies, gourmets and anyone with more than a passing interest in food, being dedicated to cooking, cuisine and food. Founded in 1983, BFC stocks over 8,000 tasty titles, but it's the shop's tiny café at the rear of the store that merits its place in this book.

It's here that the books' recipes are tested by co-owner Eric Treuillé and his staff, the results of which are sold in the charming inexpensive café. There's a no-choice lunch – until it comes to pudding, when there's an array of delicious cakes – but the standard of cooking is high and the coffee is great. Arrive early (before noon) for lunch.

Books for Cooks, 4 Blenheim Crescent, W11 1NN (020-7221 1992, booksforcooks.com, Ladbroke Grove tube, Tue-Sat 10-6).

The Brew House Café

A good brew plus art and stunning views

Tucked away in beautiful landscaped parkland on Hampstead Heath, Kenwood House (Grade II* listed) is one of the most magnificent estates in London, managed by English Heritage (see website for information). The estate's former brewery and service wing houses the Brew House Café, managed by the celebrated Company of Cooks. There's seating inside where there are flagstone floors and high ceilings, but this is primarily an alfresco venue, with umbrella-shaded tables spread across the delightful, south-facing walled garden. The tiered sheltered terrace is one of the prettiest spots in north London and the perfect place to chill out on a sunny afternoon.

The food is fairly basic but consistently good. The excellent full English breakfast is large enough to share, and at lunchtimes there's a choice of hot dishes such as lamb tagine, bangers and mash, veggie tarts, salads and soups. Drinks and tasty sandwiches, cakes (try the spicy carrot cake or the gooseberry and elderflower cheesecake) and pastries are served all day, while in summer there's a outside stand serving ice cream and Pimms.

The Brew House Café, Kenwood House, Hampstead Ln, NW3 7JR (020-8341 5384; www.english-heritage.org.uk/daysout/properties/kenwood/facilities and companyofcooks.com; Archway or Golders Grn tube; daily 9am to dusk).

Caffè Vergnano 1882
Coffee with a side order of history

Part of a small chain, Caffè Vergnano dishes up some of the best coffee available anywhere in London. It was named 'Coffee Shop of the Year' in 2011 by *What's On* magazine – which isn't surprising as it's Italian owned (by three generations of baristas).

It's worth coming here for the location alone, comfortable and stylish, with outside seating for when the weather behaves. Staple Inn was built in 1545 and was one of the few buildings to survive the Great Fire of London in 1666, only to be bomb damaged in 1944. The building was restored after the war but went into steady decline until being rescued by Luciano Vergnano to become the jewel of a coffee shop you see today.

When you want a real Italian coffee – whether it's an Americano, espresso, latte, macchiato or cappuccino – this is the place to come (but don't ask for a flat white!). Vergnano also serves great croissants (try the cheese, tomato and herb), cinnamon rolls, ricotta cheesecake, *torta della nonna* (custard pie with pine nuts and almonds) and much more. The perfect place to get your caffeine kick.

Caffè Vergnano 1882, Staple Inn, 337-338 High Holborn, WC1V 7PX (020-7242 7119; caffevergnano1882.co.uk; Chancery Ln tube; Mon-Fri 7-7, Sat 7.30-6, Sun 8.30-6).

Candella Tea Room

Homely tea parlour with a French accent

The Candella Tea Room offers over 30 high-quality loose leaf teas, plus artisan cakes and tortes, cream teas and freshly-made sandwiches. They also serve wholesome gourmet lunches, including ethnic specialties, homemade soups and delicious desserts.

The cosy, stylish and romantic interior with its French Baroque accents creates the atmosphere of an enchanted hideaway, with pastel frescoes on the walls and ceiling casting a warm glow. It's a lovely spot for a cuppa with someone special.

Candella Tea Room, 34 Kensington Church St, W8 4HA (020-7937 4161; candellatearoom.co.uk; High St Kensington tube; daily 9-7).

La Cuisine de Bar

La belle France comes to Chelsea

This simple café shares its address with the Chelsea branch of Poilâne boulangerie (see page 37) and is a French classic, serving a variety of sweet and savoury pastries in a bright and airy space filled with the intoxicating aromas of freshly-baked bread. Good-value bread baskets with various spreads are popular, as are the range of *tartines* – toasted open sandwiches – prepared to order in front of you.

For those with a sweet tooth there's a variety of Viennese patisserie, gingerbread, buttery punition (shortbread) cookies and more. *Délicieux!*

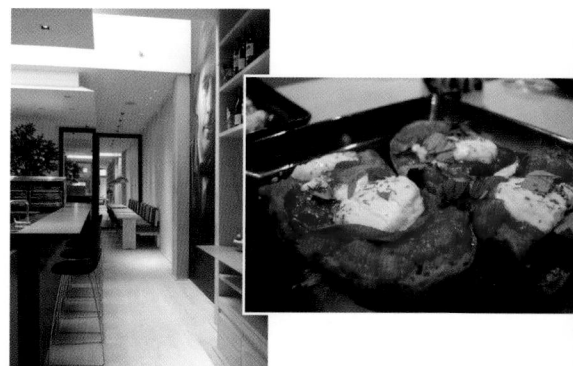

Cuisine de Bar, 39 Cadogan Gdns, SW3 2TB (020-3263 6019; cuisinedebar.fr/en; Sloane Sq tube; Mon-Fri 8-8.30, Sat-Sun 9-6.30).

Dose Espresso
Ethical coffee and a great BLT

Owned and operated by James Philips, Dose Espresso is a one-man artisan espresso bar, serving City folk with ethically sourced coffee (supplied by roasters Square Mile and sourced from farms practising biodiversity) using organic milk. Dose also make splendid sandwiches – including a terrific bacon, lettuce and tomato – fresh salads, warming porridge and great toast with a variety of toppings such as homemade pesto, Vegemite or sliced tomato/avocado.

Sweet treats are supplied by Arianna of Bittersweet Bakers, while bread and French pastries are sourced from the Seven Seeded Bakery and made with organic flour.

Dose Espresso, 70 Long Ln, EC1A 9EJ (020-7600 0382; dose-espresso.com; Barbican tube; Mon-Fri 7-5, Sat 9-4).

The Espresso Room
A shrine to espresso

The tiny hole-in-the-wall Espresso Room in Bloomsbury is a shrine to espresso, made with skill using beans from Square Mile. Established in 2009, it serves some of the best speciality coffees in London (including a great flat white) in a friendly and relaxed neighbourhood environment.

Despite its bijou size and small menu – just soup of the day, a few sandwiches and some baked goods – the Espresso Room has a loyal following. If the weather's fine, try to grab one of the small tables outside.

The Espresso Room, 31-35 Great Ormond St, WC1N 3HZ (07760-714883; theespressoroom. com; Russell Sq tube; Mon-Fri 7.30-5).

Federation Coffee

The ultimate neighbourhood coffee shop

Buzzing Brixton Market is one of London's best eating and drinking destinations (and a great place to shop for food – see page 173). It's also the home of Federation Coffee, Antipodean owned and operated, and one of the best coffee shops in south London. Federation roast their own coffee, using an ever-changing blend of coffees from Brazil, Ethiopia, El Salvador and Sumatra, and make all their own fresh food. The vast menu includes over 100 sweet and savoury options – changing daily – all made in their own kitchen (unit 46 in the market). Try the super flat white or mocha accompanied by a cherry coconut slice or cheesecake.

People flock to this attractive café which is a great place to catch up on your email or surf the web, chat with friends or simply hang out and watch the characters who frequent Brixton Village go by. There are only around a dozen tables, so you may have to share, but the locals are a friendly bunch. Great service, relaxed neighbourhood atmosphere, and excellent coffee and food in one of London's most cosmopolitan areas.

Federation Coffee, Unit 77-78, Brixton Village Mkt, Coldharbour Ln, SW9 8PS (federationcoffee. com; Brixton tube; Mon-Fri 8-5, Sat 9-6, Sun 9-5).

Fernandez & Wells

A taste of Spain at Somerset House

Fernandez & Wells started life in 2007 in Soho's Lexington Street and now boasts six outlets (see website), of which this is the largest and grandest. It occupies three impressive rooms in the east wing of 18th-century Somerset House, where Jorge Fernandez and Rick Wells have transported their signature Spanish 'street-style' café into a lovely light space with views over the fountain courtyard. The décor incorporates York stone, wood and metal; oversized geometric paintings by British artist David Tremlett decorate the walls, while a long, cool bar bisects the main café area.

Spain dominates the F&W menu, which revolves around coffee, cured meats, cheese and wine, and encompasses breakfast, lunch or dinner. There's a great

choice of tasty tapas, inventive sandwiches (try the aubergine, goat's cheese and pesto in a brioche bun) and splendid soups such as classic gazpacho. The 'ham room', where plump hams hang from the wall, dispenses slices of lomito ibérico and jamón de lampiño – ham to die for! There's also a range of enticing house-made cakes and pastries, including old-fashioned Eccles cakes.

Great service and lip-smacking, value-for-money food. *Excelente*!

Fernandez & Wells, Somerset House, Strand, WC2R 1LA (020-7420 9408; fernandezandwells. com; Temple tube; Mon-Fri 8-10, Sat 10-10, Sun 10-8).

Flat White

Great coffee from Down Under

Flat White (established in 2005) was one of the trailblazers that introduced Antipodean coffee culture to deprived Londoners. The flat white coffee – stronger, smaller and less milky than a latte, less froth than a cappuccino – is one of the best things to come out of Oz since Kylie. It's made using a Square Mile single origin blend that changes every few months (you can buy some to take home).

The food menu is small (but tasty) and the décor and seating are basic – try to bag a seat outside – but the coffee's great.

Flat White, 17 Berwick St, W1F 0PT (020-7734 0370; flatwhitecafe.com; Oxford Circus/Tottenham Ct Rd tube; Mon-Fri 8-7, Sat-Sun 9-6).

Fleet River Bakery

Baking up a storm

Part of London's new wave of excellent, innovative cafés, the Fleet River Bakery occupies a stylish corner building with high arched windows and a few outside tables. Inside it's welcoming and homely, with a large seating area decorated with reclaimed wood and vintage furniture (there's free wifi too).

This licensed café is a beacon of hospitality, offering superb coffee (from the Monmouth Coffee Company), iced lattes and a range of fancy teas, plus tasty sandwiches and baked treats – try the croissants stuffed with tomato and brie – and scrumptious cakes. Thursday and Friday are wine and cheese nights.

Fleet River Bakery, 71 Lincolns Inn Fields, WC2A 3JF (020-7691 1457; fleetriverbakery.com; Holborn tube; Mon-Wed 7-7, Thu-Fri 7-9, Sat 8.30-6, Sun 8.30-4).

Foxcroft & Ginger

You'll be nuts about (Foxcroft &) Ginger

Foxcroft & Ginger takes its name from its owners (Quintin Foxcroft and his flame-haired wife Georgina), who opened shop in 2010 after years of running other people's businesses. It's an all-day grazing spot, where you can enjoy a coffee and sandwich or a pizza with a glass of wine. Among the things that make F&G stand out are the spacious downstairs seating area with comfortable sofas (plus good wifi) and its relaxed ambience.

In addition to superb Monmouth coffee and fresh leaf tea (from Chash Tea), F&G have a passion for bread, which is baked on the premises daily. It's made with a sourdough base and includes rye, ciabatta, focaccia or 'plain' sourdough (you can buy a loaf to take home), as well as providing the base for some seriously good pizzas. F&G also make their own croissants and muffins, and a range of enticing cakes and pastries.

Great British food with an original twist made from locally-sourced ingredients – the only thing it's bad for is your waistline! There's a second branch in Whitechapel.

Foxcroft & Ginger, 3 Berwick St, W1F 0DR (020-3602 3371; foxcroftandginger.co.uk; Piccadilly Circus tube; Mon 8-7, Tue-Fri 8-10, Sat 9-10, Sun 9-7).

FreeState Coffee
A lovely spot to enjoy great coffee

Now you have even more reason to visit delightful Sicilian Avenue in Bloomsbury, as FreeState Coffee is just a few steps away from this elegant arcade. The café occupies a spacious spot with huge picture windows and an eclectic assortment of tables and pews.

The folks at FreeState use Fairtrade coffee from Union, who source their beans from around the globe; the house espresso is dark-roasted foundation blend (a mixture of Guatemalan, Indonesian and Indian beans) and there's also a 'guest espresso'. If you're hungry, there's a good selection of sandwiches, pastries, croissants, cakes, salads and quiches.

FreeState Coffee, 23 Southampton Row, WC1B 5HA (020-7998 1017; freestatecoffee.co.uk; Holborn tube; Mon-Fri 7-7, Sat-Sun 9-6).

The Gallery Café
Great food in a good cause

The Gallery Café is a tranquil hangout housed in a Georgian house in Bethnal Green (near the Museum of Childhood), part of the St Margaret's House Settlement that supports local charities (see website). The café serves large portions of homemade vegan/vegetarian food, including breakfasts, sandwiches, pizza and pasta, with most supplies sourced locally. There are also mouth-watering cakes – including cupcakes, muffins and lemon drizzle cake – plus great coffee and a range of teas.

As the name suggests, there are regular art exhibitions too.

The Gallery Café, St Margaret's House Settlement, 21 Old Ford Rd, E2 9PL (020-8980 2092; stmargaretshouse.org.uk/gallery-cafe/gallery-cafe; Bethnal Grn tube; Mon-Fri 8-9, Sat-Sun 9-9).

The Garden Café
A garden of edible delights

The Garden Café at the Garden Museum is one London's loveliest alfresco spaces, located on the Thames next to Lambeth Palace, almost directly opposite the Houses of Parliament. Managed by talented chef Sorrel Ferguson, the café is the perfect retreat from the bustling outside world, where you can relax in the 17th-century-inspired knot garden while enjoying outstanding coffee and cake (baked fresh that morning) or a delicious seasonal lunch.

In 2012 the Garden Café was ranked sixth by *Gourmet* magazine in its survey of the 'world's top 10 museum restaurants', along with the likes of the Michelin-starred Nerua at the Guggenheim Bilbao and restaurants at The Hermitage in St Petersburg and Musée d'Orsay in Paris.

This highly-rated oasis specialises in vegetarian food, including soups, salads, tarts and splendid cakes – try the scrummy orange, almond and rosemary cake. Lunch is served from noon to 3pm, while on Sundays the focus is on 'all-day' afternoon tea. The vegetarian (and often vegan) lunch menu changes daily depending on what's in season or available from the museum's vegetable patch.

The Garden Café, Garden Museum, 5 Lambeth Palace Rd, SE1 7LB (020-7401 8865; gardenmuseum.org.uk/page/café; Lambeth N tube or Waterloo tube/rail; Sun-Fri 10.30-4.30, Sat 10.30-4).

Ginger & White

Get your coffee fix in Hampstead

Since opening in Hampstead in 2009, Ginger & White has become **the** place locals go to for great coffee; it's so successful that there's now a second outlet in Belsize Park.

G&W is owned by food stylist Tonia George and restaurant managers Nick and Emma Scott, who were perplexed by the lack of decent coffee shops in Hampstead. They also wanted somewhere that celebrated artisan food from British producers, so in addition to a great flat white (beans from Square Mile roasters) you can fill up on breakfast classics (served all day), cakes, pastries, sandwiches and salads. Weekend brunches offer exciting concoctions such as roasted chorizo, avocado, lime and rocket on toasted ciabatta; smoked mackerel, fennel and Jersey Royal salad; and pear and polenta cake.

Inside there's a communal table surrounded by cool, vintage-inspired décor, but the pavement tables are the most highly prized and great for people watching. It's a child-friendly venue, so if you're allergic to kids you might want to check out the decibels first.

Friendly atmosphere, great coffee, excellent food…what's not to like? You can even take it home with you c/o *The Ginger & White Cookbook*.

Ginger & White, 4a-5a Perrin's Ct, NW3 1QS (020-7431 9098; gingerandwhite.com; Hampstead tube; Mon-Fri 7.30-5.30, Sat-Sun 8.30-5.30).

J+A Café
Comfort food like Mum used to make

Tucked away in a courtyard at the rear of a maze-like East London yard, the J+A Café occupies the ground floor of an old diamond-cutting factory. Simple and unpretentious, the large room has a warm and rustic feel with lots of natural light and exposed brickwork. Its centrepiece is a large refectory table, with smaller tables dotted around, while on sunny days you can sit in the peaceful courtyard.

Run by sisters Johanna and Aoife (J+A) Ledwidge, the licensed café majors in wholesome home cooking and baking and reflects their Irish roots. From artisan breads to organic meats, all produce is meticulously sourced from local suppliers where possible. Lunch choices include sandwiches, pies, quiches and salads – specials such as soups, pies and stews are announced on a large blackboard – while bar snacks focus on simple small plates such as ham potato cakes or organic smoked salmon and dressed crab with soda bread. Not forgetting scrumptious cakes such as chocolate Guinness cake and Irish apple.

On Wednesday to Friday evenings, J+A Café morphs into a romantic bar, with candles on the tables and great cocktails. Good value, friendly and a great atmosphere.

J+A Café, 4 Sutton Ln, EC1M 5PU (020-7490 2992; jandacafe.com; Barbican tube; Mon-Fri 8-6, Sat-Sun 9-5, Wed-Fri bar open to 11pm).

Kaffeine
Bonzer brews and terrific tucker

Another of the excellent Antipodean coffee shops that have sprouted throughout London (are there any baristas left Down Under?), Kaffeine opened in 2009 and has since been mopping up awards. Like most of London's independent cafés, great coffee (from Square Mile) is a given, but Kaffeine is also noted for its excellent food, which includes tasty salads, sandwiches (try the yummy souk lamb) and muffins. It does a nice line in cakes and pastries such as chocolate brownies, Portuguese custard tarts and ANZAC biscuits (naturally!).

Friendly, buzzy and creative, Kaffeine also runs coffee courses for budding amateur baristas.

Kaffeine, 66 Great Titchfield St, W1W 7QJ (020-7580 6755; kaffeine.co.uk; Great Portland St tube; Mon-Fri 7.30- 6, Sat 8.30-6, Sun 9-5).

Konditor & Cook
Cakes that look too good to eat!

One of London's leading cake shops, Konditor (German for 'pastry chef') & Cook was founded by German Gerhard Jenne in 1993 and now has five outlets, in Borough Market, Chancery Lane, Spitalfields Market, the Gherkin and Waterloo (listed here). There are also two cake schools (020-7633 3333) where you can learn how to bake and decorate your own celebration cakes.

K&C's creations include its legendary chocolate and vanilla curly whirly cake, gold-star winning whiskey bomb, lemon chiffon and magic cakes (fondant fancies for the 21st century) – some of which are wheat and/or dairy free. Not forgetting delicious hot food and a cold buffet.

Konditor & Cook, 22 Cornwall Rd, SE1 8TW (0844-854 9367; konditorandcook.com; Waterloo tube/rail; Mon-Fri 7.30-7, Sat 8.30-6, Sun 11-5).

Lantana Café
A ray of Aussie sunshine

The highly rated, award-winning Lantana (an Australian flowering plant) opened in Fitzrovia in 2008, since when it has gone from strength to strength and spawned two other outlets: Ruby Dock (Camden) and Salvation Jane (see page 75).

Lantana not only makes delicious coffee but is famous for its big Aussie-style breakfasts, lunches and weekend all-day brunches. There's an excellent selection of snacks and cakes (including the muffin-like raspberry friands and delicious cherry cake) and a cosy atmosphere – wooden tables, mismatched chairs and art on the white walls – with indoor and outside seating (although not enough). It's also licensed!

Lantana Café, 13 Charlotte Pl, W1T 1SN (020-7637 3347; lantanacafe.co.uk; Goodge St tube; Mon-Fri 8-6, Sat-Sun 9-5).

Lisboa Patisserie
Worth a visit just for the delicious Portuguese custard tarts

Lisboa Patisserie is a rare gem in London, an authentic Portuguese café (not an Aussie or Kiwi in sight!) that makes scrumptious cakes and pastries. This small, homely café is a treasure, serving strong espresso (*bica*) and latte (*galão*) and a wide range of tempting treats, not least their celebrated custard tarts (*pastéis de nata*). People travel far and wide for these delights, with their rich egg custard filling in a crisp puff pastry case.

You may have to queue and share a table but the experience is worth it. And it's great value too.

Lisboa Patisserie, 57 Golborne Rd, W10 5NR (020-8968 5242; Ladbroke Grove or Westbourne Pk tube; Mon-Sat 7-7.30, Sun 7-7).

Look Mum No Hands!
They also serve pedestrians...

The only place in London where you can have coffee and cake while getting your bike serviced, Look Mum No Hands! is a café/bar, repair shop and events space catering to the cool new breed of London cyclist. The café occupies a vast space with plenty of tables, excellent coffee (Square Mile) and filling food – you can even get a beer or a glass of wine.

A cyclist's Mecca, it shows cycle sports (Tour de France) on a big projector screen and there's a bike workshop downstairs – they even offer bicycle maintenance courses.

Look Mum No Hands!, 49 Old St, EC1V 9HX (020-7253 1025; lookmumnohands.com; Barbican or Old St tube/rail; Mon-Fri 7.30-11, Sat 9-11, Sun 9.30-10).

Maison Bertaux
The oldest patisserie in town

Treat yourself to a scrumptious cake at charming Maison Bertaux, an eccentric Soho landmark established in 1871. London's oldest patisserie and still one of the best, it has a lovely old-fashioned vibe, unpretentious and relaxed, with a stellar reputation for its cakes, croissants and pastries.

Maison Bertaux is endearingly quirky, a tiny room with half a dozen mismatched tables, an old piano and an eccentric accordion-playing owner. Weather permitting, most habitués prefer to cram onto the pavement tables outside. A Soho institution.

Maison Bertaux, 28 Greek St, W1D 5DQ (020-7437 6007; maisonbertaux.com; Leicester Sq tube; Mon-Sat 9-10.30, Sun 9-8).

Monmouth Coffee

Trailblazer roaster and artisan café

One of the pioneers of the new wave of coffee shops and roasters that have been brewing up a storm in London, Monmouth opened their first roast-and-retail outlet in Covent Garden's Monmouth Street (hence the name) in 1978. Roasting is now done in Maltby Street (Bermondsey), from where they supply coffee shops throughout the city, and they also have an outlet in Borough Market.

Monmouth's beans come from single farms, estates and cooperatives, with buyers travelling the world seeking out interesting varietals. They are equally fussy about their other ingredients, such as organic Jersey whole milk from Jeff Bowles in Somerset and organic whole cane sugar imported from Assukkar in Costa Rica.

Monmouth's cult shop in Covent Garden is a simple affair by today's standards, with snug tables in the back and a few benches outside. There's a tempting array of cakes and pastries – including lovely croissants and pain au chocolat – plus filled rolls and other goodies, but coffee is top dog here. You can buy coffee – whole beans or ground to your specification – in all three shops (or order by phone).

Monmouth Coffee, 27 Monmouth St, WC2H 9EU (020-7232 3010; monmouthcoffee.co.uk; Covent Gdn tube; Mon-Sat 8-6.30).

Monocle Café
Japanese breakfast anyone?

This buzzy, striking Marylebone café (think Swedish sauna meets sushi bar) opened in 2013 and is a spin-off from *Monocle* magazine, the showcase of design consultant and publisher Tyler Brûlé (founder of *Wallpaper*).

As well as tasty, full-flavour Allpress coffee, there are Swedish pastries (from Fabrique bakery in Haggerston) and scrummy cakes from Lanka, a local Japanese-run patisserie that fuses French baking with Japanese flavours such as green tea. There's also an eclectic brunch/lunch menu, which includes Japanese and German breakfasts, taco rice, chicken curry, Danish hotdog, shrimp *katsu* sandwich, *yakisoba* noodles and much more.

Monocle Café, 18 Chiltern St, W1U 7QA (020-7135 2040; cafe.monocle.com; Baker St tube; Mon-Fri 7-7, Sat 9-6, Sun 10-6).

The Nordic Bakery
Food for Vikings (and coffee lovers)

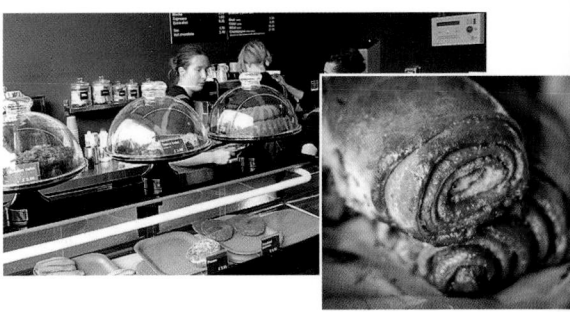

Opened in 2007 by Finn Jali Wahlsten, this delightful Scandinavian-style café is a peaceful retreat; spacious and airy, minimalist but stylish, with a combination of wood-lined and deep blue walls.

All the food is based on genuine Nordic recipes and ingredients and includes the house favourite cinnamon buns (and many other varieties), plus delicious open sandwiches on rye bread topped with prawns, gravadlax, pickled herring, hard-boiled egg and lingonberries. Cakes are scrumptious and the coffee is good and strong, but if you want something different to drink try the blueberry cordial.

Nordic Bakery, 14A Golden Sq, W1F 9JG (020-3230 1077; nordicbakery.com; Piccadilly Circus tube; Mon-Fri 8-8, Sat 9-7, Sun 10-7).

Notes Music & Coffee
Coffee that hits the right note

Arelatively new kid on the block, Notes takes its coffee very seriously – it has had its own roastery since 2013 – and there's a dedicated brew bar showcasing a rotating menu of filter coffees. And, as the name suggests, it's also an outlet for good music, with CDs and DVDs on sale.

Notes serves great artisan food, including cakes and pastries, a range of salads, sandwiches, soups and tarts at lunchtimes, and cheese and meat boards and seasonal plates in the evenings – all washed down with reasonably-priced wines.

There are other outlets in Covent Garden and Moorgate.

Notes Music & Coffee, 31 St Martin's Ln, WC2N 4ER (020-7240 0424; notes-uk.co.uk; Charing Cross tube/rail; Mon-Wed Fri 7.30-9, Thu-Fri 7.30-10, Sat 9-10, Sun 10-6).

Nude Espresso
Coffee as nature intended

This cool café on Soho Square is the second offering from Kiwi-owned Nude Espresso, whose Brick Lane outlet is the stuff of legend – the Nude team won Independent Café of the Year UK in 2010 and 2013 (awarded by the Café Society). The Soho outlet is sleek and modern, with a plush mezzanine level and outside tables on sunny days. As well as brilliant brews, Nude sells a wide range of delicious food: fresh paninis, tasty sandwiches and creative salads, plus tempting cakes and pastries.

If you want to unleash your inner barista, they host coffee cupping (tasting) and training sessions at their East End roastery.

Nude Espresso, 19 Soho Sq, W1D 3QN (07712-899336, nudeespresso.com/cafes/soho-square; Tottenham Court Rd tube; Mon-Fri 7.30-5.30).

Number 67

A feast for your eyes and your stomach

The South London Gallery is almost as famous for its independent café/restaurant as it is for its art. Occupying a huge, bright and airy space, No. 67 has two main dining areas, plus a garden with additional seating, where you can enjoy breakfast and lunch during the week and all-day brunch at weekends. In the evening, it's transformed into a relaxed, bistro-style restaurant. The robust seasonal menu includes small plates and mezze dishes, as well as daily specials, sandwiches, and delicious coffee and cakes.

A treasure – and the gallery's well worth visiting too!

No. 67, South London Gallery, 67 Peckham Rd, SE5 8UH (020-7252 7649; number67.co.uk; Peckham Rye rail; Tue 8-6.30, Wed-Fri 8-11, Sat 10-11, Sun 10-6.30).

Orange Pekoe

A temple to fine tea

Established in 2006, Orange Pekoe is a temple to tea, offering loose leaf teas in their purest form. The owners travel far and wide to find the finest handpicked leaves – the tearoom's name is taken from a top-quality grade of tea – with some 60 loose leaf and flower teas on offer. You can sip them with breakfast, lunch or an irresistible afternoon tea, or buy some to take home – they're sold in beautiful tea caddies or pouches.

There's a tea sommelier on hand to advise you and you're encouraged to open the caddies to sample the aromas and admire the leaves.

Orange Pekoe, 3 White Hart Ln, SW13 0PX (020-8876 6070; orangepekoeteas.com; Barnes Br rail; Mon-Fri 7.30-5, Sat-Sun 9-5).

Ottolenghi
London's legendary café-deli

Yotam Ottolenghi's acclaimed outlet in Islington (opposite the Almeida Theatre) showcases his trademark Middle Eastern dishes: a heavenly marriage of explosive Mediterranean and Asian flavours in a palette of vibrant colours. It's the deli chain's only 'proper' café/restaurant – unless you count NOPI (see page 224) – seating some 50 diners around communal tables in a cool, sophisticated environment.

Ottolenghi is open for breakfast, lunch and dinner, although bookings are only accepted for dinner, so if you fancy tucking into the legendary weekend brunch you'll need to arrive early. It's also a great choice for vegetarians.

Ottolenghi, 287 Upper St, N1 2TZ (020-7288 1454; ottolenghi.co.uk; Highbury & Islington tube; Mon-Sat 8-10.30, Sun 9-7).

Ozone
A breath of fresh Kiwi air in East London

Ozone is a dedicated café and roastery with its origins in New Plymouth in New Zealand, spreading its wings to Shoreditch in 2012. Nowadays their superb, freshly-roasted coffee doesn't have to travel far; like the delicious sweet and savoury treats that accompany it, it's roasted and ground on-site.

The relaxed Antipodean-style café – with its exposed brickwork, weathered tables, comfortable booth seating and huge windows – is a lovely spot to hang out and enjoy some great coffee and homemade food.

Ozone Café & Roastery, 11 Leonard St, EC2A 4AQ (020-7490 1039; ozonecoffee.co.uk; Old St tube; Mon-Fri 7.30-5, Sat-Sun 9-4).

Pavilion Café

Big breakfasts in London's first public park

Victoria Park – known colloquially as 'Vicky Park' – was London's first public park when it opened in 1845, and is still much loved by East End folk. Its old pavilion is now home to the Pavilion Café, an idyllic spot widely acknowledged as one of London's best park cafés. It occupies a lovely domed glass building overlooking the lake, although in summer all the seating is outdoors on the terrace.

This is a hearty (all-day) big breakfast destination, offering both workaday and classic dishes, from beans on toast to eggs Florentine, Benedict and Royale, in huge portions. The inexpensive organic menu is simple and short, but owners Rob Green and Brett Redman use top-quality British

ingredients such as rare-breed meat (from Ginger Pig), Cotswold eggs and fine Ceylon tea, to ensure it stands out from the crowd.

Lunch consists of fancy sandwiches (such as 'nduja and pecorino) plus the odd burger and salad. There's also excellent coffee (Monmouth) and tempting homemade cakes – try the chocolate and marmalade.

Pavilion Café, Victoria Pk, Crown Gate West, Grove Rd, E9 7DE (020-8980 0030; the-pavilion-cafe.com; Bethnal Gn or Mile End tube; daily 8.30-4).

Prufrock Coffee
Seriously good coffee

Prufrock's flagship café on buzzy Leather Lane is a shrine to coffee, founded by the legendary Gwilym Davies, 2009 UK and World Barista Champion (and no, he isn't from Down Under – he's a Yorkshireman). Davies is at the forefront of coffee's 'third wave' – a movement to raise awareness of coffee as a hand-made product, focusing as much on provenance as wine-making does. Prufrock also have their own in-house bakery – try the banana bread or cheesecake for a real treat – and sell coffee and coffee-making equipment.

This bright and bustling café is also home to the London Barista Resource and Training Centre (see page 89).

Prufrock Coffee, 23-25 Leather Ln, EC1N 7TE (020-7242 0467; prufrockcoffee.com; Farringdon tube; Mon-Fri 8-6, Sat-Sun 10-5).

Queen's Wood Café
If you go down to the woods today...

This non-profit community café is tucked away amidst 52 acres of ancient woodland in Haringey, and offers delicious organic, seasonal food (with lots of vegetarian options) in a child- and dog-friendly environment. Queen's Wood is a haven of peace and serenity from the hustle and bustle of the city, where you can chill out and enjoy a beer or a glass of wine with your meal, while the kids play on the Jungle Walkway.

You can even learn to play Himalayan singing bowls – how many other cafés offer that? Very reasonable prices too.

Queen's Wood Café, Queens Lodge, 42 Muswell Hill Rd, N10 3JP (020-8444 2604; queenswoodcafe.co.uk; Highgate tube; Mon-Fri 10-4/5, Sat-Sun 9-5/6).

Riding House Café

Come for morning coffee, stay all day!

The Riding House Café is a Jack of all trades, a café/restaurant/bar that styles itself as a modern all-day brasserie, offering breakfast, lunch, dinner, weekend brunch, Sunday roast – and everything in between. There's also a separate bar with comprehensive cocktail and wine lists. You can sit at individual settings or at the grand communal refectory table, and there's a secluded dining room and lounge too – not forgetting the bar.

Food includes full-sized brasserie meals, tapas-like sharing plates and bar snacks – or you can just have a coffee and cake or a cocktail. Fabulous.

Riding House Café, 43-51 Great Titchfield St, W1W 7PQ (020-7927 0840; ridinghousecafe. co.uk; Oxford Circus tube; Mon-Fri 7.30-11, Sat 9-11, Sun 9-10.30).

Rose Bakery

A rose by any other name...

Rose Bakery isn't a bakery but rather a classy café on the top floor of the cult designer label store, Dover Street Market. It's owned by Rose Carrarini – founder of the Villandry café-restaurant chain – who launched Rose Bakery as an English teashop in Paris and brought it to London in 2007.

The popular concession at DSM specialises in delicious salads, soups, quiches, tarts and desserts, as well as the Bakery's famous cakes and pastries. You'll have to queue at peak times and may need to sit at the long communal table, but it's worth it.

Rose Bakery, Dover Street Market, 17-18 Dover St, W1S 4LT (020-7518 0687; london. doverstreetmarket.com/dsmpaper/rose_bakery. html; Green Pk tube; Mon-Sat 11-5, Sun 12-4).

St David Coffee House
Like having coffee with old friends

This charming, wisteria-clad café in Forest Hill is more like an eccentric aunt's front room than a coffee house; the walls are lined with well-thumbed books (the café runs a book exchange) and work by local artists. The décor may be slightly kitsch but the folk who run St David are serious about their coffee (Square Mile), tea and delicious food – much of it homemade or sourced from artisan producers.

There's a large communal table by the open window for sociable sipping or grab one of the small pavement tables on a sunny day. A local treasure.

St David Coffee House, 5 David's Rd, SE23 3EP (020-8291 6646; stdavidcoffeehouse.co.uk; Forest Hill rail; Tue-Fri 8-5, Sat 9-6, Sun 10-4).

Salt WC2
Salt that is (very) good for you!

Yet another super café in Covent Garden (where you're spoilt for choice), Salt caters equally to coffee and tea lovers. Styling itself an 'espresso, lunch and tea bar', Salt serves excellent Square Mile coffee and award-winning loose-leaf teas from Waterloo Tea in Cardiff, plus delicious juices and tasty food.

The creative menu is based on fresh seasonal produce and changes weekly, plus daily specials; dishes may include organic porridge with date syrup, chickpea and chorizo stew, rare beef with truffle cream baguettes and raspberry almond tart.

Salt WC2, 34 Great Queen St, WC2B 5AA (020-7430 0335; saltwc2.co.uk; Covent Gdn tube; Mon-Fri 7.30-7, Sat 10-7).

Salvation Jane
A taste of Oz in the City

From the same stable as the Lantana Café (see page 64) and named after another Australian plant, Salvation Jane is a highly-acclaimed, all-day café/restaurant in Shoreditch with a laid-back Aussie atmosphere, great coffee and delicious comfort food. It's noted for its superb brunch (try the bubble and squeak with pork and leek sausages or the house-cured salmon on organic dark rye toast with pickled beetroot), although the lunch and dinner menus are just as good.

There are also fantastic cakes and inventive cocktails.

Salvation Jane, Unit 2, 1 Oliver's Yd, 55 City Rd, EC1Y 1HQ (020-7253 5273; salvationjanecafe. co.uk; Old St tube/rail; Mon 7.30-4, Tue-Fri 7.30-11, Sat-Sun 9-4).

ScooterCaffe
Wheelie good fun

A honeypot for scooter lovers, this tiny former Vespa workshop near Waterloo station is chaotic and unpretentious – retaining much of its scooter-infused charm – with a small garden and great (often live) music.

Owned by Kiwi scooter fanatic Craig O'Dwyer, the old-school Italian ScooterCaffe caters for all and is great fun. The excellent coffee is from Londinium and there are also great cakes (though not much else), but this place is all about the vibe. A laid-back café during the day, it mutates into a cool, buzzy bar in the evenings.

ScooterCaffe, 32 Lower Marsh, SE1 7AE (020-7620 1421; Lambeth N/Waterloo tube/rail; Mon-Thu 8.30-11, Fri 8.30-1am, Sat 10-1am, Sun 10-11).

Shoreditch Grind

Espresso, cocktails and more

Established in 2011, Shoreditch Grind (there's also a Soho Grind) is an eclectic mix of espresso/cocktail bar and recording studio (for hire). They serve their own blend of (excellent) coffee along with a mouth-watering selection of croissants, pastries, muesli, granola pots, sandwiches, salads, rolls, toasties, salads and homemade soups. Everything is made fresh in-house daily, using organic ingredients where possible. By night (actually from 5pm), Shoreditch Grind becomes a cocktail bar, serving a range of seasonal and coffee-based cocktails, some great beers and a selection of (mostly) Aussie wines.

Shoreditch Grind, 213 Old St, EC1V 9NR (020-7490 7490; shoreditchgrind.com; Old St tube/rail; Mon-Thu 7-11, Fri 7-1am, Sat 8-1am, Sun 9-7).

Speakeasy Espresso & Brew Bar

No liquor but coffee worth shouting about

Split between the ground floor and basement, the Speakeasy off Carnaby Street has an espresso bar upstairs and a brew bar downstairs. Part of the Department of Coffee and Social Affairs (see page 88), in addition to great coffee there's a range of specialist teas and tempting cakes, pastries and sandwiches from some of London's best bakers (the chocolate cherry cake is heavenly).

A unique feature of the Speakeasy is its drop-in Barista Bar sessions on Thursdays (5-7pm), where you can get free tips on how to improve your coffee-making skills.

Speakeasy Espresso & Brew Bar, 3 Lowndes Ct, W1F 7HD (020-7434 3340; speakeasycoffee. co.uk; Oxford Circus tube; daily – see website for hours).

The Table Café
Definitely the top table

The Table Café is one of Southwark's hidden gems, serving great breakfasts, grills, salads and burgers to all-day diners, ethically sourced from sustainable stocks – it even gets its herbs and veggies from the allotments of the capital's homelessness charity, St Mungo's.

The Table consists of a large Scandi-style room with clean modern lines, floor-to-ceiling glass windows, communal oak tables, and stools at the counter. Its breakfast is good but the weekend brunch is legendary and tasty enough to lure foodies from nearby Borough Market. There are also good coffee and cakes, wine and beer. Deservedly hugely popular.

The Table Café, 83 Southwark St, SE1 0HX (020-7401 2760; thetablecafe.com; Southwark tube; Mon 7.30-4.30, Tue-Fri 7.30-10.30, Sat-Sun 8.30-4).

Tap Coffee
Great coffee on tap

Tap Coffee – formerly known as Tapped & Packed – have three outlets (the original in Fitzrovia, featured here, plus Tottenham Court Road and Wardour Street), identified by the outsize street number and old-fashioned grocer's bike outside.

Tap offer an impressive variety of coffees and different brewing methods, including siphon, pour-over, AeroPress and cafetière, as well as a range of beans sourced from top roasters such as Climpson & Sons, Has Bean, Square Mile and Union. Food is homemade but limited and includes cakes and pastries, accompanied by sandwiches and salads at lunchtime. Friendly, relaxing and satisfying...

Tap Coffee, 26 Rathbone Pl, W1T 1JD (020-7580 2163; tapcoffee.co.uk; Tottenham Court Rd tube; Mon-Fri 8-7, Sat 10-6).

The Tea Box
Just potty about tea

Jemma Swallow's charming Tea Box was established in 2007 as an antidote to the plethora of coffee shops that had sprung up in the Richmond area (although Monmouth coffee is also served). The cosy and homely 'colonial boutique-style' room, festooned with weighty chandeliers and furnished with an eclectic collection of antique-style furniture, offers comfortable seating and cosy corners.

The Tea Box is serious about its beverages and has one of London's largest collections of loose leaf tea; a whole wall is devoted to decorative tea canisters filled with prime pickings from the world's most famous tea plantations. There are over 60 teas and blends, including traditional favourites, fruity infusions such as blackcurrant and hibiscus, green tea scented with jasmine, tipsy tea cocktails, Moroccan mint tea, chai latte and the exotic sounding Ms Saigon.

High or afternoon tea (with an optional glass of champagne) comprises a choice of sandwiches, 12 varieties of scone and an abundance of scrumptious cakes (including gluten-free), not forgetting the wide choice of loose leaf teas. In the evenings there's regular entertainment such as jazz and swing sessions, comedy, storytelling, poetry and more.

The Tea Box, 7 Paradise Rd, TW9 1RX (020-8940 3521; theteabox.co.uk; Richmond rail/tube; Mon-Thu 10-6.30, Fri 10-10, Sat-Sun 9-6.30).

The Tea Rooms
Tea and a good book – perfect!

Step off the streets of Stoke Newington into this old-fashioned oasis where the antique mirrors and vintage fashion prints, bunting, china and bric-a-brac are all designed to transport you back to a gentler bygone age.

All the food at the Tea Rooms is hand-made, homemade and locally sourced – with the emphasis on quality and taste – by Isabelle Allfrey and Bethaney Rose, who between them have over 16 years' experience as pastry chefs at Claridge's Hotel, Michelin-starred restaurants and private Royal households. In addition to scrummy afternoon tea, the Tea Rooms also serves great hot lunches. There's a book club too.

The Tea Rooms, 153-155 Stoke Newington Church St, N16 0UH (020-7923 1870; thetearooms.org; Stoke Newington rail; Mon-Fri 11-6, Sat-Sun 11-6.30).

Timberyard
Office, playroom, coffee shop...

Timberyard occupies a huge 'versatile lifestyle space' over two floors in Old Street, with eclectic furnishings ('distressed' furniture and mismatched suitcases) and counters equipped with iPads for customers' use. Coffee is the main draw, made with Has Bean's signature Jabberwocky blend, although the specialist teas also score highly. There's always a good range of baked goods, sandwiches and salads, plus granola and porridge for breakfast – and it's licensed.

Timberyard bills itself as a place to work and play; there's good wifi, plenty of sockets, and no-one will complain if you linger over your drink. There's a second outlet in Covent Garden.

Timberyard, 61-67 Old St, EC1V 9HW (020-3217 2009; timberyardlondon.com; Old St/Barbican tube; Mon-Fri 8-8, Sat-Sun 10-6).

Tried & True
Breakfasts worth getting up for

Tried & True in Putney specialises in all-day breakfast/brunch. In 2014, it scooped an award for the UK's Most Innovative Breakfast (Big Breakfast Awards) for its BBQ pulled pork Benedict (homemade smoky barbecue sauce on jalapeño and cheddar cornbread, topped with a couple of poached eggs). And there's plenty more where that came from!

Owned by Kiwi Rob Kelly, Tried & True brings a touch of Auckland's relaxed breakfast/café culture to west London with amazing coffee (Square Mile) and delicious food, using the freshest ingredients to create original twists on tasty classics. God's own café!

Tried & True, 279 Upper Richmond Rd, SW15 6SP (020-8789 0410; triedandtruecafe.co.uk; Putney rail; Mon-Fri 8-4, Sat-Sun 8.30-4.30).

Troubadour Café
A treat in a time warp

Put your feet up at the legendary Troubadour Café – established in 1954 – a multi-faceted café/wine bar/art gallery and live music venue. The bohemian Troub hosted Jimi Hendrix, Joni Mitchell and Bob Dylan in the '60s and is still cluttered with paraphernalia from its hippie days. Nowadays, though, it's one of London's most charming and relaxing hangouts, with an idyllic garden.

It puts emphasis on the provenance of its 'fare' and its vast menu features great coffee, breakfasts and lunches, including fresh salads, soups and 'one pot wonders', plus Troub classics such as omelettes, burgers, steaks and daily specials.

Troubadour Café, 265 Old Brompton Rd, SW5 9JA (020-7370 1434; troubadour.co.uk; Earls Court tube; daily 9-midnight).

Urban Tea Rooms

Tearoom with a twist

A modern twist on the traditional tearoom, Urban serves gourmet tea, Fairtrade coffee and artisan grub by day, while in the evening the basement becomes a funky wine-cum-cocktail bar. Teas are supplied by the Rare Tea Company – including tea from the Tregothnan estate in Cornwall – and are served in individual teapots with bone china cups.

The food is British, organic where possible, and includes superior sandwiches and salads, artisan cakes, pastries and breads. In the evening the menu showcases British 'tapas'. With ample seating, friendly staff and quality refreshments, Urban Tea Rooms is a gem.

Urban Tea Rooms, 19 Kingly St, W1B 5PY (020-7434 3767; urbantearooms.com; Oxford Circus tube; Mon 7.30-6, Tue 7.30-10, Wed-Fri 7.30-11.30, Sat 10-11.30, Sun 12-7).

White Mulberries

A brew with a view

N estling in a quiet corner of St Katharine Docks – minutes from the Tower of London – is White Mulberries, a cosy, friendly café with panoramic views over the marina. It serves excellent Allpress Coffee, including drip-to-order filter coffee and AeroPress brews. Food-wise there are scrummy cakes and pastries, such as chocolate melts, walnut and cappuccino cake and caramel macarons, plus brilliant breakfasts and tasty savoury treats.

But the biggest draw is the view and on sunny days you can sit outside on the boardwalk and watch the world go by. Divine.

White Mulberries, D3 Ivory House, St Katharine Docks, E1W 1AT (07507-572600; whitemulberries. com; Tower Hill tube; Mon-Fri 7.30-5, Sat 8-5, Sun 9-5).

Workshop Coffee Co.
An all-round winner

This highly regarded coffee roasting company opened its first café on Clerkenwell Road in 2011 and has been scooping up awards ever since, including Best Independent Café at the 2012 Café Society Awards. It has evolved into a thriving destination, not only for coffee lovers but also for foodies, adding breakfast, lunch and dinner to its repertoire.

The décor is contemporary industrial chic, light and spacious with high ceilings, bare floorboards, and exposed brick and pipes, plus long wooden tables and an elegant bar. It's a cool all-day dining spot serving innovative breakfasts, such as toasted banana bread with date and orange jam, espresso mascarpone and hazelnuts – the *Observer Food Monthly* awarded it Best Veggie Breakfast. Meanwhile, the upstairs dining room serves a fusion menu of small and large plates that happily combine Asian and Mediterranean flavours with a dash of Middle Eastern magic.

The food may be scrumptious but it's the coffee that really matters here, and you can buy Workshop Coffee Co's excellent beans (sourced from Columbia and Ethiopia) online or sign up for a masterclass on how to brew brilliant coffee at home.

Workshop Coffee Co., 27 Clerkenwell Rd, EC1M 5RN (020-7253 5754; workshopcoffee.com; Farringdon tube; Mon 7.30-6, Tue-Fri 7.30-10, Sat-Sun 8-6).

The Wren

A heavenly place to sip a latte

The Wren boasts one of the city's best locations, inside St Nicholas Cole Abbey, a Grade I listed church with a history dating back to the 12th century. It was rebuilt by Sir Christopher Wren (hence the name) and again after the Second World War, and its soaring stone columns and lovely stained glass windows make a heavenly background to the delicious coffee (Workshop Coffee Co.) and tea (Brew Tea Co.).

The Wren also does delicious breakfasts – sourdough toast, granola, pastries, etc. – plus sandwiches, quiches, salads and soups – and all at bargain prices. There's an outside terrace too.

The Wren, St Nicholas Cole Abbey, 114 Queen Victoria St, EC4V 4BJ (thewrencoffee.com; Mansion House/St Paul's tube; Mon-Fri 7-5, Sat-Sun 12-4).

Yumchaa

A great cup of cha

From small beginnings as a stall in Portobello Market, swiftly followed by one in Camden Lock, Yumchaa ('drink tea' in Cantonese) now has four teashops (Camden Market – featured here – plus Camden Parkway, Soho and Tottenham Street). Although it's at the heart of a busy market, the intimate, rustic teashop is a haven from the surrounding clamour, with a covered balcony overlooking Regent's Canal and West Yard market.

The quaint shop serves a wide variety of leaf teas and delicious cakes, muffins, scones, sandwiches and salads. Yummy indeed!

Yumchaa, 91/92 Camden Lock Pl, Upper Walkway, West Yard, NW1 8AF (020-7209 9641; yumchaa.com; Camden Town tube; Mon-Fri 9-6, Sat-Sun 9-6.30).

3.
Coffee & Tea Specialists

'Life is a beautiful and endless journey in search of the perfect cup.'

(Barbara A. Daniels, coffee connoisseur)

Wake up and smell the coffee (and tea)!

There has been a upsurge of interest in artisan coffee and tea in recent years, with connoisseurs not only thirsting after the best quality beans and leaves, but also demanding to know their origin. The desire for knowledge about all aspects of these beverages has spawned a plethora of masterclasses for those seeking to brew the perfect espresso or cuppa cha.

Britain has traditionally been a tea-drinking nation, and although sales are falling we still get through over 150 million cups a day (over 50 billion per year), compared with 'only' 75 million cups of coffee. In the last decade or so, sales of green tea have soared, boosted in part by its perceived health properties, although black tea is just as good for you (both contain antioxidants which reduce the risk of heart disease).

There are an amazing over 1,500 varieties of tea and nowadays tea connoisseurs, foodies, chefs and sommeliers are exploring its myriad styles and food-pairing possibilities.

The British have increasingly been embracing café culture, both in the high street and at home, where many people choose to grind their own beans and make their own premium coffee (espresso, macchiato, latte and cappuccino) without the help of their local barista. The passion for good coffee has been fuelled by the wave of artisan roasters – pioneered by Monmouth Coffee (see page 66) and others – and independent coffee shops, where the focus is on authentic interiors, barista techniques and a wide range of crafted coffees.

This chapter highlights some of London's growing number of retailers, cafés, teashops and experts, all dedicated to teaching you everything you ever wanted to know (and more) about making and enjoying the perfect cup of coffee or tea.

Algerian Coffee Stores
Heaven in a coffee (or tea) cup

The name is a bit of a misnomer, as the Algerian Coffee Stores (plural, although there's only one!) specialises in coffee and tea. Established in 1887, this aromatic little shop still boasts many of its original features, including its rustic wooden shelving, counter and display case. Based in Soho, it stocks over 80 blends of coffee and 120 kinds of tea from around the world.

The huge range of coffees includes a large number of house blends alongside single-origin beans, organic and Fairtrade beans, as well as flavoured and spiced beans (such as Lebanese with cardamom) and rarities such as Indonesian Kopi Luwak, made from beans that have been eaten and passed undigested by civet cats!

Algerian Coffee Stores also sells drinking chocolate and cocoa, a range of confectionery (truffles, Turkish delight, etc.) and spices, plus domestic coffee machines, grinders, milk frothers, tea strainers and more. You can buy supplies online too.

It's a great-value place to drink coffee: an espresso is just £1 and a cappuccino or latte £1.20 (take-away or standing only), with an extra shot free.

Algerian Coffee Stores, 52 Old Compton St, W1D 4PB (020-7437 2480; algcoffee.co.uk; Leicester Sq tube; Mon-Wed 9-7, Thu-Fri 9-9, Sat 9-8).

Department of Coffee and Social Affairs

Coffee classes for civil servants?

The official-sounding Department of Coffee and Social Affairs is a relative newcomer on the London coffee scene. Launched in 2010, it has five 'specialist' coffee shops in London and is a leading retailer of coffee-making equipment.

However, here we are concentrating on its Coffee School, which offers two different classes: the 'Craft and Science of Espresso' teaches the key principles and techniques of espresso coffee making, while 'Brewing for Taste' offers practical instruction in various coffee-making methods, including pour over, syphon, French press and cold water dripper techniques. Classes take place at a number of its coffee shops (see website).

Department of Coffee and Social Affairs, 14-16 Leather Ln, EC1N 7SU (020-7278 4765; departmentofcoffee.com/home-barista/coffee-school; Chancery Ln/Farringdon tube).

Jane Pettigrew

Top tips from a Tea Master

Jane Pettigrew is a tea specialist, historian, writer and consultant with 30 years' experience of working in the world of tea. She has written some 15 books on the many and varied aspects of tea – its production, history and culture – and also writes for tea-related magazines and journals. Jane broadcasts on radio and TV, and acts as a consultant to tea companies, new tea businesses, and companies making teaware and tableware.

Jane hosts regular tea masterclasses and tea tastings at the Chesterfield Hotel in Charles Street, Mayfair, W1. See the website for details of upcoming classes, but book early as they fill up fast.

Jane Pettigrew (020-8672 4020; janepettigrew. com).

London Barista Resource & Training School

Join the BRAT pack

Fancy yourself as a budding barista? Learn how to brew the perfect cup of coffee at the London Barista Resource & Training School (BRAT), run by Prufrock Coffee (see page 72). Established in 2009 and famous for their ground-breaking brews, Prufrock have over 2,000ft^2 of space on two floors at their HQ and café on Leather Lane, where they host tastings, training sessions and social events designed to provide an overview of modern barista techniques.

The school was launched in 2011 to teach baristas, coffee shop owners and coffee addicts how to brew the perfect espresso. At Prufrock they teach you to approach coffee-making as a chef does cooking: weigh your ingredients, regulate temperatures, time your extractions, clean your equipment, and taste, taste, taste.

BRAT is an accredited Speciality Coffee Association of Europe (SCAE) course provider, offering half- and full-day classes (including some at weekends) structured to help amateurs attain certificated qualifications. Classes start at 10am and focus on a different aspect of coffee making each week; courses are rotated so that you can pick and choose or just work your way through each segment at your own pace.

London Barista Resource & Training School, 23-25 Leather Ln, EC1N 7TE (020-7242 0467; prufrockcoffee.com; Chancery Ln tube).

The London Coffee Festival
The greatest coffee show on earth

Although an annual event, the London Coffee Festival – held in the Old Truman Brewery in Spitalfields in East London – is an important event in the coffee world and well worthy of a mention. The festival celebrates London's bustling and vibrant coffee scene and features over 250 artisan coffee and gourmet food stalls, tastings and demonstrations from world-class baristas, interactive workshops, street food, coffee-based cocktails, live music, DJs, art exhibitions and much more.

The festival takes place at the end of April or the first week of May (see website for dates) and is the official launch event of the UK Coffee Week (ukcoffeeweek.com).

The London Coffee Festival, The Old Truman Brewery, 15 Hanbury St, E1 6QR (londoncoffeefestival.com, Shoreditch High St rail).

The London School of Coffee
How to make the perfect espresso

The London School of Coffee (LSC) was established in 2004 to offer training and education for coffee enthusiasts and professionals. The one-day 'basic barista course' is aimed at both home enthusiasts and those working in the coffee industry, where you learn how to make the perfect espresso and the drinks that accompany this base. LSC offers a range of barista courses that include a recognised City and Guilds qualification, roasting courses, cupping courses and a two-day course in how to start your own coffee shop.

As well as professional trainers, the LSC also provides expert consultants to work with new and established businesses.

London School of Coffee, Unit 2, Princeton Mews, 167-169 London Rd, Kingston-upon-Thames, KT2 6PT (020-8439 7981; londonschoolofcoffee.com; Norbiton rail).

Postcard Teas
Small tea, big flavours

Postcard Teas in Dering Street (just off Oxford Street) is at the forefront of the capital's renewed fascination for tea, from sampling unusual and exotic leaves to taking afternoon tea. It's the brainchild of Timothy d'Offay whose fascination for tea and tea culture was nurtured when he lived in Kyoto (Japan) over 20 years ago. Since then his passion has taken him throughout Asia and his knowledge of tea is immense.

This postcard-sized shop stocks rare teas from across the globe and specialises in 'small tea', i.e. sustainably produced leaves from small, family owned and run farms that produce tea (among other crops), ideally without hired help. Surprisingly, these small producers are responsible for over half the tea in Asia, and all authentic examples of the most famous teas of China, Japan, Korea, Taiwan and Vietnam are grown by 'small tea' specialists. Every packet of tea sold by Postcard Teas contains its provenance, so that you know exactly where it was grown and picked.

On Saturdays (10am) Tim hosts a relaxed one-hour tea tasting (booking essential) complete with illustrated tasting notes. Whether your taste is for black, white, green or blue (e.g. aromatic Oolong) tea, you'll be spoilt for choice at Postcard Teas. There's also an excellent website for tea aficionados.

Postcard Teas, 9 Dering St, W1S 1AG (020-7629 3654; postcardteas.com; Bond St tube; Mon-Sat 10.30-6.30).

Taylor Street Baristas
Learn from Aussie coffee masters

Taylor Street was founded in 2006 by Aussie siblings Nick, Andrew and Laura Tolley (who also set up the Harris and Hoole coffee-shop chain) and now has eight outlets in the city, so it goes without saying that their coffee is excellent.

Now you can learn how to brew coffee the Taylor Street way as they offer an intensive three-hour 'home barista course' (using home coffee brewing equipment) on Saturdays at one of their City locations. The course includes coffee tasting, the fundamentals of espresso milk foaming, an overview of equipment and general advice (see website for bookings).

Taylor St Baristas, 125 Old Broad St, EC2N 1AR (020-7929 2207; taylor-st.com/home-barista-course; Bank tube).

Tea Palace
Tea fit for an emperor

Tea Palace has two lovely tea emporiums in London (the other one's in Chelsea), each with its own unique character, offering some 150 varieties of loose-leaf tea and infusions – all Fairtrade or ethically sourced – along with tea-making equipment, tea sets and accessories. Teas are beautifully packaged in purple caddies and range from hand-tied lotus flower and Dragon Phoenix pearls to Imperial Ceylon and lemon shimmer green tea. There's even a special Covent Garden blend to celebrate the shop's opening, made from Chinese Yunnan, organic peppermint and cobalt blue cornflowers.

Unfortunately, you can't take tea at the Palace, as it's only a retail outlet.

Tea Palace, 12 Covent Garden Mkt, WC2E 8RF (020-7836 6997; teapalace.co.uk; Covent Gdn tube; Mon-Sat 10-7, Sun 11-6).

Teanamu Chaya Teahouse

Where taking tea is an art form

The Teanamu Chaya Teahouse is a serene and calm hideaway off the bustling Portobello Road, offering tea masterclasses, tastings, afternoon tea using the Chinese *gongfu cha* tea ceremony and 'tea cuisine' cookery classes, as well as a selection of exotic and rare teas and teaware for sale.

Taking tea in tea master Pei Wang's quaint teahouse is an intimate and ceremonial experience. The unique tea masterclasses include sessions for beginners and more specialised classes for those with some insight into oriental teas. There's also a popular one-hour 'flight of tasting' event for those wishing to dip their toes into tea culture.

Teanamu Chaya Teahouse, Coach House, 14A St Luke's Rd, W11 1DP (020-7243 0374; teanamu. com; Westbourne Pk tube, Sat-Sun 12-6).

Twinings Tea Shop & Museum

The granddaddy of tea importers

Twinings was founded in 1706 when Thomas Twining bought the old Tom's Coffee House and daringly introduced tea, which was then an exotic oriental drink. Today Mr Twining's shop (opposite the Royal Courts of Justice) is the oldest in the City of Westminster and incorporates a museum telling the 300-year-old story of the Twining family.

In addition to selling the complete range of Twinings teas, from the everyday to the exotic, the shop offers a loose tea bar where you can handle, smell and taste dry tea, and a sampling counter where you can enjoy free tastings. You can even become a 'Twinings tea taster' (see website).

Twinings Tea Shop & Museum, 216 The Strand, WC2R 1AP (020-7353 3511; shop.twinings.co.uk/ shop/strand; Temple tube; Mon-Fri, 9.30-7.30, Sat 10-5, Sun 10.30-4.30).

Le Cordon Bleu

4.
Cookery
Classes

To paraphrase the Chinese proverb: 'give a man a slap-up meal and he'll eat well for a day; teach him how to cook and he'll feast like a king for the rest of his life'.

Masterchef for the masses

The British buy a wealth of cookbooks – one of the few areas of publishing where sales are flourishing – yet many of these glossy tomes end up gathering dust on shelves, unthumbed and unspattered.

> Many Britons are proud to declare that they 'can't cook, won't cook'; it's hard to imagine continentals happily admitting to that!

Fortunately not everyone is content to eat processed ready meals and takeaways, and as our appreciation for good-quality food increases, so too does our appetite for learning new kitchen skills. It's no longer enough to watch Hugh or Rick wrestling with sourdough or scallops on the telly, or reading their latest spin-off cookery book – people want to learn first-hand from the professionals – and eat the results!

Understanding artisan processes such as baking and butchery, sharpening your knife skills or mastering the pasta maker or wok, all produce a gratifying sense of achievement. While there has long been professional courses for those wishing to pursue a career in the catering industry, nowadays more and more cookery schools and individuals are offering short (from a few hours to a number of weeks) beginners' courses for enthusiastic amateurs wishing to hone their skills.

London is especially rich in cookery schools, masterclasses and food artisans who are only too willing to share their knowledge with the masses. In the capital you can learn to butcher a pig, fillet a plaice, bake brioche, roll sushi, grind curry paste, pull noodles, ice cupcakes and temper chocolate. And that's just a taste of the banquet of opportunities available; not only can you eat it all in London, you can also learn how to cook it all!

The Angela Malik Cook School
Demystifying Asian cuisines

After training at Leiths School of Food & Wine (see page 108) and gaining experience at Bibendum, Vong and with chef Tom Kime, Angela Malik founded her cookery school in 2009 with the aim of demystifying Asian cuisine. There's an emphasis on Indian food (there are classes entitled Perfect Indian Breads, Perfect Indian Chicken Curry and Indian Street Starters) as well as Chinese, Thai and Vietnamese cuisines.

Beginners are catered for and there are masterclass courses for more experienced cooks. The school also has a deli where you can stock up on hand-made spice blends and chutneys.

The Angela Malik Cook School, 6 Churchfield Rd, W3 6EG (020-8992 5011; angelamalik.co.uk; Acton Central tube).

The Avenue Cookery School
A cookery 'finishing school'

The Avenue Cookery School in Putney is run by a 'bevy of blondes' – all qualified and experienced cooks – who teach a wide range of cookery courses in a relaxed and friendly atmosphere. Courses cater for everyone from beginners to experienced cooks, particularly teenagers, undergraduates and gap-year students, with full-time, part-time and evening courses.

The school also stages themed cooking days and evenings, including some exclusively for men who prefer not to embarrass themselves in front of the ladies! You can even design your own course for a group of friends or colleagues.

The Avenue Cookery School, The Mission Hall, Walkers Pl, SW15 1PP (020-8788 3025; theavenuecookeryschool.com; Putney Br tube/ Putney rail).

Bake With Maria
Learn to bake like Mary Berry

Bake with Maria is run by passionate home baker Maria Mayerhofer, who started out teaching bread-making classes at home that proved so popular she established The Baking Lab in 2011. Maria offers a unique programme of baking courses and baking-related experiences for everyone, presented by a team of professional pastry chefs and bakers.

There are classes devoted to all types of bread – including a beginners' class and courses dedicated to brioches, French and Italian bread and sourdough – as well as a tasty menu of cake and pastry-making classes covering cupcakes, macarons, French croissants and more. There are even classes for young bakers.

Bake With Maria, The Baking Lab, 81 Loudoun Rd, NW8 0DQ (020-7998 1634; bakewithmaria. com; S Hampstead rail/Swiss Cottage tube).

Billingsgate Seafood School
Scaling the fishy heights

Billingsgate Fish Market (see page 171) is the UK's largest inland fish market and takes its name from Billingsgate Wharf in the City of London, where it was established in the 16th century; it moved to the Isle of Dogs in 1982. The Billingsgate Seafood Training School is based at the market and provides courses for students and workers in the food industry, as well as amateur cooks. Tuition covers such essentials as knife skills (filleting), presentation, cooking and nutrition.

Many courses include guided market tours that help you to identify different species of fish and assess its quality, and to understand the merits of both wild and farmed fish.

Billingsgate Seafood School, Trafalgar Way, E14 5ST (020-7517 3548; seafoodtraining.org; Poplar DLR).

Blackheath Cooks
Cookery classes for all ages

Blackheath Cooks is an innovative modern cook shop and cookery school owned and run by Amanda Keyzers. The custom-built school hosts a wide variety of courses and events for cooks of all abilities and ages, including after-school clubs and holiday workshops for 4-11 year olds ('munchkins'), and courses aimed at teens and students. Adult courses cover a broad range of culinary skills and styles, which include back-to-basics, skills classes (knife, pasta making, meats and marinades, etc.), baking, and Indian and pan-Asian cooking.

Blackheath Cooks also hosts pop-up dinner parties and caters for private parties.

Blackheath Cooks, 13 Old Dover Rd, Blackheath, SE3 7BT (020-8465 5292; blackheathcooks.com; Westcombe Pk rail).

Cactus Kitchens
Learn with a Michelin Masterchef

Run in partnership with Michel Roux Jr and the producers of BBC's *Saturday Kitchen* and other hit cookery shows, Cactus Kitchens offers an array of unique and intimate cookery classes and workshops with Michel, his protégés and some of the nation's top chefs.

Classes include 'A Taste of Saturday Kitchen', where you experience all the elements of the hit show in a fun-packed afternoon, and the 'Monica Galetti Experience', which brings you face to face with the formidable judge from *Masterchef: the Professionals*. The 'Michel Roux Jr Premier Experience' gives you a whole day with the 2-Michelin-starred chef – a once-in-a-lifetime experience.

Cactus Kitchens, Cactus Studios, 1 St Luke's Ave, SW4 7LG (020-7091 4800; cactuskitchens. co.uk; Clapham Common tube).

Central Street Cookery School
Great tastes and good value

The charity-run Central Street Cookery School is a unique award-winning learning facility located in the renovated St Luke's Centre at the heart of the City. The school was established in 2012 to provide a place where the community could cook together, learn about health through food and cooking, and gain essential skills for life.

It offers affordable evening classes and has a state-of-the-art kitchen run by cookery teacher and food anthropologist Sofia Larrinua-Craxton. Classes encompass a multitude of subjects ranging from knife skills to street food, led by a diverse team of tutors.

Central Street Cookery School, St Luke's Community Centre, 90 Central St, EC1V 8AJ (020-7549 8176; centralstreet.org; Old St tube/rail).

The Cinnamon Kitchen
Spice up your life

If you're serious about Indian food sign up for a masterclass with Vivek Singh, executive chef at three renowned London restaurants: the Cinnamon Club, Cinnamon Kitchen and Cinnamon Soho. Vivek and his team take Indian food to another level and these sell-out sessions focus on both contemporary and traditional Indian cuisine, with classes ranging from modern Indian street food and South Indian cooking to all the elements of a Bengali wedding feast. They're aimed at everyone from beginners to experienced cooks and are deservedly popular.

Vivek also hosts cocktail masterclasses at the Cinnamon Kitchen's cocktail bar, Anise.

The Cinnamon Kitchen, 9 Devonshire Sq, EC2M 4YL (020-7626 5000; cinnamon-kitchen.com/cooking-course-london; Liverpool St tube/rail).

Cookery School
An A to Z of cookery skills

Cookery School does exactly what it says on the tin – one of the best and longest-running cookery schools in London, it offers a wide range of day and evening classes aimed at beginners, foodies and those wishing to work in catering. The school is headed by Rosalind Rathouse who has worked as a professional cook, run her own cookery business, and taught adults and children for many years.

Classes are informal and relaxed, and range from single sessions with a specific theme, e.g. sauces, chocolate, Spanish or Thai, to courses taking place over several days or evenings aimed at different levels of skill. Absolute beginners start at level one, mastering soups, stews and roasts – particularly popular with students – before progressing on to dinner party

dishes and home-cooking skills. Level four (for advanced cooks) takes in chocolate, soufflés, pickles and ice cream. If you plan on making a living out of food, the school runs an intensive six-week certificated course that sets you up to run a café, cater on a yacht or even work as a sous chef.

All the courses involve a high degree of hands-on experience designed to provide students with the necessary skills to become confident and independent cooks.

Cookery School, 15b Little Portland St, W1W 8BW (020-7631 4590; cookeryschool.co.uk; Oxford Circus tube).

La Cucina Caldesi
Like mama used to make...

La Cucina Caldesi is the only purely Italian cookery school in central London, run by Giancarlo and Katie Caldesi, stars of BBC2's foodie reality show *Return to Tuscany*, who teach their native Tuscan cuisine. It's a lovely place to perfect your fresh pasta and learn regional specialities in a convivial atmosphere – nobody enjoys their food (and wine) more than Italians! Classes are fun and very hands-on; you get to cook and eat a lot, so come hungry.

To see how the pros do it, visit the couple's nearby café-restaurant (Caffè Caldesi), one of central London's best Italian eateries.

La Cucina Caldesi, 4 Cross Keys Cl, W1U 2DG (020-7487 0750; caldesi.com; Bond St tube).

Culinary Anthropologist
Food for thought

Anna Colquhoun – aka the Culinary Anthropologist – is a cookery teacher, food writer and consultant on BBC Radio 4's *The Kitchen Cabinet*. A self-confessed food nerd, she's fascinated about food's place in different cultures and societies, and has travelled far and wide to research her subject.

Her cookery classes are mostly run from her home in Highbury, north London, and include everything from Moroccan and Turkish feasts to French classics and new Nordic cuisine. Anna also offers workshops on preserving, seasonal vegetarian cooking, knife skills, bread-making, pastry, pasta, seafood and much more. Classes are small and hands-on, and culminate in a convivial meal around the kitchen table. If you prefer eating to cooking, there's a monthly supper club.

Anna Colquhoun, Culinary Anthropologist (culinaryanthropologist.org/cooking-classes; anna@culinaryanthropologist.org).

Divertimenti
Culinary escapism in South Ken

Divertimenti is one of London's most engrossing cookware shops, with two outlets (in Brompton Road and Marylebone High Street) selling just about everything a keen cook could possibly need or want. They also operate one of London's best cookery schools, with a range of classes for novice and experienced cooks alike. Classes take place at the Brompton Road store, where there's a beautifully designed 'theatre' as well as a cookery 'island' where participants can interact with some of today's top chefs.

Classes include demonstrations, hands-on masterclasses and even guided gastro tours such as a walk around Borough Market. The demos take in such diverse subjects as kosher food, celebration cakes and even how to get the best out of your AGA (range cooker), while hands-on classes include everything from sushi to sauces, pizza to dim sum. China is just one of the locations covered in a world tour of food that takes in France, Lebanon, southern India, Iran, Thailand and others. Multi-part courses such as 'Cooking with Confidence' are brilliant if you want a career in the catering industry.

Attend a class and you get 10 per cent off your purchases in the Divertimenti stores.

Divertimenti, 227-229 Brompton Rd, SW3 2EP (020-7486 8020; divertimenti.co.uk/cookery-school; S Kensington tube).

E5 Bakehouse
Learn the secrets of sourdough

The E5 Bakehouse is an artisan bakery and coffee shop in East London (E8, strangely), where the staff have a passion for sourdough and the 'lost' traditions of baking. E5's bakers share their knowledge and expertise in a one-day bread-making class suitable for all skill levels, focusing on the essentials of sourdough baking. During the class you'll prepare four different breads (pain de campagne, ciabatta, rye and bagels), incorporating a variety of techniques – be prepared to take home lots of bread!

E5 also hold special pizza-making classes and home cookery classes, led by chefs Ruth Quinian and Despina Flouri.

E5 Bakehouse, Arch 395, Mentmore Ter, E8 3PH (020-8525 2890; e5bakehouse.com; London Fields rail).

Food at 52
Life begins at 52

Food at 52 offers hands-on tuition in the heart of Clerkenwell. This beautifully appointed cookery school is run by chef John Benbow and is like learning to cook at a friend's house – albeit a sophisticated and talented friend.

Courses cover an atlas of flavours, the cuisines of Morocco, Spain, Thailand and Vietnam, as well as tackling subjects such as Fish and Seafood or the Stress Free Dinner Party – the latter focusing on gastropub-style food that can be prepared in advance, leaving you free to mingle with your guests. Each session ends with a mouth-watering feast of the food you've cooked, accompanied by complementary wines. Good value and great fun.

Food at 52, 96 Central St, EC1V 8AJ (07814-027067; foodat52.co.uk; Old St tube/rail).

Forage London
Eat for free in London's parks

Forage London is the brainchild of John Rensten who lives in north London and spends his time foraging for free food. John used to run a gastropub where he added foraged food items such as mushrooms, wild garlic and sorrel to the menu, but he now spends his time studying, picking and obsessing about wild food, and sharing what he's learned with other enthusiasts.

John organises regular foraging trips around the UK, such as mushroom hunting in the New Forest, and set up Forage London to give city dwellers a chance to discover and enjoy some of the amazing wild foods that grow all around them in the capital's parks. See his excellent website for details of courses and walks.

Forage London (foragelondon.co.uk).

Ginger Pig
Nose to tail meat preparation

One of the few places in this book that warrants two entries (the other is for its butcher's shops – see page 22), Ginger Pig is one of London's leading butchers and offers a number of highly rated masterclasses at its Marylebone shop.

The hands-on tuition provides a good grounding in butchery skills and also teaches you how to choose meat and get the most from each cut. Classes are small and take an in-depth look at one type of meat or skill: beef, lamb, pork or sausage-making. They culminate in a two-course supper with wine – and you get to take home your freshly-butchered cuts.

Ginger Pig, 8-10 Moxon St, W1U 4EW (01751-460802; thegingerpig.co.uk/butchery-classes; butcheryclasses@thegingerpig.co.uk; Baker St tube).

L'atelier des Chefs Cookery School

The studio for aspiring culinary artists

Unleash your inner Gordon Ramsay at L'atelier des Chefs, one of Europe's leading cookery schools. Whether you want to make the perfect hamburger or cook up a six-course Cordon Bleu meal, L'atelier can show you how. The school has two immaculate kitchens – in the West End and the City – and offers a smorgasbord of classes at different times throughout the day. These range from the ever-popular 30-minute Cook, Eat and Run lunchtime course to a four-hour gourmet feast.

All classes are hands-on and interactive and cover all manner of themes, from global cuisines and food trends to favourite recipes, so that you can learn how to make macaroons, cook a flawless steak or take a deeper look at French, Italian or (for a change) British food. The Sunday roast class is especially popular. Classes are taught by professional chefs with top restaurant experience and are suitable for cooks of all abilities. Prices are reasonable, with the 30-minute classes costing from just £15.

Each kitchen has its own dining space and a bar where wine, soft drinks and beverages are available. There's also a cookery shop stocked with a range of kitchen utensils and equipment chosen by L'atelier's chefs.

L'atelier des Chefs Cookery School, 19 Wigmore St, W1U 1PH (020-7499 6580; atelierdeschefs. co.uk; Bond St tube).

Le Cordon Bleu
The pinnacle of cookery schools

With over 100 years of teaching experience, world-famous Le Cordon Bleu is the world's premier cookery school, operating an international network of educational institutions dedicated to providing the highest level of culinary, hospitality and management tuition. It's considered to be the guardian of French gastronomic technique and continues to preserve and pass on the mastery and appreciation of the culinary arts that have been the cornerstones of French gastronomy for over 500 years.

Less well known is that Le Cordon Bleu isn't just for budding Michelin-star chefs and those pursuing a career in food and hospitality. It also offers a wide range of short courses designed especially for enthusiastic home cooks wishing to discover new techniques and improve their cooking skills, ranging from one-day workshops to four-day courses. There are also ten-day courses targeted at home cooks who want to hone a specific area of their cooking expertise. No prior knowledge is required to participate in these courses, which are a great way to learn more about cuisine and patisserie in entertaining and informal classes.

The ultimate amateur cook fest is the intensive three-week summer course, Summer Essentials, designed for those who love good food and cooking and want to learn practical skills and gain confidence in the kitchen. *Magnifique!*

Le Cordon Bleu, 15 Bloomsbury Sq, WC1A 2LS (020-7400 3900; lcblondon.com; Holborn tube).

Leiths School of Food and Wine

Learn to cook like Prue

The grande dame of London cookery schools, Leiths School of Food and Wine was founded in 1975 by Prue Leith, noted restaurateur, caterer, TV presenter/broadcaster and food writer. Leiths offers courses for professionals and amateurs alike, and has produced generations of accomplished chalet girls, home cooks and even some well-known professional chefs such as Gizzi Erskine, Lorraine Pascale and Henry Harris (Racine).

Leiths' purpose-built west London premises offer the ideal environment for learning everything from knife skills or basic baking to healthy eating and chocolate workshops, from discovering the flavours of the Pacific Rim to working with wild yeasts.

The teaching staff are all professional chefs with experience in the real world of restaurants and commercial catering, augmented by cookery writers and Masters of Wine who regularly demonstrate or lecture at the school.

Leiths isn't restricted to career cooks and welcomes enthusiastic amateurs on its varied courses, which include holiday and part-time courses that provide scope for interested amateurs of all ages, plus a wide range of special events. The school's guiding principle is to impart enthusiasm for the food and wine trade, and instil a life-long love of good food and wine. We'll drink to that…!

Leiths School of Food and Wine, 16-20 Wendell Rd, W12 9RT (020-8749 6400; leiths.com; Stamford Brook tube).

London Vegetarian School
Life beyond lettuce and lentils

The London Vegetarian School in southeast London is the capital's premier meat-free cookery school, offering courses in both vegetarian and vegan cuisine. The concept of the school embraces vegetarian food as a lifestyle choice, and there's a wide range of classes such as fine dining, wheat- and dairy-free, and some sophisticated geographical cuisines, including those of France and the Middle East. There's even a class targeted at busy Londoners.

There are no nut roasts here but rather a rich seam of creative and chic veggie food that has no need for meat.

London Vegetarian School, PO Box 70366, SE1P 4FT (0844-8842 699; londonvegetarianschool. co.uk).

Madame Gautier
It's all in the technique

Madame Gautier is a 'method and technique' cookery school where you learn, hands-on, the skills of classic French cuisine. They offer a wide range of small and intimate classes, from Les Classiques – two hours to learn a classic dish such as bouillabaisse or tarte tatin – to La Grande Technique, a five-hour masterclass to cook up a French feast. There are courses suitable for all standards of cooks, from total beginners to budding professional chefs.

Madame Gautier is also a classic French *traiteur* (catering business), producing restaurant-standard food to eat at home, which is sold at farmers' markets throughout London (see the website for information).

Madame Gautier Cookery School, 6 Enterprise Way, NW10 6UG (020-8964 5511; madamegautier. com; Willesden Jct tube/rail).

Paul A Young
Adventures with chocolate

Since opening his first shop on Camden Passage in Islington in 2006, Paul Young has become one of the world's best chocolatiers. He has a reputation as an alchemist with chocolate, developing flavour combinations that are original, experimental, sometimes daring, but always perfectly balanced. His 2009 book *Adventures with Chocolate* won the World's Best Chocolate Book award at the Gourmand Cookbook Awards in Paris.

Paul holds regular chocolate tasting/ making events and workshops at his Islington and Soho shops where you can learn how to temper chocolate, make ganache and discover the secrets of his sea salted caramel. There are children's workshops too (see website for dates). Scrummy!

Paul A Young, 33 Camden Passage, N1 8EA (020-7424 5750; paulayoung.co.uk/events; Angel tube).

Raw Freedom
There's more to raw food than salad

Author and life coach Saskia Fraser provides an accessible approach to raw food that can fit in with a busy lifestyle. Through her company, Raw Freedom, she aims to inspire and encourage us to incorporate raw food recipes into our diets to boost energy, mental clarity and mood. Saskia runs raw food coaching and detox programmes, as well as a number of one-day workshops (at various locations) that explain how to source, prepare and even 'cook' raw food.

There's more to raw food than salad – Saskia's recipes feature pasta, tarts and even ice cream – and you can get more ideas through the online raw community, Raw Freedom Friends (and Saskia's *Raw Freedom* book).

Raw Freedom (07733-107811; rawfreedom.co.uk).

Recipease

Pukka tucker from the Naked Chef

Jamie Oliver's name is synonymous with down-to-earth eating, so it isn't surprising that the 'Naked Chef' – never one to pass up a business opportunity – should open his own foodie hub to get people more involved with food. Recipease is a café-cum-shop-cum-cookery school with London branches in Clapham and Notting Hill.

The café serves a menu of wholesome, imaginative food, while the shop offers tasty takeaways, treats and kitchen apparatus. But it's the cookery school we're interested in here, and Recipease – 'where anyone can learn to cook and make great food' – is all about making cooking fun rather than a chore. Whether you're a complete novice or a seasoned pro, it's a great place to gain inspiration and learn some new skills. Recipease offers a wide range of lessons, from knife skills to Vietnamese street food, risotto to beef Wellington, bread-baking to rolling sushi. And Jamie's obsession with children's nutrition means there's lots of fun foodie activities for kids as well.

You're encouraged to get your hands dirty and make mistakes – an ethos aided by a complimentary wine or beer – while learning the tricks of the trade from highly trained kitchen pros (or 'food champions' as they're called).

Recipease, 92-94 Notting Hill Gate, W11 3QB (020-3375 5398; jamieoliver.com/recipease; Notting Hill Gate tube).

Rock Bakehouse
Have your cake and eat it!

Rock Bakehouse is a boutique bakery in West Hampstead specialising in baking and cake-decorating courses. Rock offers a wide range of small group and individual cake classes, from beginners to advanced level, whether you want to learn cake skills for fun or aim to turn your hobby into a career. Classes are small, so you get the most out of each session, and last from two hours to a full day.

As well as learning how to bake cakes large and small, there are also classes on decorating cupcakes, making sugar roses, and even starting a cake business from home.

Rock Bakehouse, Gascony Ave, NW6 4ND (07999-783784; rockbakehouse.co.uk; W Hampstead tube).

Sarah Moore
Learn fast, cook slow

Sarah has worked with food all her life, from supplying the Japan Centre in Piccadilly with bento boxes to running the restaurant at Sir George Martin's Air Studios and catering for the US Ambassador. She now runs a thriving catering company in north London supplying local shops with gourmet dishes, and is well qualified to offer private cookery lessons, either one-on-one tuition or in small groups.

Classes (private classes are held in your own home) cover a range of subjects such as menu planning, student survival cooking and ethical, sustainable food. The latter is close to Sarah's heart – she's an avid supporter of Slow Food (slowfood.org.uk) and Sustain (sustainweb.org).

Sarah Moore Caterers (07931-373646; sarahmoore.co.uk; sarah@sarahmoore.co.uk).

School of Wok
Stir fry magic

Founded in 2012 by celebrated Chinese chef Jeremy Pang, the School of Wok is a leading cookery school in Covent Garden with a passion for Oriental cuisine. It presents a variety of classes covering cuisines from across Asia – including Chinese, Indian, Japanese, Korean, Thai and Vietnamese – focusing on particular skills such as making dim sum and sushi and pulling noodles.

Classes are suitable for everyone from novices to experienced cooks, and are fully hands-on, including the preparation and cooking of ingredients and, most important of all, mastering the wok. There are also tasting tours of Chinatown.

School of Wok, 61 Chandos Pl, WC2N 4HG (020-7240 8818; schoolofwok.co.uk; Leicester Sq tube).

Sozai Cooking School
Make sushi like a master

London has an unusually large number of Japanese restaurants, which isn't surprising considering that Japanese food is one of the world's most popular cuisines, renowned for being as healthy as it is delicious. Sozai was the first cookery school in the UK dedicated to authentic Japanese food, catering for everyone from absolute beginners to those wishing to improve their Japanese food skills.

In addition to well-known dishes such as sushi and tempura, the school offers a wide variety of classes covering traditional cuisine, such as *kaiseki* (the traditional multi-course meal), *shojin* (vegan food), and street food (including ramen noodles and savoury *okonomiyaki* pancakes). *Itadakimasu!*

Sozai Cooking School, 5 Middlesex St, E1 7AA (020-7458 4567; sozai.co.uk; Aldgate tube).

Waitrose Cookery School
Super lessons from a supermarket

Waitrose (see page 123) don't just sell you fine produce, they'll also show you how to cook it at their celebrated cookery school in north London. The school lives up to the supermarket's reputation for quality and reliability with a team of chefs who've worked in top restaurants alongside chefs such as Rick Stein and Gary Rhodes, and between them have earned several Michelin stars. They teach a broad menu of impressive, hands-on courses, lasting from two hours to a day, including modern vegetarian cookery, French brasserie favourites and how to make the ultimate afternoon tea.

Courses are suitable for all standards and abilities, and the school's chefs ensure that you have the guidance necessary to enjoy the day and learn a new skill (or three). If you're a beginner, it's worth starting with a 'skills' course, e.g. knife skills or bread-making, while experienced cooks will enjoy the Art of Michelin Star Cookery course.

There are scores of inviting courses, from the perfect steak to classic Italian; beginner's filleting and cooking fish to perfect tray bakes; gluten-free bread and pastry to sauces. See the website for a full list.

Waitrose Cookery School, Goldhurst Ter, 199 Finchley Rd, NW3 6NN (020-7372 6108; waitrose. com/home/inspiration/waitrose_cookeryschool. html; Finchley Rd tube).

William Curley Chocolate Classes

A marriage made in chocolate heaven

One of the world's foremost chocolate experts, William Curley has been crowned Britain's Best Chocolatier by the Academy of Chocolate no less than four times, in addition to receiving numerous other awards; his book *Couture Chocolate* won the Guild of Food Writers' Cookery Book of the Year Award in 2012. Curley started his chocolate business in 2004 with the opening of his first 'boutique' in Richmond (he now has his flagship store in Belgravia and another in Harrods). He works with his Japanese wife Suzue, a highly respected pâtissière.

Drawing on a range of global experiences, together with a small team of young pastry chefs, William and Suzue have created a truly unique brand of chocolates, cakes,

patisseries and other treats. They work exclusively with chocolate from Amedei, a Tuscan company producing artisan chocolate, using the finest ethically-sourced beans from Trinitario and Criollo cacao trees: many believe Amedei makes the best couverture chocolate in the world.

The Curleys' unique chocolate-making classes are held on Saturdays at their Belgravia store and make for an extravagant day out. Here you'll learn how to pipe and roll chocolate truffles, make your own sea salt caramels or create a decadent Venezuelan Chocolate Cadeaux. Divine indulgence!

William Curley, 198 Ebury St, SW1W 8UN (020-7730 5522; williamcurley.com; Sloane Sq tube).

Fortnum & Mason

5.
Food Halls &
Emporiums

Rediscover how your grandparents shopped before supermarkets took over the world.

Temples to the food gods

London is famous for its palaces, castles and cathedrals, but it also has some terrific temples to the food gods, catering to every palate and pocket. Some are located in major department stores while others serve local shoppers, but there's one thing all food halls and emporiums have in common: they bring together an amazing range of produce and allow you to experience how your ancestors shopped before supermarkets were invented.

Unlike many supermarkets, the capital's food halls host a number of separate departments such as a baker, butcher, fishmonger and cheesemonger, so you can obtain expert advice and enjoy some social interaction along with your shopping. Larger stores also have specialist confectionery, patisserie and wine sections, and any manner of food concessions.

Food emporiums such as Harrods and Fortnum & Mason are designed to tempt you at every turn. Their counters groan with luxury foods from all corners of the globe: artisan cheeses, Beluga caviar, exotic

Most food halls have at least one café or restaurant, while some have bars (sushi, cocktail, etc.), ice cream parlours and even a Willy Wonka-style sweet shop.

charcuterie, luxury chocolates, truffles, foie gras… Some, especially Harrods, have spectacular displays of produce that can make a visit an end in itself. They cater to shoppers with **very** deep pockets and are (for most people) somewhere to buy a treat rather than do the weekly shop. However, there are smaller neighbourhood stores that offer huge choice, in-depth knowledge and artisan quality at more affordable prices.

All the establishments included in this chapter are committed to the quality and provenance of their produce and to the pleasure of truly excellent eating, from the seasonal to the stylish.

Fortnum & Mason

Her Majesty's local convenience store

This world-famous food emporium in Piccadilly is a compelling combination of delicatessen, department store, restaurant and living museum. This quintessential upmarket food retailer, established in 1707 by William Fortnum and Hugh Mason, is recognised internationally as a British icon, proudly displaying its royal warrant above the door.

Founded as a grocery store, Fortnum's reputation was built on supplying top-quality food, and its fame grew rapidly throughout the Victorian era. In time it developed into a department store, although its renown rests almost entirely on its food hall situated on the lower ground and ground floors. Today it continues to stock a wide range of exotic, speciality and 'basic' (comparatively speaking) provisions – wonderful food, impeccably sourced and beautifully presented. It's also noted for its luxury food hampers – just the job for Ladies' Day at Ascot, the Henley Regatta, Glyndebourne or a *fête champêtre* (posh garden party). Not the place to do your weekly shop – unless your surname happens to be Windsor – but wonderful for the occasional treat.

Fortnum's also has a celebrated teashop and no fewer than five restaurants.

Fortnum & Mason, 181 Piccadilly, W1A 1ER (0845-300 1707; fortnumandmason.com; Green Pk/Piccadilly tube; Mon-Sat, 10-9, Sun 12-6).

Greensmiths

An independent supermarket with a difference

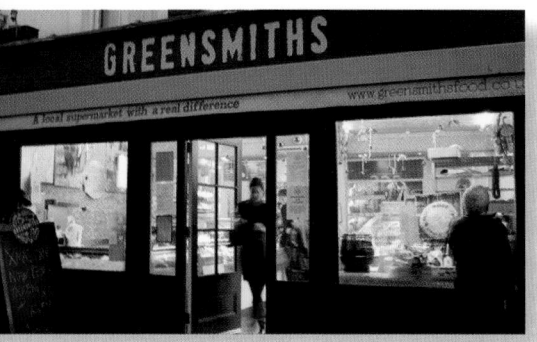

Pig – see page 22), a baker (The Old Post Office Bakery), a greengrocer (Solstice), a coffee/beverages specialist (Caffe Antica) and a wine merchant (Waterloo Wine Company). Thus your shopping experience is seamless, with the advantage of being able to buy from specialists and profit from their expert advice – so much more satisfying than pushing a trolley around the aisles.

A range of delicious dishes is prepared in Greensmiths' kitchen, either to eat in the lovely café or take away – great prices too!

Greensmiths, 27 Lower Marsh, SE1 7RG (020-7921 2970; greensmithsfood.co.uk; Lambeth N tube; Mon-Fri 8-8, Sat 8-6).

Greensmiths is an example of how good a local supermarket can be if it puts provenance over profit and works in partnership with artisan producers. Established in 2008 by Chris Smith who wanted to create something special, Waterloo-based Greensmiths has been winning plaudits ever since for its combination of superb food, excellent service and stylish interior.

It looks small from the outside but is something of a Tardis, opening up to reveal a number of levels. As well as the products you'd expect to find – groceries, general goods and dairy goods, there's a cheesemonger plus a number of concessions (both producers and merchants) which include a butcher (Ginger

Harrods' Food Hall

A feast for the eyes... and a trial for the wallet!

Set within one of the best-known department stores in the world, Harrods famous Food Hall is a gourmets' Mecca and a tourist attraction as much as food store. Harrods in Knightsbridge (established 1824) has 330 departments and around 30 restaurants and food outlets, but its pièce de résistance is its wonderful Art Nouveau food hall.

These opulent rooms are more salon than supermarket, from the mosaic frieze and magical tile-work (by W J Neatby), depicting farming and hunting scenes, to the chandeliers sparkling off the stained glass ceilings. The glorious décor makes a wonderful background for the artful displays of mouth-watering food, notable for its variety, luxury – and eye-watering prices!

In Harrods you can buy everything from artisan cheeses to Beluga caviar, exotic charcuterie to divine chocolates, truffles and foie gras to the finest champagne, much of it in Harrods distinctive 'own brand' green livery. It's all temptingly displayed in charming, old-fashioned, glass-fronted counters. For sheer magnificence, Harrods is hard to beat.

If such an excessive display of edible delights makes you hungry (which it will), there are a number of places to refuel, including a sushi bar, steakhouse and tea room.

Harrods, 87-135 Brompton Rd, SW1X 7XL (020-7730 1234; harrods.com; Knightsbridge tube; Mon-Sat 10-8, Sun 12-6).

Harvey Nichols Foodmarket
Where fashion meets food

The younger, more fashionable cousin of Harrods, Harvey Nichols ('Harvey Nicks') started life in 1831 as a linen shop and grew into a nationwide chain of prestigious department stores. The store is best known for its fashionable clothes and accessories, but it also has a reputation for on-trend food. Its celebrated restaurant, bar and café are destinations in their own right and favourite meeting places for savvy shoppers.

The fifth-floor Foodmarket at the Knightsbridge store vividly illustrates Harvey Nicks' commitment to high-quality, carefully-sourced, great-tasting food. It boasts an impressive range of national and international produce from some of the UK's – and the world's – very best suppliers. The butchery section offers salt-marsh lamb and Gloucester Old Spot pork; the deli features cheese from Alex James (past and, on occasion, present bass player with Blur) and Imperial caviar; the bakery has celebration cakes from Fancy Nancy and marshmallows (the weightwatchers' cupcake) from the Marshmallowists; while desserts include hand-crafted chocs from Marc Demarquette and Yee Kwan's Far Eastern-inspired ice cream. Fortunately, there's also a detox kitchen for when you've overdone the chocs and ice cream!

There are regular tasting evenings and product launches too.

Harvey Nichols, 5th Floor, 109-125 Knightsbridge, SW1X 7RJ (020-7235 5250; harveynichols.com/restaurant/knightsbridge-dining/foodmarket; Knightsbridge tube; Mon-Sat 10-8, Sun 12-6).

John Lewis Food Hall

The best Waitrose in town

John Lewis' department stores routinely top surveys of the UK's most popular retailers and the company scores especially high for its range of products and customer service. It offers excellent value (the JL motto is 'Never knowingly undersold'), an unconditional returns policy and a general sense of good taste rather than showy fashion.

The food hall at the Oxford Street store is run by Waitrose ('Quality food, honestly priced'), the supermarket division of the John Lewis Partnership that is the foodies' favourite supermarket chain. It occupies part of a vast basement and is a paradise for food lovers, bursting with fresh seasonal produce and inviting artisan foods. Here you'll find everything from dressed lobsters to venison and wild game, exotic fruit and vegetables, luxury preserves and honey, delicious charcuterie and terrines, plus all the usual everyday essentials. Special mentions go to the excellent delicatessen section, walk-in cheese room, in-house bakery, expansive meat and fish counters, wine and spirits department, and an olive bar, plus its wealth of tempting food to go.

John Lewis/Waitrose also provides a home delivery and party service, and online shopping.

John Lewis Food Hall/Waitrose, 300 Oxford St, W1A 1EX (020-7629 7711; waitrose.com/bf_home/bf/456.html; Oxford St tube; Mon-Fri 9.30-8/Thu 9pm, Sun 12-6).

Partridges
Posh nosh for the Chelsea set

Established in 1972, Partridges is one of only a handful of family-run food emporiums remaining in central London. One of London's poshest food stores, with a royal warrant, it's up there with Fortnum & Mason and Harrods' Food Hall (only smaller) – as are the prices! You'll find everything you need to entertain royally (or royalty!), from duck liver paté to truffles, Beluga caviar to oysters, Belgian hand-made chocolates to exotic teas and coffee. There's also a superb selection of vintage champagnes and fine wines, plus a wine bar and café.

There's even a superior Saturday market (see page 179).

Partridges, 2-5 Duke of York Sq, SW3 4LY (020-7730 0651; partridges.co.uk; Sloane Sq; daily 8-10).

The People's Supermarket
Social enterprise for shoppers

The People's Supermarket is a sustainable, environmentally-friendly, non-profit co-operative established in May 2010 to provide the people of WC1 with good food at fair prices. Although anyone can shop at the store, you can become a member for an annual fee of £25, although you must commit to working in the shop for four hours each month (no experience required). In return you get a 20 per cent discount off food purchases and a say in how the shop is run.

A spin-off, the People's Kitchen, offers food to take away.

The People's Supermarket, 72-78 Lambs Conduit St, WC1N 3LP (020-7430 1827; thepeoplessupermarket.org; Russell Sq tube; Mon-Sat 8-9, Sun 10-6).

Phoenicia Mediterranean Food Hall
A taste of the Eastern Med

Founded in 2003, the Phoenicia Mediterranean Food Hall in north London is a family-run business and a labour of love. It specialises in high-quality food from the Eastern Med – Greece, Italy, Lebanon, Morocco and Turkey – especially products that are difficult to find elsewhere at reasonable prices, such as *freekah* (green wheat, made popular by Ottolenghi – see page 70).

There's a delicatessen stocked with marvellous mezze dishes such as *tabbouleh* and *baba ganoush*; mouth-watering handmade bread, cakes and pastries (including Turkish pita and fresh baklava); a superb halal butcher; fantastic olives and olive oil; and much more. There's also a café that sells great wraps.

Phoenicia Mediterranean Food Hall, 186-192 Kentish Town Rd, NW5 2AE (020-7267 1267; phoeniciafoodhall.co.uk; Kentish Town tube; Mon-Sat 9-8, Sun 10-4).

Planet Organic
A world of organic pleasure

The UK's largest certified organic supermarket, Planet Organic believes in ethical and sustainable farming and places emphasis on the provenance of its products. Founded in 1995, there are now six outlets around London (see website), offering some of the widest ranges of organic and artisan food available, including food to go.

It's certainly not the cheapest food store around – some claim it's overpriced – but Planet Organic stocks many items that are difficult, if not impossible, to find in major supermarkets. It also has a good café/restaurant with lots of vegetarian options.

Planet Organic Islington, 64 Essex Rd, N1 8LR (020-7288 9460; planetorganic.com; Angel tube/Essex Rd rail; Mon-Sat 7.30-9, Sun 9-9).

Selfridges Food Hall
Possibly London's best all-round food emporium

Selfridges is a chain of department stores founded by American entrepreneur Harry Gordon Selfridge, who opened his flagship store on Oxford Street in 1909 and coined the phrase 'the customer is always right'. Today the store offers one of the most exciting and fashionable shopping experiences in town – and its food hall is no exception.

Selfridges sells all manner of edible treats and is noted for its vast range and superb quality. Although not as famous as Harrods' Food Hall (see page 121) – nor as grand and intimidating – many believe that 'Sellys' is the best all-round food hall in London. It's a honey pot for serious cooks and a great place to keep abreast of the latest food trends, which are promoted through demonstrations and tastings.

Every possible cuisine is represented (raw ingredients, artisan and prepared foods) from all corners of the globe, including Persian caviar, succulent jamón ibérico, fresh lobster, Wagyu beef, biltong, exotic spices and much more. There's even a section of hard-to-find American foods, a kosher department, and an oyster and champagne bar, plus lots of great places to eat.

Selfridges Food Hall, 400 Oxford St, W1A 1AB (0800-123400; Selfridges.com; Bond St tube; Mon-Sat 9.30-9, Sun 12-6.15).

Villandry
A grand café and much more

Villandry on Great Portland Street is a large food emporium encompassing a restaurant, grand café, bar and deli – with alfresco seating. The mouth-watering deli section sells chocolates, Villandry teas, coffee, honey and preserves, wine, vinegars, packaged bakery goods and more, while the patisserie counter offers a tempting selection of cakes and pastries, such as colourful berry tarts, blackberry éclairs, chocolate mousses, muffins and scones.

There's also a frozen yoghurt and ice cream counter, juice bar and an 'express' area serving a selection of hot and cold prepared food to go.

Villandry, 170 Great Portland St, W1W 5QB (020-7631 3131; villandry.com/locations/great_portland_street; Gt Portland St tube; Mon-Fri 7.30-10, Sat 8-10, Sun 9-6).

Whole Foods Market
One of the best organic retailers in London

Whole Foods Market is a small chain of five organic food emporiums, of which the Kensington outlet (housed in the former Barkers department store) is the largest, extending to some 80,000ft². Everything here is organic and/or locally sourced, free from artificial preservatives, colouring, flavourings, sweeteners and hydrogenated fats. The store offers a vast choice of food, from fruit and vegetables to meat and dairy products, and is one of the finest organic retailers in London.

The market also offers a wide range of eating options, from salad bars to sushi, omelettes to pizza. You're spoiled for choice!

Whole Foods Market, The Barkers Building, 63-97 Kensington High St, W8 5SE (020-7368 4500; wholefoodsmarket.com/stores/kensington; High St Kensington tube; Mon-Sat 8-10, Sun 12-6).

The Crabtree

6.
Gastropubs

If your steak is rare breed, butchered locally, aged for 28 days, and matched with a pint of good ale or a glass of superior wine, chances are you're eating in a gastropub.

Foodie heaven in a pub

British pubs and bars are famous for their unique atmosphere, bonhomie and great beer, but an increasing number are also noted for the excellence of their food and wine. The days when all you could get to eat in a pub was a stale pork pie or a packet of crisps are long past. Nowadays most need to offer tasty homemade fare just to survive, and those that thrive serve gourmet cuisine.

Pubs that specialise in high-quality food are often referred to as 'gastropubs' – a combination of the French word *gastronomique* and pub – although not all pubs that serve excellent food make this claim and some that do fail to live up to it. But what exactly is a gastropub? It's easier to say what a gastropub **isn't** rather than what it is; it isn't, for example, a pub that's been turned into a 'fine dining' restaurant with a posh bar. Most gastropubs have a dining room for diners and a bar for drinkers, although you can usually also eat in the bar, often from a more limited (and cheaper) bar menu.

While the concept of a restaurant in a pub has reinvigorated both pub culture and dining out, it has also attracted criticism for altering the character of traditional pubs. However, the best gastropubs are 'proper' pubs, serving craft beers in a 'pubby' atmosphere alongside gourmet food and fine wines.

> The quality of pub food is highlighted by the increasing number with Michelin stars.

We've included almost 60 of London's best gastropubs in this chapter. They don't usually serve food all day (the times shown are the pub's opening hours), so check the website for meal times, although there are usually bar snacks available when the kitchen is closed. And most can still rustle up a bag of crisps!

The Admiral Codrington
Burgers to die for!

One of Chelsea's best gastropubs, the much-loved Admiral Codrington (the 'Cod') features regularly in the *Michelin Pub Guide* and has a reputation for high-quality, modern food. The seasonal menu is constantly evolving, but its famous Ad Cod (rare breed) burger, chilli squid and dry-aged steaks are regulars. The superb food is accompanied by an excellent choice of ales and wines, chosen by Master of Wine Tim Atkin.

In addition to the large bar and restaurant, there's also a covered/heated beer garden.

The Admiral Codrington, 17 Mossop St, SW3 2LY (020-7581 0005; theadmiralcodrington.co.uk; S Kensington tube; Mon-Tue 11.30-11, Wed-Thu 11.30-midnight, Fri-Sat 11-1am, Sun 12-10.30).

The Alma
Gastropub meets boutique hotel

Built in 1866, this archetypal Victorian pub was named after the Battle of Alma in 1854, the first conflict in the Crimean War. It's an imposing pub that was extended in 2010 to provide 23 boutique-style hotel rooms. Food is important here, with a large dining area serving seasonal British fare such as Barnsley lamb chops and English asparagus, while mouth-watering Sunday roasts include Dingley Dell pork belly and roast sirloin of West Country beef.

Drinkers are well served with ales from Sambrook's, Twickenham, Wells and Young's, plus over 30 wines.

The Alma, 499 Old York Rd, SW18 1TF (020-8870 2537; almawandsworth.com; Wandsworth Town rail; Mon-Fri, 11-12, Sat 10-12, Sun 12-10.30).

The Anchor & Hope
Fine fare for London's workers

Close to the Young Vic theatre, the Anchor & Hope is one of London's best-known gastropubs. It's a no-frills venue, with minimal decor, bare wooden tables and art to brighten the walls, while the menu is chalked on a board. The food is tasty, modern British fare, served in hearty portions and reasonably priced – the 'workers' lunch menu' is good value, starting from £15 for two courses (£17 for three). Sample dishes include grilled lemon sole with asparagus and buttered almonds; pappardelle with girolles, beet greens and ricotta; and longhorn beef ragu with red wine, grilled semolina gnocchi and parmesan.

The Anchor is generally busy, and the 'no reservations' policy (except for Sunday lunch) means that you may have to wait for a table, although you can relax in the bar and enjoy something from the comprehensive wine list, which includes a reasonable choice by the glass. There are also bargain cocktails priced around £5 and real ales such as St Austell Tribute, Wells Bombardier and Young's.

If you're planning an intimate tête-à-tête, be aware that you may be seated at one of the Anchor's communal tables, which are either sociable or noisy, depending on your viewpoint.

The Anchor & Hope, 36 The Cut, SE1 8LP (020-7928 9898; anchorandhopepub.co.uk; Southwark rail; Mon 5-11, Tue-Sat 11-11, Sun – see website).

The Atlas
Take a foodie tour of the Med

The Atlas is a plain-looking pub in a Fulham back street, although appearances can be deceptive, as it's an award-winning gastropub – and not a trendy yuppie venue but a friendly traditional local. Its imaginative menu offers a tour of the Mediterranean, with Italian, Moroccan and Turkish influences; mains are priced around £12-£18 – around average for gastropub fare. The Atlas is also serious about its drinks and offers four real ales plus an excellent wine list (tasting notes are provided), including many available by the glass. Indeed, the Atlas is sufficiently interested in the grape to host wine workshops by the London Wine Academy (see page 264).

The simple, spacious bar area – split into eating and drinking sections – has been renovated but retains original features such as glazed tiles, wood panelling, wall benches and stone fireplaces, and an assortment of 'school' chairs and well-spaced tables. Outside is an attractive walled garden with an overhead awning and heaters for cool evenings.

In short, the Atlas is a civilised and relatively peaceful place to enjoy great food, beer and wine.

The Atlas, 16 Seagrove Rd, SW6 1RX (020-7385 9129; theatlaspub.co.uk; W Brompton tube; Mon-Sat 12-11, Sun 12-10.30).

The Builder's Arms
A hidden delight in Chelsea

There's nothing rough and ready about this popular Chelsea gastropub, which belies its workaday name with a stylish interior and excellent food. Occupying a handsome Georgian building, the Builder's Arms has a relaxed and inviting atmosphere, with a cosy main bar – featuring unusual artwork, bookcases and comfy banquettes – a dining area and outdoor seating.

They take their food seriously here, serving imaginative bar snacks and a brief but tempting modern British menu. There's also an excellent wine list and a wine club on Wednesdays, while beer drinkers have a choice of ales on tap.

The Builder's Arms, 13 Britten St, SW3 3TY (020-7349 9040; geronimo-inns.co.uk/ thebuildersarms; S Kensington tube; see website for opening times).

The Bull & Last
Head to Highgate for Sunday lunch

Situated close to the verdant sweep of Hampstead Heath and housed in a Grade II listed Victorian building, this renowned gastropub builds on its good looks and location by providing fine food, ales and wines. Artisan produce is championed ceaselessly, with daily-changing menus and an award-winning Sunday lunch – the *Observer* Food Monthly bestowed its 'Best Sunday Lunch' gong on the Bull in 2011.

The menu is a carnivore's delight, featuring hearty hunks of meat cooked with skill – and it also serves irresistible homemade ice cream. Dog- (and child-) friendly, they also provide tasty doggy treats.

The Bull & Last, 168 Highgate Rd, NW5 1QS (020-7267 3641; thebullandlast.co.uk; Kentish Town tube/rail; Mon-Thu 12-11, Fri-Sat 12-12, Sun 12-10.30).

The Canton Arms
Gastro genius at work

Stockwell isn't somewhere you'd expect to find one of London's best gastropubs, until you learn that the kitchen is run by Australian chef (and author) Trish Hilferty, formerly of the renowned Eagle (see page 139). The revamped traditional bar remains dedicated to drinkers, while Trish creates her culinary fireworks – seriously good rustic food – in the dining room.

The short British menu (with a few continental influences) is big on meat and offers flavoursome dishes such as foie gras and haggis toasties, game terrine, roast venison *tagliata* (sliced steak) and treacle tart. There's a gutsy wine list and four ales on tap.

The Canton Arms, 177 S Lambeth Rd, SW8 1XP (020-7582 8710; cantonarms.com; Stockwell tube; Mon 5-11. Tue-Sat 11-11, Sun 11-10.30).

The Carpenter's Arms
Hammersmith h(e)aven

Looking more like a shop than a pub, the Carpenter's Arms in Hammersmith is a gem of a gastropub serving great food. The good-value menu offers a mixture of pub classics and more complex foreign-influenced dishes. Thus pub staples like burgers and beer-battered haddock feature alongside more elaborate offerings such as saffron risotto with artichokes, squash and parmesan, and Brazilian fish stew with chilli and coconut milk.

There's also a great beer garden, a pleasing wine list and some excellent ales, plus friendly efficient service.

The Carpenter's Arms, 91 Black Lion Ln, W6 9BG (020-8741 8386; carpentersarmsw6.co.uk; Stamford Brook tube; Mon-Sat 11-11, Sun 12-10).

The Chapel
Worship at this temple of fine food

One of London's earliest gastropubs, the Chapel has won many awards since opening in 1995. Its interior is typical of the genre – light and airy with wooden floors – but it also boasts a walled garden and terrace, a rare bonus for a central London pub. There's a choice of menus – including antipasti and canapés if you want a lighter bite (see website) – with main dishes including the likes of griddled wild sea trout, confit duck leg and seven-hour Swaledale lamb shoulder.

There's also a comprehensive and reasonably-priced wine list and a good choice of ales, including Adnams and IPA on draught.

The Chapel, 48 Chapel St, NW1 5DP (020-7402 9220; thechapellondon.com; Edgware Rd tube; Mon-Sat 12-11, Sun 12-10.30).

The Coach & Horses
Traditional meets rustic for a weekday treat

Tucked away in Clerkenwell, the Coach & Horses is a traditional Victorian pub with wood-panelled walls, etched glass windows and arty prints – along with some spectacular food, excellent ales and a classy wine list. The simple rustic menu offers tasty starters such as bacon and black pudding hash, while mains include risotto and pasta dishes, steak and burgers (including a delicious pulled pork burger with beetroot, apple and bacon relish). Finish off with an affogato, an addictive melange of coffee, booze and ice cream.

Unfortunately, the pub only opens on weekdays, but is well worth a visit.

The Coach & Horses, 26-28 Ray St, EC1R 3DJ (020-7278 8990; thecoachandhorses.com; Farringdon tube; Mon-Fri 12-11).

The Crabtree
Chill out by the Thames

The Crabtree is a vast, iconic Victorian pub, spectacularly situated on the River Thames in Hammersmith/Fulham with a lovely sprawling decked garden. Weather permitting, food is served in the garden (there's an informal barbecue menu and a rotisserie option) or daily in the 'gastro' restaurant at the rear, specialising in seafood and meat dishes including Sunday roasts with all the trimmings.

Offerings may include foie gras and chicken liver parfait; baked Camembert; crispy duck and spinach salad; char-grilled 28-day Angus rib eye; and bouillabaisse, rouille and garlic croutons. Plus a good wine list and a superb choice of beers.

The Crabtree, 60 Rainville Rd, W6 9HA (020-7385 3929; thecrabtreew6.co.uk; Hammersmith tube; Mon-Sat 12-11, Sun 12-10.30).

The Crooked Well
Eat well at this Camberwell beauty

Recommended by the *Michelin Guide*, the Crooked Well in Camberwell is a delightful foodie pub with an elegant dining space and an attractive wooden bar. It serves honest, tasty food made with local, seasonal ingredients – including sharing dishes for families and friends – in a relaxed atmosphere. The enticing weekend breakfast (served from 9-11am) is well worth getting up for.

It isn't just about the food – drinkers are well catered for at the Crooked Well, with a good selection of fine wines and ales, an extensive cocktail list and delicious non-alcoholic drinks for drivers.

The Crooked Well, 16 Grove Ln, SE5 8SY (020-7252 7798; thecrookedwell.com; Denmark Hill rail; Mon 5-12, Tue-Thu 12.30-12, Fri 12.30-1am, Sat 9-1am, Sun 9-11).

The Drapers Arms
Georgian good taste

Drinkers and diners are both well served at this superior Islington gastropub and freehouse; while the owners state their 'determination to serve rewarding food and drink', they're also keen to stress that it's a neighbourhood pub. The Drapers Arms certainly looks the gastropub part, occupying an elegant Georgian building with a classic, stripped-down interior, lots of wood, and pale blue and green décor, with the added bonus of an attractive beer garden.

The lunch and dinner menus change daily (see website) and offer such meaty treats as ox cheek terrine and roast grouse.

The Drapers Arms, 44 Barnsbury St, N1 1ER (020-7619 0348; thedrapersarms.com; Highbury & Islington tube/rail; Mon-Fri 11-12, Sat 10-12, Sun 10-11).

The Duke of Cambridge
The greenest pub in London?

This back-street Islington pub was one of the UK's first to be certified organic by the Soil Association (soilassociation.org) and remains one of only a handful to hold this accolade. Its organic credentials apply to the drinks as well as the food – from home-baked bread to Fairtrade coffee – even the electricity is provided by wind or sun!

Some 80 per cent of the fresh produce is sourced in the Home Counties and the excellent menu includes plenty of vegetarian options, served in a large, airy bar with shabby chic décor that manages to be both fashionable and cosy.

The Duke of Cambridge, 30 St Peter's St, N1 8JT (020-7359 3066; dukeorganic.co.uk; Angel tube; Mon-Sat 12-11, Sun 12-10.30).

The Eagle
In and out of the Eagle...

This trail-blazing local on Farringdon Road was arguably the UK's first-ever gastropub. It started serving posh pub grub in 1991 and has stayed true to its principles while many imitators have fallen by the wayside. The Eagle does the gastropub 'model' perfectly, offering a good pint or glass of wine with well-cooked food at reasonable prices in a pared-back space of plain walls and wood, with large windows providing plenty of natural light.

Around six beers are available (including real ales) and there's a short wine list and even a few cocktails. The menu is chalked on blackboards and consists mainly of well-executed Mediterranean fare cooked in an open kitchen. Typical dishes may include *pappa al pomodoro* (Tuscan bread and tomato 'porridge'); linguine with clams; braised peas, jamón and aioli; and pan-fried scallops with chorizo on toast. The superb steak sandwiches are also hard to resist.

Friendly, efficient staff oversee proceedings and while it isn't a venue for an intimate date – it can be crowded and noisy, with some shared tables – the Eagle has a great vibe. There's no booking, so arrive early or late to ensure a seat.

The Eagle, 159 Farringdon Rd, EC1R 3AL (020-7837 1353; theeaglefarringdon.co.uk; Farringdon tube/rail; Mon-Sat 12-11, Sun 12-5).

The Earl Spencer
Lively local with great-value food

The Earl Spencer in Southfields was given a gastro makeover in 2003, but has managed to remain a 'proper' pub (with a log fire in winter) and a destination for drinkers as well as diners – not always an easy compromise. It's housed in an attractive Edwardian building with a long, low bar connecting two large, high-ceiled spaces, with outdoor tables for sunny days.

Food is reasonably priced and has attracted excellent reviews for its quality, value and thoughtful touches, such as the freshly-baked bread on the bar counter. The menu changes daily (see website) and features hearty seasonal dishes. Typical options may include home-smoked Atlantic prawns; devilled kidneys on toast; beef, bacon and pearl onion stew; smoked haddock kedgeree; and salt caramel and honeycomb ice-cream with biscotti.

Three cask ales are stocked such as Fuller's London Pride, Hook Norton's Old Hooky and Sharp's Doom Bar, and there's a well considered list of around 30 wines starting from just £3-£4 a glass.

Needless to say, the Earl is usually packed with locals and booking is essential if you wish to eat.

The Earl Spencer, 260-2 Merton Rd, SW18 5JL (020-8870 9244; theearlspencer.co.uk; Southfields tube; Mon-Thu 4-11, Fri-Sat 11-12, Sun 12-10.30).

The Empress

Hackney's jewel in its foodie crown

The Empress is one of London's best gastropubs. Chef Elliott Lidstone has over 12 years' experience working in Michelin-starred kitchens and uses quality produce from local suppliers including meat from Ginger Pig, fish from Jonathan Norris and bread from the E5 Bakehouse. One look at the mouth-watering menu (see website) is all you need to hotfoot it to Hackney.

If you're looking for good value, try the Monday night £10 dinner (main course with a glass of wine or pint of ale) or the ever-popular Frugal Feast: three courses for £20 – and you can bring your own bottle. Perfect!

The Empress, 130 Lauriston Rd, E9 7LH (020-8533 5123: empresse9.co.uk; Cambridge Heath rail or Bethnal Gn tube; see website for opening times).

The Engineer

Tuck in at Brunel's local

This elegant canal-side hostelry in Primrose Hill was built by English engineer extraordinaire Isambard Kingdom Brunel between 1845 and 1850 for the brewers Claverts. Recently refurbished, the fine Italianate building still has some original Brunel touches such as the striking wrought-iron 'dragon' light fixtures alongside the entrances. It's a relaxed, neighbourhood gastropub with friendly service, specialising in seasonal food.

Try the smoked haddock, poached egg and hollandaise for brunch, or a ribeye, chuck and bone marrow burger for lunch – or simply graze on Scotch quails' eggs at the bar. There are also some good ales and a carefully selected wine list.

The Engineer, 65 Gloucester Ave, NW1 8JH (020-7483 1890; theengineerprimrosehill.co.uk; Camden Town tube; see website for opening times).

The Fox
Hunt down this den of delights

The Fox is a laid-back gastropub in Shoreditch with an attractive large central bar – park yourself here for some tasty bar food – and a lovely first-floor restaurant with a terrace for sunny lunches and balmy-evening suppers. Cooking is fairly simple and straightforward, but nonetheless delicious, including spiced chicken livers with green wheat and yogurt; *panzanella* (Tuscan salad of bread and tomatoes); rib steak grilled on the bone; and salmon and haddock fish cakes.

There are some good ales, such as Harvey's Sussex Best, and a fine choice of wines – check out the monthly wine dinners (four courses with matching wines).

The Fox, 28 Paul St, EC2A 4LB (020-7729 5708; www.thefoxpublichouse.co.uk; Old St tube/rail; Mon-Fri 12-11, Sat 6-11pm, Sun 12-5).

The Fox and Grapes
Rural idyll meets Michelin magic

The Fox and Grapes occupies a fine position on Wimbledon Common where you feel as if you're deep in the countryside rather than on the edge of London. The pub was taken over in 2011 by Claude Bosi of Hibiscus and is now a superior gastropub with a seasonal British menu managed by Claude's brother Cedric. It's an unashamedly exclusive venue, as befits one overseen by a two-Michelin-starred chef, and isn't cheap; however, the quality of the cooking means it's still good value.

There are also some great real ales for CAMRA fans and a short but excellent wine list chosen by Berry Bros & Rudd.

The Fox and Grapes, 9 Camp Rd, SW19 4UN (020-8619 1300; foxandgrapeswimbledon.co.uk; Wimbledon tube/rail; Mon-Sat 11-11, Sun 11-10.30).

The Guildford Arms

An oasis of culinary calm

Food is the focus at the Guildford Arms, a friendly gastropub housed in a striking Georgian building in Greenwich, with an elegant restaurant, a private dining room and a stunning sunken garden. The ground floor bar is relaxed and informal, offering a good selection of cask beers, lagers and wines, along with a bar menu featuring light bites, seasonal dishes and popular pub classics.

Upstairs, the fine-dining restaurant is where chef-proprietor Guy Awford presents his modern British menu, showcasing the best of local and seasonal produce. Typical offerings include new-season English lamb, Scottish salmon and wild sea bass from Cornwall, while the wine list includes a wide choice from Europe and the New World, many available by the glass. The midweek lunch is a steal: three courses for just £22.

The spectacular sunken garden features both lawn and decked terrace areas, where white birch, grasses and kitchen herbs combine to create an oasis of calm. It's the perfect place to chill out with a jug of Pimm's while tucking into delicious grub from the barbeque.

The Guildford Arms, 55 Guildford Grove, Greenwich, SE10 8JY (020-8691 6293; theguildfordarms.co.uk; Deptford Br DLR; Tue-Sat 12-11.30, Sun 12-10.30).

The Gun
Fine dining in Horatio's love nest

Housed in a striking (Grade II listed) 18th-century building, the Gun overlooks the Thames in Docklands, just a short walk from Canary Wharf. For many years it was a run-down boozer for local foundry and river workers; Horatio Nelson was said to be a regular patron and allegedly enjoyed assignations with Lady Emma Hamilton in an upstairs room. After a fire in 2001 it was given a makeover by brothers Tom and Ed Martin and is now a celebrated gastropub.

The Gun serves award-winning modern British cuisine, including such delights as pheasant, oysters and salt-marsh lamb. Main courses are priced between £15 and £30 – prices more in tune with City traders than dockers – although bar grub is relatively inexpensive. In summer an alfresco bar serves Portuguese classics from a barbecue. There's a good choice of beer, with the likes of London Pride and Adnams ales as regulars, plus an extensive wine list.

High-backed leather armchairs, smartly turned-out waiters and panoramic views across the river from the large terrace are further draws for this popular venue, where booking is recommended.

The Gun, 27 Coldharbour, E14 9NS (020-7515 5222; thegundocklands.com; Canary Wharf DLR; Mon-Sat 11-12, Sun 11-11).

The Harwood Arms
A pint and wild game pie

Agenuine pub on a back street in Fulham, the Harwood Arms has received numerous accolades for its cooking and was the first London pub to be awarded a Michelin star. Unlike some gastropubs, the pub element hasn't been neglected; the owners are at pains to emphasise that the Harwood remains a traditional boozer and can get noisy.

At the same time, it has a rural feel – described on the website as 'where the country comes to the town' – which is reflected in the fare that includes game (such as venison, pheasant, rabbit and pigeon) and other wild produce such as signal crayfish, British snails and truffles from Berkshire. It isn't the cheapest place to eat – the set menu is £50 for three courses! – but good value considering that all-important Michelin star. Booking is recommended if you want to dine, although tasty bar snacks are also available including such tempting morsels as venison Scotch egg and rabbit rissoles.

As for drinks, there's a good choice of real ales on tap, including Black Sheep Bitter and Ruddles County, and a fine wine list, including over 30 available by the glass.

The Harwood Arms, Walham Grove, SW6 1QP (020-7386 1847; harwoodarms.com; Fulham Broadway tube; Mon 5-11, Sun, Tue-Thu 12-11, Fri-Sat 12-12).

The Havelock Tavern
Worth pushing the boat out for

Opened in 1996, the Havelock was one of London's earliest gastropubs and it hasn't forgotten its roots; it's a pub that serves food, rather than a restaurant serving beer. The distinctive, blue-tiled frontage conceals a classic gastro interior: light and airy with bare wooden floorboards and plain walls, plus outdoor tables for clement days.

The eclectic food isn't cheap but has won awards and recommendations from *Michelin* and the *Good Pub Guide*, and is worth pushing the boat out for. The Havelock also takes its beer and wine seriously, with many wines available by the glass.

The Havelock Tavern, 57 Masbro Rd, W14 0LS (020-7603 5374; havelocktavern.com; Kensington Olympia tube/rail; Mon-Sat 11-11, Sun 12-10.30).

The Horseshoe
A lucky find for foodies

Dating from the 1880s, this striking corner pub is now an outlet for Camden Town Brewery. Inside it's reminiscent of an American brewpub, as are some of its ales. However, the Horseshoe is the antithesis of the popular image of a fusty, specialist beer venue: large windows mean that it's light and airy, while the whitewashed brick and refectory tables are slick and stylish.

Food is simple but interesting (and good value), and makes the Horseshoe well worthy of the gastropub tag. There's also an affordable wine list.

The Horseshoe, 28 Heath St, NW3 6TE (020-7431 7206; thehorseshoehampstead.com; Hampstead tube; Mon-Thu 11-11, Fri 11-12, Sat 10-12, Sun 12-10.30).

The Jugged Hare
Medieval magic and fine wines

Get stuck into a robust medieval feast at the Jugged Hare, somewhere Henry VIII would have felt at home. The décor includes a lovely oak floor, red leather seating, and assorted stuffed and mounted animals, while the menu – big on roast meat and game – is a carnivore's delight.

The open 'theatre' kitchen features a state-of-the-art, eight-spit rotisserie and charcoal grill turning out spit-roast chicken, suckling pig and spring lamb, plus seasonal British game (haunch of venison, wood pigeon, grouse, etc.), fish and shellfish. There are also superior bar snacks (and a bar menu) including pork crackling with apple sauce, chips and gravy, and venison Scotch egg with Cumberland sauce. You can even come for breakfast, as the pub opens at 7am daily! It isn't somewhere to bring non-meat eaters – the menu offers only one nameless 'vegetarian' option – although there's plenty of fresh fish and seafood from Billingsgate market.

The Hare is big on wine and offers many by the glass, dispensed from its wine preservation machine; it also stages monthly gourmet wine nights. Beer fans aren't forgotten with four cask ales on tap, including their own Jugged Hare pale ale brewed by Sambrook's Brewery in Battersea.

The Jugged Hare, 49 Chiswell St, EC1Y 4SA (020-7614 0134; thejuggedhare.com; Moorgate tube; Mon-Wed 7am-11pm, Thu-Sat 7-12, Sun 7-10.30).

The Junction Tavern

Go up the Junction for great grub and ales

Beer drinkers are well catered for with Sambrook's Wandle and a list of rotating guest beers including Ascot, Brodies, East London, Exmoor, Meantime, Redemption, Timothy Taylor, Tring and Wye Walley (many from London brewers). The Junction has been voted CAMRA 'North London Pub of the Year' and stages regular beer festivals (see website for details).

The Junction Tavern, 101 Fortess Rd, NW5 1AG (020-7485 9400; junctiontavern.co.uk; Tufnell Pk tube or Kentish Town tube/rail; Mon-Thu 5-11, Fri-Sat 12-12, Sun 12-11).

A large corner establishment with an enviable reputation, the Junction Tavern caters equally to both beer aficionados and gourmets. It's a typical Victorian affair with high ceilings and elaborately carved dark wood, and a choice of places to sit, including the warm and friendly front bar area – with a stunning bar top and original fireplace – an airy conservatory, large heated garden terrace and award-winning beer garden.

The menu is modern British bistro with Italian seasoning, devised by Italian chef Jimmy Tirinzoni. Options change daily with mains in the £13-£20 range – around the London average for superior gastro fare. Weekend options include Saturday brunch (12-4pm) and all-day Sunday lunch (until 9pm). There's also a reasonably-priced and comprehensive wine list, with many available by the glass.

The Ladbroke Arms
Foodies can put their shirt on it

A free house on a tranquil street in Holland Park, the Ladbroke Arms is a destination pub for both foodies and drinkers, attracted by its eye-catching exterior, welcoming vibe, tasty food, good beer and extensive wine list. In summer the pub is festooned with an award-winning display of hanging baskets, while inside the look is pure gastropub: light and airy with wooden floors and a lovely terrace for sunny days.

The eclectic menu takes inspiration from around the globe, using fresh ingredients to produce tasty dishes such as linguine nero with octopus, clams, chilli and white wine, and beef cheek stew with roast vegetables.

The Ladbroke Arms, 54 Ladbroke Rd, W11 3NW (020-7727 6648; capitalpubcompany.com/our-pubs/the-ladbroke-arms; Holland Pk tube; Mon-Sat 11.30-11, Sun 12-10.30).

The Lady Ottoline
The hostess with the mostest

This beautifully restored gastropub is named after Bloomsbury society hostess Lady Ottoline Morrell, whose address book included Aldous Huxley and DH Lawrence. It's a classy venue that promises 'Bloomsbury's Best Sunday Roast' among other culinary attractions. The upstairs dining room serves imaginative modern British cuisine, and you can also eat in the bar which boasts a log fire in winter.

Tempting offerings from the menu include Chart Farm venison carpaccio and turnip remoulade; globe artichoke pie with toasted chestnuts and sheep's curd; and marinated clementines with white chocolate mousse and brandy snap.

The Lady Ottoline, 11A Northington St, WCIN 2JF (020-7831 0008; theladyottoline.com; Chancery Ln tube; Mon-Sat 12-11, Sun 12-5).

The Lansdowne
People-watching in Primrose Hill

One of the stalwarts of the gastropub scene, the Lansdowne has been serving roast cod and samphire to the gilded Primrose Hill set since 1992. You may even see a familiar face from television or *Hello!* magazine as you jostle to grab a spot in front of the welcoming winter fire (or an outdoor table on sunny days).

The downstairs bar offers good-quality pizzas and pasta, while the upstairs restaurant has a concise but classic menu of Mediterranean-influenced gastro grub. There's an extensive wine list and a good choice of ales on tap.

The Lansdowne, 90 Gloucester Ave, NW1 8HX (020-7483 0409; thelansdownepub.co.uk; Chalk Farm tube; Mon-Fri 12-11, Sat 10-11, Sun 10-10.30).

The Leather Bottle
Beach huts and burgers

There's been a pub on this spot for over 300 years; the current huge, sprawling Young's operation is noted for its expansive beer garden complete with beach huts ('the best pub garden in London' according to *Cosmopolitan* magazine), while in winter there are snug corners and open fires. Food is important at the Bottle, with all-British ingredients such as West Country meat and free-range eggs. Chef's specials change daily and include pub classics such as beer battered fish alongside seasonal delights (pheasant is popular).

In summer they fire up the barbecue in Tom's Bar (named after the pub's dog!).

The Leather Bottle, 538 Garratt Ln, SW17 0NY (020-8946 2309; leatherbottlepub.co.uk; Earlsfield rail; Mon-Thu 12-11, Fri-Sat 12-12, Sun 12-10.30).

The Mall Tavern

Modern food from a Masterchef

The Mall Tavern is a large, lovely Victorian corner pub in Notting Hill with a striking central bar (complete with chandeliers), a dining room, two private dining spaces (each with its own menu) and a lovely walled garden. It's owned by the Perritt brothers who in 2010 transformed what was then a run-down boozer into a modern local with great food and charming service, which still manages to retain the atmosphere of a 'real' pub.

The menu is the creation of Jesse Dunford Wood, a master of modern British food (with a twist) and sometime celebrity chef, having appeared on BBC's *Masterchef* and *The Truth about Food*. His food is imaginative and moreish. For starters, try the sharing plate of smoked salmon, chicken liver pate, smoked beetroot mousse and pork crackling, followed by salmon and herb fishcakes with parsley and sprouting broccoli or guinea fowl legs with pink firs, celeriac and aubergine. For dessert there's blood orange cheesecake, rum-soaked bubba with vanilla cream, or apple and rhubarb crumble with custard.

Drinkers aren't neglected, with three changing cask ales (such as Otter Bitter, Sambrook's Wandle and Sharp's Doom Bar), craft ciders, a classic cocktail list and some 30 wines.

The Mall Tavern, 71-73 Palace Gardens Ter, W8 4RU (020-7229 3374; themalltavern.com; Notting Hill Gate tube; Mon-Sat 12-12, Sun 12-11).

The Malt House
Leave room for the malted ice-cream

D ating back to 1729, the Malt House in Fulham occupies a building where cereal grain was once converted into malt – although nowadays it concerns itself with serving and drinking alcohol rather than brewing it. It was refurbished by Claude Bosi and reopened in 2013, quickly gaining a reputation as one of Fulham's most elegant destinations. The large dining space has high ceilings and beautiful *Period Living* décor, and there's also a charming beer garden. If you want to stay a bit longer, there are six luxurious en-suite rooms.

The seasonally inspired menu is overseen by Bosi, a two-Michelin-starred chef, and offers a selection of cheffy creations – such as cuttlefish, smoked sausage and borlotti bean stew – alongside classic English pub grub, including burgers, fish and chips, and traditional Sunday roasts. Tempting desserts include yogurt panna cotta with Alfonso mango and the Malt House's famous malted ice-cream.

For drinkers there's a choice of craft beers, an excellent wine list developed by Berry Bros & Rudd and a seasonal cocktail list. There's even a special Match Day menu when Chelsea are playing at home, but you'll struggle to get to the bar!

The Malt House, 17 Vanston Pl, SW6 1AY (020-7084 6888; malthousefulham.co.uk; Fulham Broadway tube; Mon-Thu 11-11, Fri-Sat 11-12, Sun 11-11).

The Narrow
Gordon's gastropub is just the tonic

Owned by Gordon Ramsay, the Narrow gastropub in Limehouse has an enviable riverside location in a former dockmaster's house. The delightful Grade II listed building has retained much of its period charm with original flagstones and fireplaces; it also has an attractive bar and a conservatory-cum-dining room.

The Narrow serves simple (by Gordon's standards) but elegant food sourced from the best British and European artisan producers. Sample dishes include Devon cock crab, chilli and broad beans on toast; burrata with fava beans and toasted almonds; crispy confit duck leg, grilled baby leek and tomato chutney; and Welsh lamb shank, rainbow chard, rosemary and black olives. Puds range from chocolate and Guinness cake to the perennially popular sticky toffee pudding. There's also a children's menu and Sunday roasts. Prices are reasonable for food of this quality – the set lunch is good value (£19 for two courses, £25 for three) – and a good deal cheaper than most of Gordon's other eateries. Cocktails, wine and beers can be enjoyed in the bar or the lounge. There's also a bar menu.

The Narrow is the perfect setting for lunch on a sunny day, but you'll need to book early to grab the best riverside tables.

The Narrow, 44 Narrow St, E14 8DP (020-7592 7950; gordonramsay.com/thenarrow; Limehouse DLR; Mon-Sat 12-11, Sun 12-10.30).

The Norfolk Arms

Tapas heaven!

Alongside its regular menu of reasonably-priced food, the Norfolk Arms has made a name for itself with its tapas. This friendly gastropub serves a vast choice of small dishes. Portions are generous given the prices – most cost £5.50 or under – and are complemented by an extensive, affordable wine list. Tuck into classic Spanish (Serrano ham and Manchego cheese), Mediterranean (baba ganoush) and even British (Jersey Royals with samphire) takes on the tapas theme.

If you want something more substantial, there's a small but tempting menu of mains with a (mostly) southern European influence.

Norfolk Arms, 28 Leigh St, WC1H 9EP (020-7388 3937; norfolkarms.co.uk; Russell Sq tube; Mon-Sat 11-11, Sun 12-10).

The Orange

An Orange with foodie appeel!

The Orange in Pimlico is a welcoming gastropub and boutique hotel housed in a beautifully-restored Georgian building (owned by Cubitt House). The four guest rooms are elegant and well-equipped, but food is the main draw, complemented by a good selection of guest ales, well-chosen wines and creative cocktails.

The extensive menu reflects the owners' passion for fresh, seasonal produce and sustainable sourcing. It's modern European with a rustic twist, featuring wood-fired pizzas (topped with, for example, goat's cheese, bresaola and chorizo), roasted meats and fish. Typical dishes include cider-braised pork belly and Anglesey mussels steamed with Guinness.

The Orange, 37-39 Pimlico Rd, SW1W 8NE (020-7881 9844; theorange.co.uk; Sloane Sq tube; Mon-Thu 8-11.30pm, Fri-Sat 8-12, Sun 8-10.30).

The Palmerston
Your lordship's ale house

A haven of civilisation in East Dulwich, the award-winning Palmerston has an attractive wood-panelled dining room and a large bar. Transformed into a gastropub in 2004, it's now regarded as one of southeast London's best places to eat and drink.

The food is good, if a bit pricey, although the set lunch on weekdays is reasonable and a good way to sample the kitchen's flair. There's a comprehensive choice of around 50 wines, many available by the glass, and a thoughtful selection of real ales.

Paradise by Way of Kensal Green
A foodie Eden in west London

D iscover Paradise by Way of Kensal Green, a charming, bohemian gastropub with a rabbit warren of intimate and larger spaces decorated in eclectic, shabby-chic style. The modern British menu includes treats such as Morecambe Bay shrimps, Lonk lamb and Dorset lobster – and a delicious Sunday roast.

With its bizarre, banquet-sized dining room – containing a melange of antiques, mirrors and chandeliers – a lovely courtyard garden and decked roof terrace, the über-stylish Paradise is well named.

Paradise by Way of Kensal Green, 19 Kilburn Ln, W10 4AE (020-8969 0098; theparadise.co.uk; Ladbroke Grove tube; Mon-Wed 4-12, Thu 4-1am, Fri 4-2am, Sat 12-2am, Sun 12-11.30).

The Palmerston, 91 Lordship Ln, SE22 8EP (020-8693 1629; www.thepalmerston.net; E Dulwich rail; Mon-Thu 12-11, Fri-Sat 12-12, Sun 12-10.30).

The Peasant
Very peasant food indeed!

Midway between Smithfield and the Angel, the Peasant was one of London's pioneering gastropubs (the second to earn that label, according to some) and is still pulling in the punters. It's an imposing Victorian public house – an inviting, light and airy place – with arched windows, huge mirrors, a horseshoe bar and an old mosaic floor thought to date from the 17th century.

There's a broad choice of bar food – from sharing plates, such as ploughman's or Mediterranean mezze, to roast meats and comfort puddings – while the upstairs restaurant serves an imaginative set menu (£20 for two courses, £24 for three). Typical dishes from the spring/summer menu include corn-fed chicken and ham hock terrine with mango mayonnaise; herb-crusted tuna Nicoise salad; globe artichoke stuffed with ricotta or mushroom duxelles

with asparagus, soft polenta and sauce vierge; and char-grilled whole mackerel with fennel and rocket salad. Sweets range from white chocolate fondant to pineapple tart tatin.

The Peasant also appeals to serious drinkers, with an ever-changing choice of real ales, lagers and ciders and around 50 wines. Children and dogs are welcome. Booking is recommended.

The Peasant, 240 St John St, EC1V 4PH (020-7336 7726; thepeasant.co.uk; Farringdon tube/rail; Mon-Sat 12-11, Sun 11.30-10.30).

The Pig and Butcher
Cutting-edge food at keen prices

Housed in an attractive mid-19th century building, the Pig and Butcher is a smart, well-run gastropub. It lives up to its name by butchering, smoking and curing its own rare-breed meat, which allows the chef to offer unusual cuts at keen prices. Fish is sustainable and line-caught, while vegetables are delivered farm-fresh from Kent.

The menu changes daily (see website) and is always inventive and hearty; main courses are mostly priced between £10 and £20, and include such treats as venison faggots, pearl barley risotto and guinea fowl. There are also plenty of craft beers and a good wine list.

The Pig and Butcher, 80 Liverpool Rd, N1 0QD (020-7226 8304; thepigandbutcher.co.uk; Angel tube; Mon-Wed 5-11, Thu 5-12, Fri-Sat 12-1am, Sun 12-11).

The Prince Bonaparte
A prince among gastropubs

The Prince Bonaparte is one of those gastropubs that makes drinkers feel as welcome as diners. It's a striking, large corner establishment with an Art Deco interior, neutral colours, open fires and picture windows, which somehow manages to appear spacious, uncluttered and cosy all at the same time.

The creative menu includes the likes of smoked haddock and parsnip risotto, lamb and red wine pie, wild mushroom and leek stroganoff, and 28-day aged longhorn steaks cooked on a Japanese grill. There's an interesting wine list of around 40 bins and a good selection of ales.

The Prince Bonaparte, 80 Chepstow Rd, W2 5BE (020-7313 9491; theprincebonapartew2.co.uk; Notting Hill Gate tube; Mon-Sat 12-11, Sun 12-10.30).

The Princess of Shoreditch
Pearly princess is a foodie delight

The acclaimed Princess of Shoreditch is a handsome, award-winning gastropub occupying a lovely, light-filled, 270-year-old building with a spiral staircase linking the downstairs bar and the upstairs dining room. It's a proper pub with a good choice of real ales and an interesting wine list, but the big attraction is the food.

The Princess is big on provenance and sources its venison, game birds and delicious beef from Chart Farm in Kent (the lamb is also from Kent), pork from Kilravock Farm in Nairnshire (Scotland) and fresh fish from day boats (and sustainable stocks) on the south coast.

The Princess of Shoreditch, 76-78 Paul St, EC2A 4NE (020-7729 9270; theprincessofshoreditch. com; Old St tube; Mon-Sat 12-11, Sun 12-10.30).

The Princess Victoria
Fit for a (future) Queen

The Princess Victoria is a one-time gin palace in Shepherd's Bush, built in 1829 and restored to its former grandeur: high ceilings with ornate cornices, atriums flooded with natural light and a lovely curved, white marble-topped bar. At the rear is a pretty walled herb garden, scented with rosemary, mint and lavender – the perfect place for an alfresco lunch or supper.

The PV is serious about superior food and fine wines, making most things from scratch, including bread and cakes, sausages and pies, and home-smoked and cured fish and meat. It even has its own wine shop and larder...

Princess Victoria, 217 Uxbridge Rd, W12 9DH (020-8749 5886; princessvictoria.co.uk; Shepherd's Bush Market tube; Mon-Sat 11.30-12, Sun 11.30-11).

The Queen's Head & Artichoke

A right royal feast in a classic Victorian pub

The Queen's Head and Artichoke was once a 16th-century royal hunting lodge in what later became Regent's Park. Relocated to its present site in 1811, the current classic Victorian corner pub dates from around 1900 and has been attractively restored, retaining its wood panelling and leaded windows.

One of London's more recent gastropubs, it offers a daily menu of modern British dishes alongside an exhaustive list of Mediterranean tapas – including breads and dips, salads and vegetarian plates, cured meats, meat and seafood dishes – many priced at around a fiver. The bar offers a wide range of real ales and beers, a comprehensive list of some 50 wines and creative cocktails.

The Queen's Head & Artichoke, 30-32 Albany St, NW1 4EA (020-7916 6206; theartichoke.net; Great Portland St tube; Mon-Sat 11-11, Sun 12-11).

St John's Tavern

Patron saint of good eating?

One of north London's first gastropubs and still one of the best, St John's Tavern consists of an intimate and sumptuous dining room and an atmospheric bar. It serves hearty British cuisine – alongside a healthy showing of European regional cooking using seasonal, locally-sourced produce; flame-grilled steak with béarnaise sauce, seasonal risottos and fish and chips regularly appear, alongside more exotic and unfamiliar dishes.

The back-to-basics kitchen makes all its own stocks from scratch, bakes sourdough bread daily, does all its own butchery and makes all its dishes in-house. There's also an impressive wine list and an excellent choice of beers.

St John's Tavern, 91 Junction Rd, N19 5QU (020-7272 1587; stjohnstavern.com; Archway tube; Mon-Thu 5-11, Fri-Sat 12-11, Sun 12-10.30).

The Sands End
The best Scotch eggs in Fulham

Although secreted away in a corner of Fulham with few transport links, the friendly Sands End is well worth a visit. It claims to bring a slice of the countryside to southwest London and has earned several awards.

The kitchen offers creative nose-to-tail eating and daily menus incorporate vegetables from its allotment, fish from day boats and meat butchered in-house, plus the best British seasonal farm produce. The Sands' signature dishes include its famous Scotch eggs, 12-hour slow-cooked lamb, roast rib of beef, and whole chicken with lemon and herb stuffing. Seriously good food and fine wines to boot.

The Sands End, 135-137 Stephendale Rd, SW6 2PR (020-7731 7823; thesandsend.co.uk; Parsons Grn tube/Imperial Wharf rail; Mon-Sat 12-12, Sun 12-11).

The Seven Stars
The real star is in the kitchen

The Seven Stars is a tiny pub, tucked away behind the Royal Courts of Justice in an early 17th-century building – one of the few to survive the Great Fire of London in 1666 – which celebrated its 400th anniversary in 2002.

The splendidly-named landlady Roxy Beaujolais has a cookbook to her name – *Home from the Inn Contented* – so you can rest assured that you'll be well fed. There's an inviting real ale choice (Sussex's Dark Star features regularly) and a short wine list by the glass, but punters come for the glorious food listed on a blackboard menu.

The Seven Stars, 53 Carey St, WC2A 2JB (020-7242 8521; Chancery Ln tube; Mon-Fri 11-11, Sat 12-11, Sun 12-10.30).

The Ship
Rambling riverside refuge

Conveniently located near the station and next to Wandsworth Bridge, the Ship is a much-loved riverside pub. There's been an inn on the site since 1786, although the current building dates from the early 19th century and was first leased by Young's brewery in 1832. It's a large pub with a comfortable interior – lots of nooks and crannies – as well as a conservatory and a large deck overlooking the Thames. On sunny days, these are usually packed while the bar areas remain relatively quiet.

On one side of the conservatory the dining area serves respectable gastro fare, for which booking is recommended; the pub also hosts barbecues when 'the temperature creeps above 14 degrees C'. The Ship is famous for its hearty and traditional seasonal food, with almost everything prepared daily from the simplest fresh ingredients. There's also a fantastic Sunday roast and a children's menu.

As well as Young's beer, there are up to four guest cask ales, including offerings from Sambrook's. There's also a reasonable wine list, designed to appeal to the pub's clientele of young professionals who flock here to enjoy the buzzy atmosphere. Regular live music events include jazz, blues and Irish acoustic sessions.

The Ship, 41 Jew's Row, SW18 1TB (020-8870 9667; theship.co.uk; Wandsworth Town rail; Sun-Wed 11-11, Thu-Sat 11-12).

The Somers Town Coffee House

From British tapas to cocktails and cake

Somers Town is an inviting place with a rabbit warren of rooms, including a spacious front bar and a restaurant, a series of dining spaces on the first floor, a front terrace and a rear courtyard. It's noted for its British tapas menu – from Stilton dumplings and pigs in blankets to smoked kipper fish cakes and game pie – plus staples such as burgers, salads, sandwiches and fish and chips. They also serve cocktails and homemade cakes.

Despite all these delicious distractions – and its odd name – Somers Town is first and foremost a pub, with around ten cask ales and an excellent wine list.

The Somers Town Coffee House, 60 Chalton St, NW1 1HS (020-7387 7377; thesomerstowncoffeehouse.co.uk; Euston tube/ rail; Mon-Fri 8-12, Sat 10-12, Sun 10-11.30).

The Stonemasons Arms

Builder-sized portions of tasty grub

A Fuller's pub, the Stonemasons Arms is a friendly hostelry in Hammersmith and one of the area's best pubs, managing to be both a friendly local and a noted gastropub. Inside, it's sleek, airy and modern, with wooden furniture, bare brick walls, a roaring log fire, large windows that flood the bar with light and a terrace for sunny days.

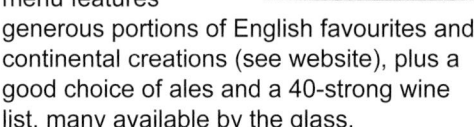

The seasonal menu features generous portions of English favourites and continental creations (see website), plus a good choice of ales and a 40-strong wine list, many available by the glass.

The Stonemasons Arms, 54 Cambridge Grove, W6 0LA (020-8748 1397; stonemasons-arms. co.uk; Hammersmith tube; Mon-Sat 11-11, Sun 12-11).

The Sussex Arms

Ale house supreme

Just off Twickenham Green, the Sussex Arms is full of olde-worlde charm that's absent from many suburban pubs. As you'd expect from a pub that styles itself an 'ale & cider house', it offers a multitude of draft beers and ciders, plus a choice of wines by the glass.

It also does a great line in home-cooked food – more pub grub than gastro but tasty nonetheless – including its famous signature pies and burgers, baby back ribs, braised lamb shank with sweet potato mash, and inviting blackboard specials – all at reasonable prices.

The Sussex Arms, 15 Staines Rd, TW2 5BG (020-8894 7468; thesussexarmstwickenham.co.uk; Strawberry Hill rail; Mon-Sat 12-11, Sun 12-10.30).

The Three Crowns

Drink, dine and dance the night away

Recently given a new lease of life as a gastropub-cum-nightclub, the Three Crowns has a cosy atmosphere with battered sofas, candlelit tables and a sleek wooden bar. The menu changes every two days and may include the likes of grilled, 28-day, rib-eye steak or steamed linguini with wild mushrooms. There are also some great beers on tap and a decent wine list.

The pub has an intimate basement space (called the Waiting Room) that hosts live music and DJ nights until the wee hours (2am Thu, 4am Fri-Sat).

The Three Crowns, 175 Stoke Newington High St, N16 0LH (020-7241 5511; threecrownsn16.com; Old St tube/rail; Mon-Wed 4-11, Thu 4-12, Fri 4-2am, Sat 12-2am, Sun 12-11).

The Truscott Arms
Making magic in Maida Vale

The Truscott Arms is a large, imposing Victorian pub with high ceilings, large windows and three lovely places to eat: a huge bar, an open restaurant and a decked garden. The award-winning restaurant specialises in locally-sourced ingredients, seasonal (sustainable) produce and gluten-free dishes (and drinks). Food ranges from bar snacks such as Scotch quails egg with salsa verde and Wagyu beef burger, to a hearty 35-day, dry-aged, rib-eye steak with girolle mushrooms and fondant potatoes.

There's a good range of ales on tap, a choice of beers (some gluten-free) and a thoughtful wine list.

Truscott Arms, 55 Shirland Rd, W9 2JD (020-7266 9198; thetruscottarms.com; Warwick Ave tube; Mon-Thu 10-11, Fri-Sat 10-12, Sun 10-10.30).

The Victoria
West London's queen of gastropubs

Voted 'Best Gastro Pub in London' at the Great British Pub Awards 2011, the Victoria is situated in a quiet road close to Richmond Park and feels more like a country house (there are also rooms available) than a London pub. It's co-owned by TV chef Paul Merrett, so the emphasis is firmly on fine food, both in the bar and the conservatory dining room.

It isn't cheap but is excellent value for the quality on offer; mains are around £14-£28 (for 28-day rib-eye steak). There's a good choice of ales and an extensive wine list.

The Victoria, 10 West Temple Sheen, SW14 7RT (020-8876 4238; thevictoria.net; N Sheen or Mortlake rail; Mon-Sat 8.30-11, Sun 11-10).

The Wells

A warm welcome for those on two legs or four

A short walk from Hampstead Heath, the Wells dates back to the early 18th century when Hampstead was the location of several spas (or wells). A run-down boozer when rescued in 2003, it has been transformed into an acclaimed 'pub-with-food' and is a highlight of the Hampstead gastro scene. Some original Georgian features remain and are combined with modern decorative touches to make for an eye-catching venue.

A diverse menu offers both lunch and dinner, plus roasts on Sundays. Sample starters include fig, gorgonzola and prosciutto salad or ham hock terrine; mains range from pan-fried Icelandic cod with crispy globe artichoke and romesco sauce to venison meatballs with linguini and chilli ragu. If you have room for a pud, you can dig into passion fruit pavlova or a dark chocolate pot. Prices are at the top end for gastro fare, but not excessive for food of this quality.

The wine list is well considered, categorised by character rather than grape (a few are available by the glass), while beer drinkers can enjoy solid favourites such as London Pride and Black Sheep. Dogs are welcome and there's even a menu for your four-legged friend!

The Wells, 30 Well Walk, NW3 1BX (020-7794 3785; thewellshampstead.co.uk; Hampstead tube; Mon-Sat 12-11, Sun 12-10.30).

The White Horse
First past the post for beer and food

The White Horse (aka 'The Sloaney Pony'), a lovely historic pub overlooking Parsons Green, is a magnet for both foodies and beer lovers. There's been a coaching inn on the site since at least 1688, but the current building is a model of Victorian elegance with a pleasing blend of traditional polished mahogany wall panels, wood and flagstone floors, large windows, open fires and contemporary lighting. The main space extends around three sides of a vast horseshoe bar, with the dining room in the old coach house at the rear. In the bar, Chesterfield-style sofas surround huge tables, ideal for families and groups, although the outdoor tables bordering the green are the most coveted.

The White Horse manages to be both one of the UK's best beer pubs – with a magnificent choice of cask and bottled beers from around the globe – and a serious foodie destination. It serves homemade British pub grub with a regional European influence, plus a selection of inexpensive, tasty bar snacks and canapés, plus Sunday roasts and BBQs (when the weather permits). Not cheap but good value for this neck of the woods.

The White Horse, 1-3 Parsons Green, SW6 4UL (020-7736 2115; whitehorsesw6.com; Parsons Grn tube; Sun-Wed 9.30-11.30, Thu-Sat 9.30-midnight).

The White Swan
Fine fare for City bankers

The White Swan (Pub & Dining Room) is an attractive gastropub near Chancery Lane, where the emphasis is on hearty British fare. The set lunch may be aimed at City bankers (£29 for two courses, £34 for three) but it does include the likes of Cumbrian veal cheek and wild Brixham sea bass. However, a more affordable bar menu offers enough to keep most people happy – try the Dexter beef burger or haddock and chips, both priced at under £16.

There are a number of draught ales on offer and a well-chosen wine list, with around two dozen available by the glass.

The White Swan, 108 Fetter Ln, EC4A 1ES (020-7242 9696; thewhiteswanlondon.com; Chancery Ln tube; Mon-Thu 11-12, Fri 11-1am).

The Woodman
A country pub in south London

The Woodman is a secluded, rustic south London pub steeped in history, with a spacious front bar (Chesterfields, gilt mirrors and old barrels), a dining room with vaulted ceilings and candles, and a delightful walled garden.

Styling itself a 'beer & food house', the Woodman serves award-winning food and ales. The seasonal menu – overseen by chef/proprietor James Rogers – offers a wealth of tasty delights including Dorset-reared rib eye, slow-braised wild venison and roast, free-range Suffolk pork. There are also daily specials, bar snacks, burger and steak nights, Sunday roasts and a reasonably priced, thoughtful wine list. Excellent value.

The Woodman, 60 Battersea High St, SW11 3HX (020-7228 2968; woodman-battersea.co.uk; Clapham Jct tube/rail; Mon-Sat 12-11.30, Sun 12-10.30).

7.
Markets

Artisan, organic and fresh – direct from farm to fork – food markets bring a delicious taste of country living to local communities throughout the city.

Fabulous foodie favourites

London's colourful food markets cater to people of all tastes, including purists seeking organic, local and sustainably-produced foods, cooks in search of rare or exotic ingredients, foodies wishing to sample the latest artisan flavours, and hungry folk yearning for something more satisfying than a sandwich. Here you'll find an abundance of seasonal fruit and vegetables; a wealth of meats, fowl and charcuterie; fresh fish; hand-made cheeses and other dairy products; bread, cakes, honey and preserves; herbs, spices and much, much more – not just from around the UK but from all corners of the globe.

For those for whom only the best is good enough, there are specialist markets such as the gourmet's paradise of Borough Market, the carnivore's Mecca of Smithfield and the fishy nirvana of Billingsgate, which cater to professional chefs, caterers and foodies alike. Those wanting the finest products must usually pay accordingly, but families on a tight budget can also find bargains on the streets.

In addition to replenishing your larder you can also fill your stomach at London's food markets, most of which are home to a battalion of street-food vendors (see Chapter 9).

London has retained many of its authentic 'Albert Square-style' markets, flogging no-nonsense fruit and veg, while some – such as Brixton and Whitechapel – offer more exotic ethnic fare reflecting the tastes of the local immigrant populace. In addition, all corners of the capital host vibrant farmers' markets, where local producers – not just farmers – sell direct to the public.

London's food markets are great places to browse, particularly when seeking inspiration for a dinner party or a special occasion, or when you just wish to give your taste buds a treat. So whether you're seeking fresh fruit and veg, meat or fish, unusual ingredients, or just fancy indulging in some homemade treats, the city's wealth of markets will fill your basket. There's only one simple rule: arrive early for the best choice.

Berwick Street Market

A rare surviving traditional street market

Berwick Street Market is one of London's oldest, created in the 18th century when shopkeepers started (illegally) displaying their wares outside their shops; it wasn't officially recognised until 1892. It's primarily a produce market, selling fresh fruit and vegetables, but has expanded in recent years to include an abundance of street food – you can pick up a great lunch for less than a fiver.

Stallholders also sell some fabrics and clothes (this was once a centre of the rag trade) and are noted for 'shouting' their wares to attract the attention of passers-by.

Berwick Street Market, Berwick St & Rupert St, W1F 8TW (berwickstreetlondon.co.uk; Oxford Circus tube; Mon-Sat 9-6).

Billingsgate Market

Shop at dawn if you want fresh fish for supper

The UK's largest inland fish market takes its name from its original location at Billingsgate – originally known as Blynesgate and Byllynsgate – on the Thames, where it was a centre of the fish trade from the 16th century onwards. It moved to East London in 1982 and is the capital's only dedicated fish and seafood market, selling some 25,000 tonnes of fish and related products annually. Billingsgate is open to the general public and is an interesting place to visit, although if you're shopping for fish you need to arrive early (it opens at 4am) for the best choice.

There's also an excellent Seafood School (see page 98).

Billingsgate Market, Trafalgar Way, E14 5ST (020-7987 1118; billingsgate-market.org.uk; Poplar DLR; Tue-Sat 4-9.30).

Borough Market
Foodie nirvana!

Borough Market in Southwark was first recorded in 1276, although some claim a market has existed in the area since the 11th century and possibly much earlier. Despite changing locations a number of times, and even being temporarily abolished in the 18th century, the market has thrived and today is the largest wholesale and retail artisan food market in London, selling a huge variety of food sourced from throughout Britain and around the globe. It's run by a charitable trust and is the only fully independent market in London

Since its renaissance as a retail market in the early 21st century – it still operates as a wholesale market from 2-8am on weekdays – Borough Market has become a mecca for those who care about the quality and provenance of the food they cook, sell or eat, including chefs, restaurateurs, gourmets, foodies and keen amateur cooks. It seems that anyone who's anyone in London's artisan food world has an outlet at Borough Market, including Artisan du Chocolat, Ginger Pig, Konditor & Cook, Monmouth Coffee and Neal's Yard Dairy, all of whom are featured in this book.

If anywhere in the capital illustrates our fascination with good food, it's Borough Market.

Borough Market, 8 Southwark St, SE1 1TL (020-7407 1002; boroughmarket.org.uk; London Br rail/tube; retail market, Wed-Thu 10-5, Fri 10-6, Sat 8-5).

Brixton Market
London's Caribbean treasure trove

Brixton Market is actually a number of markets thrown together in a gloriously haphazard manner. It comprises a vibrant street market and three elegant covered arcades: Reliance Arcade, Market Row and Granville Arcade (rebranded as 'Brixton Village' and packed with culinary treats) which are open daily. A more recent addition is Brixton Station Road, hosting both a food market on Fridays and a Sunday farmers' market.

After the huge wave of immigration in the '50s, Brixton Market became an important focal point for the black community, selling a wide range of ethnic goods. It's Europe's largest Afro-Caribbean food market, where you'll find specialities such as flying fish, goat and breadfruit, reflecting the diverse communities of Brixton and the surrounding area. In addition to a wide choice of world produce at modest prices with minimum frills, you can also tuck into a symphony of street food (see page 249).

Most markets are interesting to wander and browse, but Brixton Market is a much busier affair. It has a heaving atmosphere that you won't find elsewhere in London and is clearly the heart of a community that hasn't lost sight of its roots.

Brixton Market, Electric Ave, Pope's Rd and Brixton Station Rd, SW9 (020-7926 2530; brixtonmarket.net; Brixton tube; see website for times).

Broadway & Netil Markets
East London's foodie Mecca

Spend Saturday at Broadway and Netil Markets in East London, where Broadway Market – running from London Fields south to Regent's Canal – has been welcoming shoppers since the 1890s. It has gone from strength to strength since the Saturday food market was launched in 2004 and now boasts over 100 stalls selling delicious cheeses, bread, coffee, rare-breed meat, spices, cakes and much more.

Neighbouring Netil Market – an altogether more sedate affair – is located on Westgate Street, where you'll find more food stalls plus vintage homewares, jewellery designers, illustrators, original artwork, vintage clothing, accessories and more.

Broadway Market, E8 (broadwaymarket.co.uk; London Fields rail; Sat 9-5) and Netil Market, 13-23 Westgate St, E8 3RL (netilmarket.tumblr.com; Sat 11-6).

Brockley Market
South London's artisan honeypot

Open all-too-briefly on Saturdays, Brockley Market is one of London's leading outlets for artisan and small producers, with a reputation extending far beyond the local area. The host of traders reads like a who's who of the movers and shakers of the slow food revolution, offering everything from seasonal fresh fruit and veg to meat, fish and poultry; ice-cream and coffee to artisan bread, cakes and charcuterie.

Like all good food markets, the pleasure is in browsing; feeding your eyes and imagination, and just going where your stomach takes you.

Lewisham College Car Park, Lewisham Way, SE4 1UT (brockleymarket.com; St John's rail; Sat 10-2).

Farmers' Markets
The food lovers' best friend

London pioneered the late 20th century rise of farmers' markets and they can now be found throughout the capital, from Walthamstow to Wimbledon, providing a lifeline for small producers and vendors selling fresh, often organic and (most importantly) locally-produced food.

grown fruit and vegetables (often organic) to hand-made foods such as cakes, preserves and sauces. There's a rule that everything on sale should have been grown, reared, caught, brewed, pickled, baked, smoked or processed by the stallholder (with the exception of imported foods) – or as the London Farmers' Markets organisation states, 'we grow it, we sell it'.

Produce on sale usually includes fresh

For the uninitiated, a farmers' market is a venue where food is sold directly to the public by farmers, growers and producers, with no middleman. Ranging in size from well-established food fairs to a small collection of stalls, they're united by the premium produce they sell: from locally-

fruit and vegetables; fish, meat and poultry; eggs, cheese and other dairy products; bread, juices, preserves, olives/olive oil, wine, cider and cakes; plus more unusual things such as edible flowers, raw honey and buffalo mozzarella. Because it's

Farmers' Markets (cont.)

> Take the opportunity to speak to stallholders and find out how their food is grown and produced – you may even get some cooking tips or recipe ideas.

seasonal, produce varies throughout the year, but you'll often find unusual varieties that aren't available in supermarkets, such as Tatsoi salad greens, striped or golden beetroot, and heritage varieties of fruit and veg.

As well as being a source of quality food, farmers' markets are good for the environment: everything is 'locally' produced, thus reducing food miles. To trade at one of the capital's farmers' markets, producers must be located within 100mi (160km) of the M25, although many are much closer. Some of the farms are organic, while others use minimal amounts of chemicals.

There are over 30 farmers' markets across London, most held weekly on Saturdays or Sundays, although some are held on weekdays and some only once a month. Many of the best are certified by FARMA, the National Farmers' Retail & Markets Association (farma.org.uk/certification-farmers-market), which independently assesses and certifies farmers' markets around the country to make sure that they're the 'real deal'.

There are two main organisations for farmers' markets in London: London Farmers' Markets (www.lfm.org.uk), with around 20 markets, and City & Country Farmers' Markets (weareccfm.com), with around ten. Their aims are to increase farm incomes; promote local and seasonal foods; encourage sustainable agriculture, traditional animal breeds and heritage fruit and vegetable varieties; and further understanding between rural and urban communities. The websites contains a list of markets, while the LFM website contains a roll call of regular stallholders, maps and other information.

London Farmers Markets (www.lfm.org.uk) and City & Country Farmers' Markets (weareccfm. com).

Hackney Homemade Market
A Hackney love affair

Hackney Homemade Saturday market – the brainchild of local travel and food writer Jane Egginton – is held in the glorious grounds of St John's Church, opposite Hackney Central station. Like all good markets, it isn't just a shopping experience but an opportunity for local people to socialise in a pleasant environment.

Market stalwarts include a bevy of artisan producers selling bread, cakes, cheese, cured meats, game, fruit and veg, chutneys and pickles, etc., alongside stalls offering ready-to-eat treats such as homemade sausages, salt beef burgers, Japanese *katsu* curry and quesadillas.

Hackney Homemade, St John's Church grounds, Lower Clapton Rd, E5 0PD (hackneyhomemade. com; Hackney Central rail; Sat 11-5, 4pm in winter).

Lower Marsh Market
From cheap eats to artisan treats

Steeped in history, Lower Marsh is one of London's oldest and best-loved market streets, less than five minutes from Waterloo, Southwark and Lambeth North stations.

Starting as a weekday street food market offering cheap eats to local office workers, the market has now expanded to include a Saturday artisan food market (10am to 3pm) where traders sell speciality ingredients and produce. These include award-winning steaks from Boarstall Meats, fruit and veg from Brambletye Farm, bread and cakes from Raffo & Ridgeway and Italian goodies from the Seriously Italian Company.

Lower Marsh Market, Lower Marsh, SE1 (020-7620 1201; lowermarshmarket.co.uk; Lambeth N tube; Mon-Fri 10.30-5, Sat 10-3).

Maltby Street/Ropewalk Market

Possibly the city's coolest food market

Maltby Street in Bermondsey is fast becoming London's latest foodie destination, where the indie foodie spirit thrives. The area between Maltby Street and Millstream Road and the nearby Ropewalk hosts a lively, informal weekend street market, with a combination of railway arch shops, open stalls, pop-up bars and eateries. It's a more laidback and relaxed affair than nearby Borough Market (see page 172) and has a burgeoning reputation among chefs and foodies.

The market (known variously as Maltby Street Market or Ropewalk Market) grew from an informal Saturday community after the Monmouth Coffee roastery decided to open its doors for a few hours each week.

They were swiftly followed by Neal's Yard Dairy, the Kappacasein Dairy and the Ham & Cheese Co. A few years on some of the old traders have moved down the road to the Spa Terminus and newcomers have moved in.

At weekends, trestle tables heave with everything from cupcakes and brownies to seafood and charcuterie, gourmet gelato to oven-fresh bread and a profusion of vegetables and fruit. You can also enjoy a local gin-based cocktail, artisan beers from the Kernel Brewery, wine and sherry from José Pizarro's tapas bar, and – of course – great Monmouth coffee.

Maltby Street Market, Rope Walk, Maltby St, SE1 3PA (maltby.st and www.spa-terminus.co.uk; Bermondsey tube; Sat 9-4, Sun 11-4).

Partridges Food Market
Ambrosia for Sloane Rangers

bread and cheese; fish and seafood; homemade pies; specialist coffees and teas; and a wide range of international specialities and street food. Traders include Blue Mountain Coffee, the Maldon Oyster Company, Neustift Goat Dairy Cheeses, Pieminister pies, Simply Handmade (chocolates), Tartufi Sibillini (Umbrian truffles), Wapping Sourdough Bakery and many, many more (see the website for a full list).

Partridges (named after the nearby upmarket food emporium – see page 124), West London's most popular food market, began life in 2005 and has grown rapidly in popularity ever since, so much so that it now has a waiting list for would-be stallholders. The aim was to celebrate the diverse and evolving world of fine local British and international foods, and also to offer small producers, start-up businesses and farmers the chance to share their passion and expertise with the public. Starting with just 15 stalls it now attracts an average of 70 traders every Saturday.

Held on the Duke of York Square (close to Sloane Square tube station), the market offers a wide range of produce including free-range meats; patisserie, pastries and cakes; organic juices and produce; artisan

Partridges Food Market, Duke of York Sq, SW3 4LY (020-7730 0651; partridges.co.uk/foodmarket; Sloane Sq tube; Sat 10-4).

Portobello Road Food Market
Not just for antiques

Although most famous for its Saturday antiques bazaar, Portobello Road also hosts one of London's best fruit and veg markets (mainly between Elgin Crescent and Talbot Road), where Londoners flock from miles around to buy their produce. Prices are generally much lower than in supermarkets and you can find seasonal varieties that are rare elsewhere, such as heritage tomatoes, 'donut' peaches and *cavolo nero* (black cabbage).

There's also a wide range of specialist food stalls, particularly on Fridays and Saturdays, when you can choose from baked goods, oils, olives, gourmet cheeses, meat, fish/seafood, tea and coffee and much more. Near the corner of Talbot Road, the Bread Stall has bread, cakes and pastries throughout the week, but save their biggest selection for Fridays and Saturdays when 20 different kinds of bread go on sale. There's also at least one discount food stall (Fri-Sat) selling cheese, confectionery, biscuits and pantry foods; real bargain hunters should arrive late on Saturday when boxes of ripe produce go on sale for around a pound.

As if that wasn't enough, Portobello Road is home to a vast choice of cafés, restaurants, artisan food shops and stalls selling delicious street food (see page 254).

Portobello Road Market, Elgin Cres to Talbot Rd, W11 (portobellomarket.org and shopportobello. co.uk; Notting Hill Gate tube; Mon-Wed 9-6, Thu 9-1, Fri-Sat 9-7).

Real Food Market

Real food from real people at affordable prices

Fill your larder (and stomach) with artisan food at the Real Food Market in Southbank Centre Square (behind the Royal Festival Hall), held weekly Friday to Sunday. The market was created in the shadow of this Modernist landmark to provide an outlet for small artisan producers and bring high quality 'real food' at affordable prices to the masses.

The Real Food Market hosts some of the capital's best artisan food producers selling unique and delicious seasonal produce including some of the freshest fish in London (sourced from the nearby Kent coast), high-quality beef, artisan bread, tasty cheeses and charcuterie, all manner of delicious cakes and desserts, superb coffee and tea, the finest craft beers and wines, plus some of the city's most creative street food vendors. You can fill up on brioches stuffed with duck confit, Spanish *churros* (pastries not dissimilar to doughnuts) dunked in hot chocolate, and even artisan ice lollies.

There are also quarterly street food festivals on Queens Walk on the South Bank (between the London Eye and Hungerford Bridge) presenting a line-up of London's most passion-driven street food traders, along with a live music stage – see website for information.

Real Food Market, Southbank Centre Sq, Belvedere Rd, SE1 8XX (020-7370 8624; realfoodfestival.co.uk/markets; Waterloo rail/ tube; Fri 12-8, Sat 11-8, Sun 12-6).

Smithfield Market
A cathedral for carnivores

This landmark for the meat trade dates back over 800 years and is the last surviving historical wholesale market in central London. It's housed in an imposing Victorian (Grade II* listed) edifice and is worth visiting for its architecture as much as its food. The Italian-inspired market building was designed by Sir Horace Jones (1819-1887) – the man who built Tower Bridge – and opened in 1868. The main wings (the East and West Market) are separated by the Grand Avenue, a wide roadway roofed by an elliptical arch: the whole is a vast cathedral-like structure of ornamental cast iron, stone, Welsh slate and glass.

Although Smithfield is primarily a wholesale market, anyone can buy meat here, although to get the best choice you need to arrive before 7am. The market's website advises that before buying anything you should have a good look around and ask questions – prices aren't normally displayed – and, if you're going to be buying regularly, get to know the traders too. But it's a fascinating place to visit even if you don't plan on shopping.

After your visit treat yourself to a hearty breakfast in one of the local pubs, which open early to accommodate the market traders.

Smithfield Market, East Market Building, EC1A 9PS (020-7332 3092; smithfieldmarket.com; Barbican tube; Mon-Fri 3am until mid-morning).

Spitalfields Produce Market
Spitalfields goes back to its foodie roots

Old Spitalfields Market is one of London's finest surviving Victorian market halls, situated just outside the City. Today it's a popular fashion, food, vintage and general market, open seven days a week, but in June 2013 it returned to its roots and added a produce market.

Held every other Friday and on the second Saturday of the month from 10am until late in the evening, it offers a wide range of seasonal and locally produced goods, including fruit and veg, meat, chicken, fish, cheese, eggs, juice, bread, cakes, preserves and much more.

Spitalfields Produce Market, Old Spitalfields Market, 16 Horner Sq, E1 6EW (020-7375 2963; oldspitalfieldsmarket.com/events/spitalfields-produce-market: Liverpool St rail/tube; 10am to late, see website for dates).

Whitechapel Market
Full of East End promise

Situated between Vallance Road and Cambridge Heath Road, Whitechapel Market is a long-established local market and social hub that unites the area's different cultures. A visit to this bustling market with its exotic sights, smells and sounds is like being deposited in Dhaka or Delhi.

It offers a wealth of Asian herbs and spices, from cumin to coriander, cardamom to cloves, plus a wide range of exotic fruit and vegetables and other Asian foods. You can also buy cut-price toiletries, cheap fashion, ethnic jewellery, flowers and fabrics. Great value!

Whitechapel Market, Whitechapel Rd, E1 1DT (Whitechapel/Aldgate E tube; Mon-Sat 9-6).

Brasserie Zedel

8.
Restaurants

'Nothing would be more tiresome than eating and drinking if God had not made them a pleasure as well as a necessity.'

(Voltaire)

The world on a plate

The days when London's restaurant scene was the subject of international derision are long gone. The city has seen a gastronomic revolution in the last few decades and is widely considered to offer some of the best and most varied dining in the world. Indeed, many critics now rate it on a par with Paris, New York and Hong Kong as one of the gourmet capitals of the world. The city is now home to many of the planet's most highly acclaimed chefs, and its vast choice of innovative and exciting restaurants caters for all tastes and budgets.

This chapter spans the gamut of London's dining experiences, from Michelin-starred 'fine dining' to pie and mash, with cuisines ranging from French and Italian to Indian and Vietnamese, modern British to Mediterranean, steak house to vegetarian, dim sum to tapas – and everything in between. There's something to suit every foodie's palate and pocket.

> 'Pull up a chair. Take a taste. Come join us. Life is so endlessly delicious.'
>
> (Ruth Reichl, American food writer)

With a few exceptions, we have omitted London's most celebrated and lauded restaurants – although we have included around a dozen with one Michelin star – not because they aren't excellent, but because they don't always offer the best value for money, you often need to book weeks (or months) in advance – and there's frequently an understudy in the kitchen.

Instead, we've tried to find a compromise between price and quality. We've featured cheap eats and expensive restaurants – almost 100 of our favourites – with the emphasis on value for money. All provide good (if not great) food, friendly service and an agreeable atmosphere. Most have also stood the test of time and will be around long after today's faddish places have gone.

Bon appétit!

L'Absinthe

Every neighbourhood should have one

This attractive traditional French bistro (plus coffee shop, deli and caterer) in Primrose Hill opened in 2007 and quickly became a favourite destination for the local community.

Fronted by charming expat Burgundian and 'Grand Fromage' Jean-Christophe (JC) Slowik, L'Absinthe offers a bright and cosy dining room, conservatory and small courtyard. Here you can enjoy great French cooking such as classic fish soup with rouille and croutons, duck confit with braised red cabbage, and crème brûlée with blackcurrant sauce. There's a well-chosen (mostly French) wine list or you can even bring your own. *Magnifique!*

L'Absinthe, 40 Chalcot Rd, NW1 8LS (020-7483 4848; labsinthe.co.uk; Chalk Farm tube; Tue-Sun – see website for times; French; ££).

Al Waha

Simply the best Lebanese food in town

The award-winning Al Waha ('oasis') is a relaxing Lebanese restaurant in Notting Hill, serving some of the best Middle Eastern cuisine in London. It's the perfect place to enjoy the fresh, spicy food of Lebanon, one of the great unsung cuisines of the world. Al Waha is renowned for its mezze – a parade of small dishes, including falafel, hummus and sambousek (stuffed pastries) – followed by delicately marinated and grilled meat and poultry, and mouth-watering homemade baklava.

There's also a wide choice for vegans and vegetarians, plus a selection of Lebanese wines, some of which are surprisingly good.

Al Waha, 75 Westbourne Grove, W2 4UL (020-7229 0806; alwaharestaurant.com; Bayswater or Royal Oak tube; daily 12-11.30; Lebanese; ££).

Amaya
Indian food that's out of this world

From the MW Eat group (www. realindianfood.com) – which also owns Chutney Mary in Chelsea and the venerable Veeraswamy (Regent Street), plus the Masala Zone brasserie chain – Amaya offers cutting-edge, contemporary Indian cuisine that breaks the mould. The stunning interior complements the theatrical open-grill kitchen which employs three traditional Indian styles of cooking: the tandoor (a furnace-like clay oven), *sigri* (cooking over a coal-fired barbecue) and *tawa* (searing and griddling on a very hot plate).

Amaya is London's most avant-garde Indian restaurant – with a Michelin star and many other awards – and its fresh, fragrant and flavoursome food has been described as 'gourmet theatre from another stratosphere'. The seasonal menu includes delectable kebabs – such as a succulent row of smoky, clove-infused lamb nuggets – finger-licking Punjabi chicken-wing lollipops, scrumptious masala lobster served in the shell, and much more. The wines (some available by the glass) have been chosen by award-winning wine author and respected journalist Matthew Jukes to accompany the complex and varied flavours of Amaya's cuisine.

Don't expect curry-house prices, but there are a number of (more) affordable set-meal options including the Amaya platter (the equivalent of three courses), business and weekend lunch specials, plus a host of multi-cultural events (see website for details). The restaurant offers wheelchair access and a disabled WC.

Amaya, Halkin Arcade, Motcomb St, SW1X 8JT (020-7823 1166; amaya.biz; Knightsbridge tube; Mon-Sat 12.30-2.15, 6.30-11.30, Sun 12.45-2.45, 6.30-10.30; Indian; ££-£££).

L'Anima

Exceptional Italian food, beautifully presented

An acclaimed, award-winning Italian restaurant and bar in the heart of the City, L'Anima (Italian for 'soul') offers fine contemporary Italian cooking (and a superb wine list) in elegant surroundings. The sophisticated ambience is more than matched by the creative cuisine of chef Francesco Mazzei, whose passion for food was cultivated while working for some of the most famous restaurants in the world.

You can choose to dine in the bar, which has live music from 7pm (Tue-Sat). Francesco also offers cookery classes (see website).

L'Anima, 1 Snowden St, Broadgate West, EC2A 2DQ (020-7422 7000; www.lanima.co.uk; Shoreditch High St rail or Liverpool St tube/rail; Mon-Sat – see website for times; Italian; ££-£££).

Apero

I'm not sharing my sharing plate!

Apero – named for the blessed hour when Italians precede their dinner with an *aperitivo* – is a superb Italian brasserie/ bar with leather snugs, Spanish tiles and exposed bricks, nestled in the vaulted cellars of the Ampersand Hotel in South Kensington.

Chef Chris Golding creates unpretentious Mediterranean cuisine packed with flavour using fresh seasonal ingredients, from breakfast through to supper. The sharing menus of small plates – think Italian 'tapas' – are a house favourite, as is the great-value set lunch (£12 for two courses, £15 for three). There are interesting wines and cocktails too.

Apero Restaurant & Bar, Ampersand Hotel, 2 Harrington Rd, SW7 3ER (020-7591 4410; aperorestaurantandbar.com; S Kensington tube; open daily – see website for times; Mediterranean; ££).

L'Autre Pied
Magical, masterful cuisine

C hic and contemporary modern European cuisine in fashionable Marylebone, L'Autre Pied is the sister restaurant of highly acclaimed Pied à Terre. Since opening in 2007 – with talented young head chef and part-owner Marcus Eaves creating his magic in the kitchen – it has received a string of accolades, including a Michelin star.

Marcus has been replaced by Andy McFadden, whose culinary artistry conjures up dainty yet intense dishes with a cornucopia of fresh ingredients packed into every mouthful – and at slightly more affordable prices than its aristocratic sibling. The set menus are particularly good value.

L'Autre Pied, 5-7 Blandford St, W1U 3DB (020-7486 9696; lautrepied.co.uk; Bond St/Baker St tube; Mon-Sat 12-2.30/6-10.30, Sun 12-3.30; modern European; ££-£££).

Barrica
As good as tapas get outside Spain

I f you love tapas then you'll be passionate about Barrica, an authentic Spanish eatery – awarded a Michelin Bib Gourmand in 2014 – which wouldn't be out of place in Barcelona or Madrid. Whether you want a coffee and pastry, some olives, jamón or queso manchego with a glass of fino, or a full-blown Iberian feast, Barrica fits the bill.

With its friendly atmosphere and reasonable prices, it's a great place for a snack, a leisurely lunch, or an evening lingering over tapas and sherry. *Bravo!*

Barrica, 62 Goodge St, W1T 4NE (020-7436 9448; barrica.co.uk; Goodge St tube; Mon-Fri 12-11.30, Sat 1-11.30; Spanish tapas; ££).

Bibendum
A star turn from the Michelin Man

Dining at Bibendum is a visual feast as well as a treat for the taste buds. You'll be as charmed by the venue's spectacular windows and elegant spaciousness as by Matthew Harris' classic French cuisine (which, alas, has no Michelin star).

The landmark Michelin House opened in 1911 as the UK HQ of the Michelin Tyre Company. Its design is Art Nouveau meets Art Deco: a riot of decorative ceramic tiles, mosaics and stained-glass windows depicting racing cars, maps and – not least – the Michelin Man. Since 1987 it has been home to Bibendum – named after the original Michelin Man – encompassing a restaurant, oyster bar and a more informal bistro-café.

The restaurant's classic French food has a strong British influence with a contemporary edge, using the best seasonal ingredients to produce flavourful and stylish dishes of sophisticated simplicity. The informal oyster bar focuses on all kinds of fruits de mer, plus salads, pasta and simple mains, or you can relax with a coffee or glass of wine in the café. There's also a 'crustacea stall' where you can buy fresh lobster or crab for your supper.

Bibendum, Michelin House, 81 Fulham Rd, SW3 6RD (020-7581 5817; bibendum.co.uk; S Kensington tube; open daily – see website for times; French; ££-£££).

The Bingham Restaurant
Divine – and a bargain to boot

The handsome boutique Bingham Hotel occupies two elegant Georgian townhouses – built in 1740 and combined in the 1830s by Lady Anne Bingham – tucked away beside the river in Richmond-upon-Thames. The acclaimed Bingham is a chic retreat, although thanks to its dining room it's more of a destination restaurant with rooms than a hotel.

Head chef Mark Jarvis' superb modern British cuisine uses the finest locally-sourced sustainable ingredients, including herbs and vegetables from the hotel's own garden. The resplendent light and airy dining room, with its abundant gold leaf and wooden floors, has French doors opening onto a covered balcony for alfresco summer dining, with impeccable service provided by attentive and knowledgeable staff.

In summer the 'market lunch' menu (Mon-Sat) is a bargain at just £15 for three courses, which may include the likes of cod brandade, velouté of celeriac, Cornish ling, Telmara Farm duck and mascarpone cheesecake with strawberry sorbet. You can also choose from the tempting à la carte menu, plus a special Sunday lunch and a mystery menu (vegetarian options available) – or even afternoon tea. There's a lovely lounge bar for pre-dinner drinks.

Bingham Restaurant, Bingham Hotel, 61-63 Petersham Rd, TW10 6UT (020-8940 0902; thebingham.co.uk/our-restaurant; Richmond tube/rail; open daily – see website for times; modern British; ££).

Bistrotheque
East End hipsters' hangout

Occupying a converted factory in an uninspiring East End location, Bistrotheque is a breath of fresh air, managing to be both elegant and contemporary at the same time, with sparkling white décor, high ceilings and industrial chic. The menu is more French-style than truly Gallic, offering the likes of mackerel paté and steak tartare alongside cod and chips and cheeseburgers.

The prix fixe menu (available before 7pm) is good value at £20 for three courses and there's a popular weekend brunch. Drop-ins can eat at the large oval bar (the Manchichi), which also serves divine cocktails.

Bistrotheque, 23-27 Wadeson St, E2 9DR (020-8983 7900; bistrotheque.com; Cambridge Heath rail; open daily – see website for times; modern French; ££).

Blue Elephant
A tantalising taste of Thailand

Blue Elephant is a grand Thai restaurant – one of an international chain founded by Khun Nooror Somany Steppe in Brussels in 1980 – located in Chelsea's Imperial Wharf.

Offering the best of Thai cuisine and hospitality, Blue Elephant is renowned for the authenticity and excellence of its food, its palatial Thai décor and friendly, efficient service. The chefs prepare traditional dishes using ingredients imported fresh from Thailand; diners can choose from a choice of tasting, à la carte, vegetarian and gluten-free menus, which are a feast for the eyes as well as the palate.

Blue Elephant, The Boulevard, Imperial Wharf, Townmead Rd, SW6 2UB (020-7751 3111; blueelephant.com/london; Imperial Wharf rail; open daily – see website for times; Thai; £££).

Blueprint Café
A winning design on every plate

Situated on the first floor of the Design Museum, the Blueprint Café (operated by D&D London) enjoys an enviable location on the south bank of the Thames, offering panoramic views of Tower Bridge, the City and Canary Wharf.

It's the perfect setting to experience the modern European cuisine of head chef Mark Jarvis; the daily changing menu of classic dishes (with a modern twist) includes the likes of homemade black pudding with cider vinegar, apple chutney and a poached hen's egg or French turbot, seeded quinoa, brown shrimp and chorizo. Grand designs indeed!

Blueprint Café, Design Museum, 28 Shad Thames, SE1 2YD (020-7378 7031; blueprintcafe. co.uk; Tower Hill tube; Mon-Sat 12-2.45, 6-10.45, Sun 12-4; modern European; ££).

Bocca di Lupo
The whole of seductive Italy is here

Opened in 2008, Bocca di Lupo (literally 'wolf's mouth' but also an expression for 'good luck') is a small, friendly-family trattoria specialising in authentic regional Italian cuisine. Most food is made in-house including breads, sausages, salami, pickles, mustard, gelato and, of course, pasta, with the remainder carefully sourced from Italy.

The delicious and reasonably priced cuisine – available in small and large plates – has won many awards, as has its outstanding all-Italian wine list (winner of 'Best Wine List' at the Tatler Restaurant Awards 2013).

Bocca di Lupo, 12 Archer St, W1D 7BB (020-7734 2223; boccadilupo.com; Piccadilly Circus tube; Mon-Sat 12.15-3, 5.15-12, Sun 12.30-3.15, 5-11; Italian; ££).

Boqueria
Tapas nirvana!

Boqueria is an exciting tapas restaurant located on Brixton's Acre Lane (there's another outlet in Clapham) which has received rave reviews, including the *Good Food Guide's* London Regional Restaurant of the Year 2014.

Named after Barcelona's famous food market, Boqueria aims to introduce diners to the traditional flavours of Spain in a relaxed and convivial setting. Just as important as the food is the excellent Spanish wine list – including a wide choice of cava and sherry – without which you cannot have a truly authentic tapas experience.

Boqueria, 192 Acre Ln, SW2 5UL (020-7733 4408; boqueriatapas.com; Clapham N/Common tube; Mon-Fri 5-11.30, Sat 12.30-3.30, 5.30-12, Sun 12.30-10.30; Spanish tapas; ££).

Bouchon Fourchette
Unlikely French gem in East London

Bouchon Fourchette is a welcome addition to London's menu of French restaurants, particularly in East London where French cuisine of any kind is thin on the ground.

Chef Jeremy Huguet did his apprenticeship in the kitchens of Alain Ducasse and Pierre Gagnaire and his classical training is evident, although you shouldn't expect haute cuisine. The food needs a bit of tweaking to really impress but all the ingredients are there – it's excellent value for money and the French waitresses are a delight! Bouchon also does a great brunch.

Bouchon Fourchette, 171 Mare St, E8 3RH (020-8986 2702; bouchonfourchette.co.uk; London Fields rail; Mon 5-10pm, Tue-Thu, Sun 9am-10pm, Fri-Sat 9am-11pm; French; ££).

Brasserie Zedel
The best French brasserie in town

Tuck into traditional French cuisine at buzzy Brasserie Zedel, a Parisian grand café, bar and brasserie from the prolific Chris Corbin and Jeremy King partnership. The vast subterranean dining room is a vision of La Belle Époque, with the ambience of an ocean liner during the golden era of transatlantic travel.

All the brasserie favourites are here, including classic onion soup, escargots, celeriac rémoulade, frisée with lardons, pâté de champagne, steak haché, boeuf bourguignon, duck confit, choucroute, tarte au citron, heavenly tarte tatin and much more.

Above all, Zedel is terrific value, offering a taste of the gastro palaces of Paris for the price of your local Café Rouge, including the bargain prix fixe at £8.95 for two courses (£11.75 for three) and the formule (£19.75 for three courses plus a glass of wine, water and coffee). The short wine list starts at £16 a bottle, with almost everything below £30, while cocktails start from around £6.50. The restaurant is also rated three stars by the Sustainable Restaurant Association (thesra. org), so you'll be helping save the planet! And if you want to make a night of it, there's also a glitzy cabaret and nightclub.

Brasserie Zedel, 20 Sherwood St, W1F 7ED (020-7734 4888; brasseriezedel.com; Piccadilly Circus tube; Mon-Sat 11.30-midnight, Sun 11.30-11pm; French; ££).

Brawn

Food with provenance, cooked to perfection

Designed to appeal to hip East Londoners, Brawn is on-trend with its chic industrial look of concrete floors, whitewashed walls and simple furniture. The great value French-influenced menu allows diners to pick and mix small plates – such as brawn (or head cheese, if you prefer), rillettes and varieties of charcuterie – while the Sunday fixed-price menu (3 courses for £28) is a great treat after exploring the nearby flower market.

All food is seasonal and carefully sourced, and Brawn also takes great care with its wines, which are mostly 'natural' (organic or biodynamic) and sourced from small growers working sustainably.

Brawn, 49 Columbia Rd, E2 7RG (020-7729 5692; brawn.co; Hoxton rail; open daily – see website for times; French; ££).

Buen Ayre

Steak and Malbec – a marriage made in heaven

When nothing but a big fat juicy steak will do, hotfoot it to Buen Ayre, a bona fide *parrilla* (South American grill) located in trendy Broadway Market. Occupying a rustic room with the *asado* (barbecue) at centre stage, it's a great place to have a mighty meaty feast with a group of friends.

The pièce de résistance is the Parrillada Deluxe mixed grill (£28), comprising two fantastic steaks, sausages, black pudding and provolone cheese (and a free doggy bag!). Just add a bottle of delicious Malbec and you're in carnivore heaven.

Buen Ayre, 50 Broadway Mkt, E8 4QJ (020-7275 9900; buenayre.co.uk; London Fields rail; Mon-Fri 12-3, 6-10.30, Sat-Sun 12-3.30, 6-10.30; Argentinian; ££).

Café des Amis
Authentic French cooking with a British twist

Enjoy a tasty lunch or supper at Café des Amis in Covent Garden, a haven of civilisation (with cosy corners and chandeliers) in a sometimes fraught and chaotic corner of the city. It serves solid French brasserie fare, from classic steak tartare and roast duck breast glazed in a prune and Armagnac sauce, to proper bouillabaisse and porc a la Normande. Finish with *la soupe au chocolat*, a decadent chocolate soup served with black pepper ice cream.

Good value, particularly the pre-theatre set menus. Try the cosy cellar wine bar too.

Café des Amis, 11-14 Hanover Pl, WC2E 9JP (020-7379 3444; cafedesamis.co.uk; Covent Gdn tube; Mon-Sat 12-11.30pm, Sun 12-9; French; ££).

Cambio de Tercio
Paying homage to el Bulli

Founded in 1995, Cambio de Tercio is a vibrant, award-winning restaurant in Kensington, offering modern and innovative Spanish cuisine in the style of the legendary el Bulli alongside more traditional dishes.

One of London's most authentic restaurants – it was once declared 'the best Spanish restaurant in any country outside Spain' by the Spanish Minister of Agriculture, Fishing and Food – Cambio is best-known for its modern take on classic tapas. A feast for the eyes and taste buds, it's expensive, but then you don't find food of this quality on every menu.

Cambio de Tercio, 163 Old Brompton Rd, SW5 0LJ (020-7244 8970; cambiodetercio.co.uk; Gloucester Rd tube; open daily – see website for times; Spanish; ££-£££).

Caravan
Comfort food to die for

You can eat your way around the world at Caravan, a cool, trendy café-restaurant, bar and coffee roastery in Farringdon's bustling Exmouth Market. With huge windows overlooking the market, the restaurant has an outdoorsy feel, which is enhanced during fine weather when the doors fold back to allow alfresco dining. The room has a casual vibe and funky industrial design – wooden tables, white pipework and trendy light fittings – although the mouth-watering food is the star attraction.

There are three menus – breakfast (weekdays, 8-11.30), brunch (weekends 10-4) and an all-day lunch and dinner menu offering small and large sharing plates – employing seasonal ingredients to create inventive dishes featuring flavours from around the globe. The fashionable term is fusion food, but this is like no fusion food you've ever tasted – in a good way!

Breakfast treats include banana caramel porridge, and smoked black pudding with roast apples and a fried egg, while the main menu includes miso-cured salmon with pickled daikon, red onion and *furikake* (Japanese seasoning), and slow-roasted rabbit with herb polenta, heritage carrots and golden raisins. It's innovative and unusual, but at Caravan unusual is the norm and the norm is fantastic!

There are also great coffee and interesting wines – all at reasonable prices.

Caravan, 11-13 Exmouth Mkt, EC1R 4QD (020-7833 8115; caravanonexmouth.co.uk; Farringdon tube; Mon-Fri 8-11.30, 12-10.30, Sat-Sun 10-4, 5-10.30; global; ££).

Cây Tre

Some of the freshest and best-value Oriental food in town

Soho-based Cây Tre – there's another branch in Shoreditch – has a fresh and creative approach to Vietnamese cooking, one of the Orient's best (but largely unsung) cuisines. Using only the very freshest ingredients, everything at Cây Tre is bursting with flavour, from the classic beef Pho, which takes over 18 hours to make, to crispy sea bass with green mango and wok-fried Devon duck. For dessert, dip your spoon into basil and coriander ice-cream, made by Gelupo (see page 21).

There's the bonus of a surprisingly good wine list and they also offer takeaway.

Cây Tre, 42-43 Dean St, W1D 4PZ (020-7317 9118; caytresoho.co.uk; Leicester Sq tube; Mon-Thu 11-11, Fri-Sat 11-11.30, Sun 11-10; Vietnamese; £).

Chabrot Bistrot d'Amis

Bijou bistro with grandes flavours

Chabrot Bistrot d'Amis opened to critical acclaim in 2011, showcasing the elegant simplicity of its classic French bistro fare. The décor of this charming restaurant – wood panelling, red and white table linen and waiters' aprons – conjures up images of southern France, while the seriously skilful cooking and high-quality ingredients only serve to strengthen the illusion that you are indeed in *la France profonde*.

There's a good value prix fixe lunch menu (£14.50 for two courses, £19.50 for three) and an excellent all-French wine list, with a wide selection available by the glass (12.5cl) or carafe (50cl).

Chabrot Bistrot d'Amis, 9 Knightsbridge Green, SW1X 7QL (020-7225 2238; chabrot.com; Knightsbridge tube; Mon-Sat 12-11, Sun 12-10; French; ££).

Chez Bruce
Well worth a trip south of the river

You can expect a magnificent meal at the Michelin-starred Chez Bruce, a restaurant with fine foodie credentials. In an earlier incarnation this was Harvey's, where Marco Pierre White, the enfant terrible of celebrity chefs, cut his teeth, and although two decades have passed since Bruce Poole and Nigel Platts-Martin took over, it remains one of London's very best places to eat. In 2014, readers of *Harden's London Restaurants* guide voted Chez Bruce their favourite restaurant for the 10th consecutve year!

The cuisine is based loosely on classical and regional French/Mediterranean cooking, and may lack the histrionic flourishes, showmanship and theatricality that many restaurants indulge in nowadays, which some may view as old-fashioned. However, foodies and gourmets delight in

the wonderful food, relaxed ambience and superb service.

Specialities include homemade charcuterie, slow-cooked braises, offal dishes, warm and cold salads, classical desserts and an impeccable cheeseboard. It also has an excellent wine list, including many great and rare fine wines. The set lunch and dinner menus are a bargain for food of this quality. Chez Bruce's sister restaurant The Glasshouse also features in this chapter (see page 211).

Chez Bruce, 2 Bellevue Rd, SW17 7EG (020-8672 0114; chezbruce.co.uk; Wandsworth Common rail; open daily – see website for times; French/ Mediterranean; ££-£££).

Clarke's
A delight at any time of day

Opened in 1984 by trail-blazing chef Sally Clarke, this award-winning café-restaurant and bar has been a Kensington landmark for 30 years, and is a firm favourite with critics and foodies alike. Clarke's serves breakfast, lunch and dinner, and its menus change daily to showcase Sally's passion for using the very best and freshest seasonal produce (organic where possible). Everything is delicious, simple and elegant, and the staff are charming too.

Clarke's also has a delightful shop and operates a commercial bakery which supplies many of the capital's top restaurants and hotels.

Clarke's Restaurant, 124 Kensington Church St, W8 4BH (020-7221 9225; sallyclarke.com; Notting Hill Gate tube; Mon-Sat – see website for times; modern British; ££).

Clos Maggiore
London's most romantic restaurant

An oasis of calm in the heart of Covent Garden, Clos Maggiore has a string of awards – including London's 'Most Romantic Restaurant' (Hardens 2014) – and a menu of beautifully presented, contemporary French cuisine. The creative Provençal-inspired food includes such delights as slow-cooked Gloucester pork cheek, venison with chestnuts and slow-roasted rabbit, followed by decadent desserts like tiramisu wrapped in dark chocolate and pear frangipane tart.

It's also great value – the pre- and post-theatre menus are a particular bargain at under £20 for two courses – and the wine list was voted (joint) 'Wine List of the Year 2014' by Imbibe magazine.

Clos Maggiore, 33 King St, WC2E 8JD (020-7379 9696; closmaggiore.com; Covent Gdn tube; Mon-Sat 12-2.30, 5-11, Sun 12-2.30, 5-10; French; ££-£££).

Club Gascon

Haute cuisine at its highest

jus; cappuccino of black pudding, lobster and asparagus; and squab pigeon with glazed kumquats.

Alternatively you can opt for Pascal's five-course seasonal 'Le Marché' menu or – if time is pressing – choose the lunchtime version, a more affordable introduction to Gascon's cuisine with two courses from the 'Le Marché' menu for £26.50. There's also a comprehensive selection of wines from southwest France.

The Gascon group includes Comptoir Gascon – a gourmet bistro and delicatessen – and a wine bar, Cellar Gascon.

Club Gascon, 57 West Smithfield, EC1A 9DS (020-7600 6144; clubgascon.com; Barbican tube; Mon-Sat – see website for times; French; ££-£££).

Since opening in 1998, Club Gascon has received numerous accolades, including a Michelin star awarded in 2002. It specialises in authentic haute cuisine from the Gascony region of southwest France; executive chef Pascal Aussignac hails from Toulouse, where foie gras, sausage, cassoulet and Armagnac are the order of the day.

Situated close to Smithfield market, Club Gascon boasts a delectable menu focussing on the very finest seasonal produce. The à la carte menu changes frequently and includes the likes of cured yellow fin tuna, crispy pork and Bearnaise sabayon; 'royale' of duck, seared langoustine and sea urchin

Cocochan
A masterclass in pan-Asian cuisine

Enjoy a taste of the Orient at award-winning Cocochan restaurant and bar in the West End, offering affordable pan-Asian cuisine and classy cocktails. The bold contemporary interior features geometric screens, moody lighting, mirrored origami-lattice work décor and black table tops.

The vast eclectic menu includes light meals such as dim sum and sushi from the canapé menu, along with classic dishes drawn from Chinese, Indian, Japanese, Thai and Vietnamese cuisines. Favourites include soft shell crab *futomaki* (fat sushi rolls), Thai green curry, and sea bass with chilli bean dumplings. Set menus start from £35 a head, cocktails from £8.

Cocochan, 38-40 James St, W1U 1EU (020-7486 1000; cocochan.co.uk; Bond St tube; daily 12-12; pan-Asian; ££-£££).

The Dairy
Worth moving to Clapham for

Chef Robin Gill and his wife Sarah previously worked at Le Manoir aux Quat'Saisons, so it isn't surprising that The Dairy (bar and bistro) has received voluminous praise for its superb modern British cuisine and attention to detail. The menu varies depending on the season and what's available in the restaurant's own urban garden (other produce is impeccably sourced), with daily specials for both lunch and dinner. The four-course lunch (served Wed-Fri) is a snip at £25.

Don't let the venue's unremarkable (but cool) appearance fool you, this is seriously good cooking.

The Dairy, 15 The Pavement, SW4 0HY (020-7622 4165; www.the-dairy.co.uk; Clapham Common tube; Tue 6-10, Wed-Sat 12-3, 6-10, Sun 12-4; modern British; ££).

Daquise
A Polish home from home

This landmark restaurant in South Kensington has been serving traditional Polish cuisine to homesick Poles since 1947. It was taken over by the legendary Gessler family of restaurateurs in 2008 and is now a light and airy space with shabby-chic décor: wooden floorboards, bare plaster walls, white tablecloths and fresh flowers. However, it's the food that's the real attraction.

The menu changes daily and always includes traditional fare such as steak tartare, marinated herring, rabbit in mustard sauce and roasted duck stuffed with apples. It's the place expatriate Poles go to reminisce over favourite dishes such as *barszcz* (a Polish version of borscht), *golonka* (pickled ham hock with sauerkraut), *pierogi* (dumplings filled with minced pork, mushrooms and cabbage) and *bigos*, a rich and savoury soup with cabbage and meat which is Poland's national dish. Desserts are rich and filling – try dumplings stuffed with fresh strawberries or pancakes filled with cheese – and best of all, courses are interspersed with vodka shots.

Daquise offers wholesome, flavoursome, authentic cuisine, charming and friendly service, and is great value. Who ever knew Polish food could be so good?

Daquise, 20 Thurloe St, SW7 2LT (020-7589 6117; daquise.co.uk; S Kensington tube; daily 12-11; Polish; ££).

The Delaunay
Dine like a Euro-millionaire

Indulge yourself at the elegant Delaunay café-restaurant in Covent Garden, which takes its inspiration from the grand cafés of Europe; its glamorous and sophisticated dining room echoes a sumptuous European brasserie with a vibrant cosmopolitan buzz.

The menu is diverse, offering everything from crustacea platters to salads and steaks, and takes in Euro classics such as moules frites and choucroute à l'Alsacienne, as well as a selection of wieners and schnitzels. There's also a tempting array of cakes, pastries and desserts, making the Delauney the perfect place for a decadent Viennese-style afternoon tea.

The Delaunay, 55 Aldwych, WC2B 4BB (020-7499 8558; thedelaunay.com; Holborn or Covent Gdn tube; open daily – see website for times; modern European; ££).

Dinings
Where sushi meets tapas

Dinings is a contemporary sushi and Japanese 'tapas' restaurant occupying an unassuming converted townhouse in Marylebone. The food is based on the traditional Japanese *izakaya* style of dining – not dissimilar to a Spanish tapas bar – and combines both traditional Japanese and modern European cuisine.

Executive chef (and MD) Masaki Sugisaki previously cooked at Nobu, so not surprisingly the food is superb, bursting with flavour, freshness and originality. From soft-shell crab spring rolls to char-grilled Wagyu beef, everything is a taste sensation. There's also a street-level counter offering a good-value lunchtime sushi selection.

Dinings, 22 Harcourt St, W1H 4HH (020-7723 0666; dinings.co.uk; Edgware Rd tube; Mon-Fri 12-3, 6-10.30, Sat-Sun 12.30-3.30, 6-10.30; Japanese; ££-£££).

Dishoom

Vibrant comfort food from old Bombay

A wonderfully kitsch café-restaurant, Dishoom is a modern take on the old Irani (Persian) style cafés that were popular in '60s Bombay. Based in Shoreditch (there's another in Covent Garden), its faded retro design incorporates ceiling fans, vintage advertising, family photos and droll slogans ('All chai is coming strictly without opium').

The authentic Indian-fusion food is delicious, whether you opt for breakfast (bacon naan rolls with chilli jam), lunch or dinner (try the moreish lamb raan) – and all served with bottomless house *chai* (Indian spicy tea), refreshing lassi or Raj-style cocktails on the verandah.

Dishoom, 7 Boundary St, E2 7JE (020-7420 9324; dishoom.com; Shoreditch High St rail; Mon-Wed 8-11pm, Thu-Fri 8-12, Sat 9-12, Sun 9-11; Indian; ££).

Donostia

One of the world's truly great cuisines

Donostia is the Basque name for San Sebastián, considered by many to be the gastronomic capital of Spain. It's run by Tomasz Baranski (previously of Barrafina) whose passionate interpretation of Basque cuisine more than lives up to his restaurant's name. The look may be minimalist – white walls, rustic tables, open kitchen – but the food is complex, offering Basque favourites such as salt cod and Ibérico pork, as well as an enticing menu of tapas (or *pintxos* as they're called here).

The wine list features some unusual (and superb) Riojas and Basque white wines (*txakoli*) or, if you prefer, there's *sargadoa* (Basque cider).

Donostia, 10 Seymour Pl, W1H 7ND (020-3620 1845; donostia.co.uk; Marble Arch tube; Mon 6-11, Tue-Sat 12.30-3, 6-11, Sun 1-4, 6-9; Spanish; ££).

Esarn Kheaw
Fresh, zingy, spice heaven

One of London's best Thai restaurants, Esarn Kheaw specialises in north-eastern Thai cuisine and has been wowing diners (including many expat Thais) in west London for over two decades.

It serves standard Thai treats such as pad Thai noodles, Thai green curry and spicy *tom yum* soup, but it's the Esarn cuisine that sets it aside from the rest. Try the grilled catfish, spicy salads (minced chicken, pork or beef with lime leaves, coriander, chillies and fish sauce) and the wonderfully named Tiger Cry – strips of char-grilled beef served with a hot chilli sauce. Everything is delicious, authentic and inexpensive.

Esarn Kheaw, 314 Uxbridge Rd, W12 7LJ (020-8743 8930; esarnkheaw.com; Shepherd's Bush Mkt tube; Mon-Fri 12-3, 6-11, Sat-Sun 6-11pm; Thai; £-££).

Five Fields
Creativity runs riot in Chelsea

Run by chef-proprietor Taylor Bonnyman and head chef Marguerite Keogh, Five Fields – winner of the 2013 BMW Square Meal Restaurant of the Year award – balances luxurious indulgence with fresh and playful creativity. The cuisine focuses on modern British fare and combines carefully-sourced fish and meat with produce from the restaurant's own herb and vegetable garden in East Sussex (veggies also find their way into the desserts, e.g. butternut squash ice-cream!). The daily dinner menu (£50 for three courses) is relatively expensive, but good value.

There are also intriguing cocktails and an excellent wine list that spans the globe, although France dominates.

Five Fields, 8-9 Blacklands Ter, SW3 2SP (020-7838 1082, fivefieldsrestaurant.com, Sloane Sq tube, Tue-Sat 6.30-10pm, modern British, £££).

Franco Manca
The best pizzas in town

Enjoy London's best (and most reasonably priced) pizzas at Brixton Market's Franco Manca (there are eight other outlets around town). Franco's pays homage to the best Neapolitan pizzerias, making delicious, slow-rise, sourdough-crust pizzas topped with a simple sauce, the best Italian-style cheese, cured meats and seasonal vegetables – all baked for just 40 seconds at an inferno-like temperature (500°C/930°F!) in a wood-fired brick oven. The dough is magnificent and all the ingredients are carefully sourced from rare breed animals or made in-house. The result is a real artisan pizza – *bellissimo!*

Franco Manca also offers pizza-making masterclasses at its Chiswick branch.

Franco Manca, Unit 4, Market Row, SW9 8LD (020-7738 3021; francomanca.co.uk/pages/brixton.html; Brixton tube; Mon 12-5, Tue-Sat 12-11, Sun 12-10.30; pizza; £).

The Gate
Great veggie cuisine for allcomers

This stylish, award-winning vegetarian restaurant in Islington is the younger sibling of the original Gate in Hammersmith (opened in 1989). The food reflects the diverse cultural background of the owners (Adrian and Michael Daniel) whose grandmothers blended Indian and Arabic cuisines with traditional Jewish food. Ingredients are carefully sourced and inventively blended to create beautifully presented, original food combinations such as couscous-crusted aubergine and wild mushroom and celeriac rosti.

The Gate offers a selection of à la carte, set menus and weekend brunch, plus a children's menu for little veggies.

The Gate, 370 St John St, EC1V 4NN (020-7278 5483; thegaterestaurants.com; Angel tube; daily 12-3, 5-10.30, Sat-Sun brunch 10-3; vegetarian; ££).

Gauthier Soho

Flawless food from a French master

for dessert, a tart of Grand Cru Virunga dark chocolate (70 per cent) with a yoghurt sorbet. A novel touch is that each dish is calorie-counted, although if you're eating here then calories should be the last thing on your mind! There's also an exciting wine list, chosen to complement and elevate the classically light French cuisine. *Parfait!*

In 2013, Gauthier published his first cookbook, *Vegetronic*, described as 'vegetables for carnivores'.

Gauthier Soho, 21 Romilly St, W1D 5AF (020-7494 3111; gauthiersoho.co.uk; Leicester Sq tube; Mon 6.30-10.30, Tue-Sat 12-2.30, 6.30-10.30; modern French; ££-£££).

Occupying a charming Regency townhouse in Soho, Alex Gauthier's fine dining restaurant is a gem, while his modern French cooking is lively and refreshing with a twist of decorative kitsch. Since opening its doors in May 2010, Gauthier Soho has won many awards, including three AA rosettes and a Michelin star (which it inexplicably lost in 2013). Decorated in cream and white, the atmosphere is rarefied and genteel – somewhere for a special spoil-yourself occasion.

There's a wide range of menus, including extravagant tasting menus, a set lunch (a bargain at £18 for two courses and £25 for three) and à la carte. Menus are seasonal and may include duck egg and trompette mushrooms, English crayfish tortellini, black truffle risotto, wild Atlantic sea bass, crispy and tender piglet, Charolais beef fillet, and

The Glasshouse

A gem of a neighbourhood restaurant

Sister restaurant to the celebrated Chez Bruce (see page 201) and La Trompette, the Glasshouse opened in 1999, gained a Michelin star in 2002 and has maintained its outstanding reputation ever since. Head chef Berwyn Davies has travelled extensively and his culinary experiences in Australia, India, the Far East and New York are evident in the delicious cuisine, imbued with great flavours, flawless technique and a lightness of touch.

There are set-price menus for lunch (from £24.50 for two courses) and dinner (£45 for three courses) and a superb wine list offering rare and fine wines at reasonable prices.

The Glasshouse, 14 Station Parade, TW9 3PZ (020-8940 6777; glasshouserestaurant.co.uk; Kew Gdns tube; Mon-Sat 12-2.30, 6.30-10.30, Sun 12.30-2.30, 7-10; modern European; ££-£££).

Gokyuzu

Turk of the town

A long-established, family-run restaurant, Gokyuzu's authentic eastern Mediterranean cuisine has been enthusing diners in this north London Turkish enclave for over 15 years. This superb – and under-rated – cuisine was conceived for the tables of the Ottoman Sultans and was once the most sophisticated fare in the world.

Classic Turkish dishes are prepared in a traditional wood oven or on a charcoal grill using authentic Mediterranean ingredients and spices – such as lamb, aubergines, cumin and mint – and include amazing mezze, wonderful kebabs and *pide* (Turkish pizza) to die for. Huge portions and outstanding value for money; well worth queuing for at busy times.

Gokyuzu, 26-27 Grand Parade, Green Lanes, N4 1LG (020-8211 8406; gokyuzurestaurant.co.uk; Harringay Green Lanes rail; daily 9am-1am; Turkish; ££).

Golden Hind
The gold standard in fish and chips

In 2014 the Golden Hind celebrated a century of providing fish suppers to the spoiled residents of Marylebone, so they must be doing something right. First opened by Italians, now run by Greeks, it's a down-to-earth chippy with a gleaming vintage fryer, which does this British classic proud. Wonderful fresh fish (cod, haddock, halibut, plaice, skate, rock salmon, etc.) is coated in a light, non-greasy batter (using groundnut oil) and matched with crispy chunky chips and tangy homemade sauce tartare.

There's no alcohol license but you can bring your own, or opt for a mug of builder's tea. Generous portions and great value.

Golden Hind, 73 Marylebone Ln, W1U 2PN (020-7486 3644; Bond St tube; Mon-Fri 12-3, 6-10, Sat 6-10; fish & chips; £).

Grain Store
Putting veggies centre stage

Located on Granary Square in King's Cross – with a huge terrace for alfresco dining – the Grain Store is the brainchild of chef Bruno Loubet, who uses it to showcase his love of vegetables. Although it isn't a vegetarian restaurant, the eclectic menu gives veggies a starring role in dishes such as sprouting seeds with miso aubergine and crispy citrus chicken skin. It has great 'green' credentials too, and was voted the UK's best sustainable restaurant at the 2013 National Restaurant Awards.

The bar is a destination in its own right, with cocktails invented by Tony Conigliaro of 69 Colebrooke Row (see page 259).

Grain Store, Granary Sq, 1-3 Stable St, N1C 4AB (020-7324 4466, grainstore.com; King's Cross/St Pancras tube; Mon-Wed 10-11.30, Thu-Fri 10-12, Sat 11-12, Sun 11-4.30; global; ££)

Great Queen Street
Best of British

Despite its pub-like vibe (it's from the same stable as the Anchor & Hope and Canton Arms gastropubs), Great Queen Street in Covent Garden is a proper restaurant where bookings are almost essential. The convivial dining room offers a produce-led and mainly British menu, serving the likes of middle white pork, pistachio and pigeon terrine, confit duck leg with braised peas and lettuce, and cherry and almond sundae. The lunchtime 'sale' menu is good value (two courses for £18, three for £20).

Excellent choice of wine and craft beers, and you can also sip and snack in the cosy cellar bar.

Great Queen Street, 32 Great Queen St, WC2B 5AA (020-7242 0622; greatqueenstreetrestaurant. co.uk; Holborn tube; Mon-Sat 12-2.30, 5.30-10.30, Sun 1-4; modern British; ££).

The Green Man & French Horn
One of London's foodie bargains

A French bar-cum-bistro, the Green Man & French Horn (part of a small group that includes Brawn, Soif and Terroirs) takes its culinary inspiration from France's longest river, the Loire, from the hills of the Ardèche to the oyster beds on the coast of Saint Nazaire. The result is tasty food, an interesting wine list and reasonable prices.

It's located in the heart of Theatreland and the 'theatre' menu – offered from noon to 7pm – is one of the capital's foodie bargains at just £14.50 for two courses (£16.50 for three) and a 500ml carafe of wine for just £11.50. *Fantastique*!

The Green Man & French Horn, 54 St Martin's Ln, WC2N 4EA (020-7836 2645; greenmanfrenchhorn. co; Leicester Sq tube; Mon-Sat 12-11; modern French; ££).

Hakkasan Hanway Place

The coolest Chinese restaurant on the planet?

One of London's coolest venues, Hakkasan Hanway Place is the original Hakkasan Chinese restaurant (there's another in Mayfair), which opened in 2001 and spawned a global empire. Its Michelin star was the first ever awarded to a Chinese restaurant, and deservedly so.

The striking dining room – designed by Christian Liaigre in black and gold – provides a dramatic background for Hakkasan's brand of glitzy Cantonese cuisine. Smouldering incense, seductive spot lighting and a gentle soundtrack help create a nightclub atmosphere, while the open-plan kitchen adds to the theatrical experience.

The contemporary Chinese 'fusion' cuisine created by chef Tong Chee Hwee is the benchmark against which other Chinese restaurants are judged. The dim sum platter is a great place to start; while 'signature' dishes include silver cod roasted with champagne and honey, and seared Wagyu beef with white asparagus. If you've just won the lottery, Hakkasan's Peking duck with Qiandao caviar is, at £215 for the whole duck, a once-in-a-lifetime dish.

In addition to the à la carte menu, there are themed 'signature' and 'taste of Hakkasan' menus, 'dim sum Sundays', plus an award-winning wine list, fantastic cocktails and specialist teas. Cool, sexy, expensive – and worth every penny!

Hakkasan Hanway Place, 8 Hanway Pl, W1T 1HD (020-7927 7000; hakkasan.com/hanwayplace; Tottenham Court Rd tube; open daily – see website for times; Chinese; £££-££££).

Hawksmoor Seven Dials

London's classic 'American' steakhouse

Hawksmoor, located in the old Watney-Combe brewery near Seven Dials, specialises in generous steaks supplied by Ginger Pig (see page 22) and cooked to perfection on a charcoal grill. Start with half a native lobster with garlic butter and follow with a fillet, sirloin, rib-eye or rump steak, or – if you're really (really) hungry – a bone-in prime rib, porterhouse or chateaubriand, which is big enough for two to share.

Good-value 'express' menus cater for pre- or post-theatregoers (until 6.30pm or after 10pm, Mon-Sat), or you can drop into the bar for a burger and beer. Cocktails are also special.

Hawksmoor, 11 Langley St, WC2H 9JG (020-7420 9390; thehawksmoor.com/locations/seven-dials; Covent Gdn tube; open daily – see website for times; British; ££).

Hereford Road

Bold British cooking at its best

On the site of what was once a Victorian butcher's shop – as is evident from the shop window – Hereford Road is a comfortable neighbourhood restaurant offering simple yet innovative British cooking. Chef Tom Pemberton, formerly head chef of St John Bread and Wine, uses the best UK-sourced seasonal produce (meat, fish and vegetables) with impeccable provenance. Typical summer fare includes sea trout, samphire, Scottish girolles and native berries, while in winter there's mutton, game and middle white pork.

The set lunch (Mon-Fri) is a steal, and the wine list has been chosen with care.

Hereford Road, 3 Hereford Rd, W2 4AB (020-7727 1144; herefordroad.org; Bayswater tube; Mon-Sat 12-3, 6-10.30, Sun 12-4, 6-10; British; ££).

Honey & Co.
Full of Middle Eastern promise

Honey & Co. is a delightful small café-restaurant and bakery in Fitzrovia specialising in food from the Middle East. Run by husband-and-wife team Itamar Srulovich and Sarit Packer, both of whom have worked at Ottolenghi (Sarit was also executive chef at NOPI – see page 224) and know their *shakshouka* from their *muhamra*!

It's a tiny venue with a beautiful Moroccan-tiled floor, a clutch of tables and basic white-walled décor, but don't let the small space put you off. The food here is big and bold – a treat for the eyes and the taste buds – and also great value.

Honey & Co., 25A Warren St, W1T 5LZ (020-7388 6175; honeyandco.co.uk; Warren St tube; Mon-Fri 8-10.30, Sat 9.30-10.30; Middle Eastern; £-££).

Hunan
Feast like an emperor at Hunan

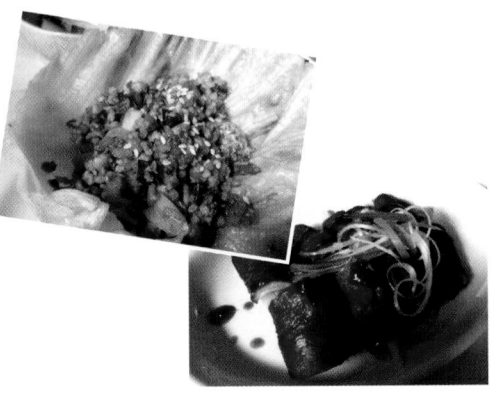

Founded in 1982, Hunan isn't your typical Chinese restaurant. For one thing there's no menu! You don't choose what you want but rather tell the waiter what you don't (or won't) eat, how spicy you like your food and how hungry you are – and wait to be pleasantly surprised. Chef Peng's cuisine is based on small portions of food with the emphasis on sharing. There's a fixed price lunch/dinner 'menu' that includes up to 18 dishes. Though some Hunanese dishes feature, such as double-cooked pork, the cuisine is actually influenced by Taiwan.

Unusually for a Chinese restaurant, Hunan is noted for its superb wine list.

Hunan, 51 Pimlico Rd, SW1W 8NE (020-7730 5712; hunanlondon.com; Sloane Sq tube; Mon-Sat 12.30-2, 6.30-11; Chinese; ££-£££).

Incanto
Vibrant southern Italian outpost

Sample the flavours of southern Italy at Incanto, an award-winning (two AA Rosettes) restaurant just a stone's throw from Harrow School. Occupying a former 19th-century post office, the front room is a delicatessen-cum-café, while the main room at the rear is a stylish dining room with simply-laid tables and leather banquettes beneath a long skylight and beamed ceiling.

This unassuming friendly restaurant is one of London's best Italian eateries, where classic dishes with robust flavours are given a contemporary twist. There's a good selection of wines from small artisan winemakers, including many organic examples.

Incanto, The Old Post Office, 41 High St, HA1 3HT (020-8426 6767; incanto.co.uk; Harrow-on-the-Hill tube; Tue-Sat 12-2.30, 6.30-10.30, Sun 12.30-4; Italian; ££).

Kathmandu Inn
Scaling the curry heights

The unassuming but magnificent Kathmandu Inn in Shepherd's Bush is, by popular consent, one of London's best curry houses. It specialises in Nepalese (and Indian) food, skilfully spiced, perfectly cooked and utterly authentic – and a far cry from the anglicised Indian food served in many eateries. Famous dishes include momo (dumplings in spicy sauce), lamb Nepal (with mango) and – if you have an asbestos-lined mouth – the ferocious chicken or lamb Gurkhali. The more familiar bhuna, dhansak and patia dishes are also delicious.

Great value for money, charming service and mouth-watering food.

Kathmandu Inn, 6-7 Seven Stars Cnr, W12 8ET (020-8749 9802; kathmanduinn.co.uk; Ravenscourt Pk tube; daily 12-3, 6-11; Indian/Nepalese; ££).

Kitchen W8

Another star turn from Philip Howard

Awarded a Michelin star in 2011, Kitchen W8 is the latest venture from Philip Howard, co-owner of the Ledbury in Notting Hill and the Square in Mayfair, both of which have two Michelin stars. At Kitchen W8 the spotlight is on the ingredients, sourced from suppliers who, Howard claims, are the true heroes of the culinary world. Chef Mark Kempson's seasonal menus make the most of their produce, with dishes ranging from simple grills to more complex and hearty offerings.

Cool, polished and friendly, with a good-value set menu offered at lunch or an early dinner.

Kitchen W8, 11-13 Abingdon Rd, W8 6AH (020-7937 0120; kitchenw8.com; High St Kensington tube; Mon-Sat 12-2.30, 6-10.30, Sun 12.30-3, 6.30-9.30; French/European; ££-£££).

Little Social

French with an English accent

Across the street from his flagship restaurant, Pollen Street Social, Jason Atherton's Little Social follows the fashion for French bistros/brasseries which has seen such venues as Balthazar and Brasserie Zedel (see page 196) open in recent years. Designed in classic speakeasy-style, the dining room has blood red leather banquettes, faux-Lalique lampshades, vintage Michelin maps, a long bar lined with stools, and neon for a dash of Manhattan chic.

With first-rate bold cooking, interesting wines, inspired cocktails, charming staff, an intimate atmosphere and affordable prices – in particular the prix fixe menu – Little Social is a winner all the way.

Little Social, 5 Pollen St, W1S 1NE (020-7870 3730; littlesocial.co.uk; Oxford Circus tube; Mon-Sat 12-2.30, 6-10.30; French; ££).

Magdalen
A masterful tour de force

Opened in 2007 to critical acclaim, Magdalen is a delightful neighbourhood restaurant. The low-key room with its bentwood chairs, burgundy walls, polished wooden floors, chandeliers and crisp white tablecloths, is comfortable, elegant and attractive, while the food is fabulous.

Magdalen is run by a trio of chefs (husband and wife James and Emma Faulks, and partner David Abbott), all with impeccable culinary credentials. The kitchen uses the best of British and European produce to create robust, modern, meaty cuisine – think St John Smithfield (see page 234) – and the menu puts the emphasis on charcuterie and proper sauces, and simple, perfectly-made puddings.

To whet your appetite, why not start with hot foie gras, roasted peach and salted almonds, or Tamworth and rabbit terrine with onion marmalade; follow this with braised Somerset kid, borlotti beans, fennel and radicchio or fried lamb's tongue, green beans, roast shallots and anchovy; rounding off with chocolate soufflé cake, cherry and red wine sorbet or elderflower jelly, gooseberry fool and meringue. There's an interesting wine list and an excellent value set lunch. The ever-changing menu is playful, creative, pitch-perfect, a dream… Magdalen is magnificent!

Magdalen, 152 Tooley St, SE1 2TU (020-7403 1342; magdalenrestaurant.co.uk; London Br tube/rail; Mon-Fri 12-2.30, 6.30-10, Sat 6.30-10pm; modern British; ££).

Mangal 1 Ocakbasi
Food fit for a Sultan

Voted the city's best Turkish restaurant by *Time Out* magazine, Mangal 1 Ocakbasi is a traditional grill restaurant with an open fire pit in the middle (the *ocakbasi*). Chargrilled meat is a speciality – *mangal* is Turkish for 'barbecue' – and is simple but stunning fare.

Starters include *lahmacun* (Turkish pizza), *sarma* (stuffed vine leaves) and *cacik* (cucumber and yogurt), but it's the kebabs that draw the punters. Try the delicious *cop sis* (marinated cubes of lamb), *tavuk beyti* (grilled minced chicken breast) and *bildircin* (grilled quail) – all guaranteed to get your juices flowing. There's no alcohol licence but you can bring your own.

Mangal 1 Ocakbasi, 10 Arcola St, E8 2DJ (020-7275 8981; mangal1.com; Dalston Kingsland rail; daily 12-12; Turkish; £).

Manuka Kitchen
A honey of a local bistro

Manuka Kitchen was founded by Kiwi chef Tyler Martin and wine expert Joseph Antippa (both formerly of the Gore Hotel). As you might expect, manuka honey features on the menu, although the name is more a nod to Martin's New Zealand roots. This stylish restaurant has high ceilings and large windows, while its rustic décor of terracotta tiles, white walls and simple wooden tables gives it a homely feel.

But it's the food that's the star here. Martin is a chef who's going places and his delicious, imaginative European cuisine is a joy. Coupled with excellent wines, superb friendly service, great atmosphere and reasonable prices – it's perfect.

Manuka Kitchen, 510 Fulham Rd, SW6 5NJ (020-7736 7588; manukakitchen.com; Fulham Broadway tube; Tue-Thu 12-11, Fri-Sat 10-11, Sun 10-5; modern European; £-££).

M Manze
As nice as pie (and mash)

Established in 1902 by Michele Manze – grandfather of the present owners – M Manze is an institution in southeast London, where it has outlets in Bermondsey (address below), Peckham and Sutton. Generations of Londoners have been brought up on Manze's traditional beef pie, mash and liquor, and its jellied (or stewed) eels.

The company uses the same recipes today as it did in 1902; everything is made by hand and cooked daily in traditional ovens. It may not have a Michelin star but Manze's pie 'n' mash is foodie heaven to many London folk.

M Manze, 87 Tower Bridge Rd, SE1 4TW (020-7407 2985; manze.co.uk; Borough tube; Mon 11-2pm, Tue-Thu 10.30-2pm, Fri 10-2.30pm, Sat 10-2.45pm; pie & mash; £).

Medlar
Punching well above its weight

The highly acclaimed and Michelin-starred Medlar is the first restaurant venture of Joe Mercer Nairne and David O'Connor, both of whom have worked in some of London's best kitchens. A small and cosy neighbourhood eatery – bare floorboards, distressed mirrors, plush green banquettes and crisp white linen – at the downmarket end of Chelsea's King's Road, Medlar punches well above its weight.

The modern seasonal French cooking, taking inspiration from a world of influences, is amazingly good, and is backed by a superb wine list, efficient laid-back service and an elegant atmosphere. The prix fixe menus (lunch and dinner) are excellent value for food of this quality.

Medlar, 438 Kings Rd, SW10 0LJ (020-7349 1900; medlarrestaurant.co.uk; Sloane Sq tube/Imperial Wharf rail; daily 12-3, 6.30-10.30; modern French; ££-£££).

Min Jiang

Brilliant Beijing duck with a cracking view

Located at the Royal Garden Hotel in Kensington, Min Jiang (named after its chef) boasts a breath-taking vista of leafy Kensington Gardens and Hyde Park and the rooftops beyond – in perfect harmony with the restaurant's relaxed atmosphere and authentic Oriental vibe. The room's tranquil cream colour scheme is enlivened with dashes of vibrant dark red and some striking blue and white Chinese vases.

Min Jiang serves some of London's best traditional Chinese cuisine using the freshest ingredients and authentic spices. It's famous for its signature dish, the legendary Beijing duck, cooked to perfection in a conventional wood-fired oven, along with spicy Sichuan classics such as double-cooked pork with celery, spicy clay pot venison, lobster and abalone. There's also delectable dim sum (a lunchtime bargain), including poached Beijing dumplings filled with chicken, prawn, chives and dried shiitake; golden-brown deep-fried yam croquettes with seafood; steamed crab meat; stir-fried turnip cake with spicy XO sauce; and baked char siu puff. Service is charming and efficient.

There's also an attractive bar where you can sip a pre-dinner cocktail or tuck into a platter of dim sum and Chinese tea.

Min Jiang, Royal Garden Hotel, 2-24 Kensington High St, W8 4PT (020-7361 1988; minjiang.co.uk; High St Kensington tube; daily 12-3, 6-10.30; Chinese; ££-£££).

The Modern Pantry

Fusion food with a touch of magic

With a relaxed, calm setting and charming ambience, the Modern Pantry in Clerkenwell is noted for its flavoursome, imaginative food and formidable wines. Chef Anna Hansen's culinary philosophy is to excite the palate by fusing everyday ideas with unusual ingredients and global inspiration. Her food is a synthesis of east meets west: experimental, playful and touched with magic. Not everything works perfectly, but when it does – which is most of the time (like her strawberry, lemon grass and black sesame trifle) – the results are sublime.

There's also a separate café on the ground floor and a delicatessen next door.

The Modern Pantry, 47-48 St John's Sq, EC1V 4JJ (020-7553 9210; themodernpantry.co.uk; Farringdon tube; open daily – see website for times; fusion; ££).

Mon Plaisir

A corner of London that remains forever France

Mon Plaisir in Covent Garden is one of London's oldest French restaurants, serving fine French cuisine for over half a century. From the pewter-topped bar (said to have come from a Lyonnais brothel!) to the waiters' accents, this is as French a bistro as you're likely to find this side of La Manche. Its authentic cuisine is amazing value if you opt for one of the lunch, dinner (*menu du mois*) or pre/post theatre menus.

The restaurant also holds cooking masterclasses, wine and cheese tastings and evenings devoted to regional French food.

Mon Plaisir, 19-21 Monmouth St, WC2H 9DD (020-7836 7243; monplaisir.co.uk; Covent Gdn tube; Mon-Fri 12-2.30, 5.45-11.15, Sat 12-3, 5.45-11.15; French; ££).

Moro
An Iberian love affair

Eat your way around the southern Mediterranean, courtesy of Moro in Exmouth Market. Established in 1997 by 'the Sams' – Sam(uel) and Sam(antha) Clark – Moro offers a delectable fusion of Spanish, Middle Eastern and North African comfort food, much of which is cooked in a wood-fired oven or char-grilled.

Moro's buzzy and sensual dining room is one of London's hottest tickets, so be prepared to book well in advance. You can also eat at the bar from the excellent tapas menu and enjoy the superb Iberian wine list. *Fantástico!*

Moro, 34-36 Exmouth Market, EC1R 4QE (020-7833 8336; moro.co.uk; Farringdon tube; Mon-Sat 12.30-2.30, 6-10.30, Sun 12.30-2.45; Spanish/N African; ££).

NOPI
Flavourful food touched by genius

NOPI is the latest brainchild of Yotam Ottolenghi (see page 70), mastermind of London's legendary deli chain, which continues his ethos of quality, innovation, freshness and abundance. The design is formal on the ground floor, with lots of marble, brass and white tiles, whilst the basement has long sharing tables overlooking the theatrical open kitchen.

NOPI is an all-day brasserie – a grown-up Ottolenghi café – with a twist, serving small plates to share, with robust, sunny flavours, typically from the Middle East and Asia. There's also an interesting (if quite expensive) wine list.

NOPI, 21-22 Warwick St, W1B 5NE (020-7494 9584; nopi-restaurant.com; Piccadilly Circus tube; Mon-Fri 8-2.45, 5.30-10.30, Sat 10-10.15, Sun 10-4; Middle East/Mediterranean; ££).

Odette's
Pride of Primrose Hill

S et among a parade of mid-Victorian shops and cafés in beautiful Primrose Hill, Odette's is one of London's original dining rooms (it opened in1978) and a much-loved local landmark. The kitchen was taken over by Welshman Bryn Williams in 2006 and has since gone from strength to strength. Inside there's a cosy split-level dining room, but it's the alfresco dining that's the main draw. Tucked away at the back is a lovely walled garden, with comfortable cushioned banquettes, ornate cast iron chairs and starched white tablecloths; tables out front have views over Primrose Hill.

Williams' modern British menu is an innovative marriage of textures and flavours that reflect his personality and heritage, using the finest produce sourced from his native Wales and elsewhere in the UK. Typical offerings include crayfish lasagne topped by little squid rings; pig's head and black-pudding terrine with crackling; saddle of rabbit with mustard gnocchi; sea bream with glazed endive and pine nut and raisin dressing; and pistachio cake with caramelised apples and Calvados cream.

Odette's is a comfortable venue with charming service and good value set lunches (starting from £13 for two courses). There's also a relaxing bar.

Odette's Restaurant & Bar, 130 Regent's Park Rd, NW1 8XL (020-7586 8569; odettesprimrosehill. com; Chalk Farm tube; Mon-Thu 12-2.30, 6-10, Fri 12-2.30, 6-10.30, Sat 12-3, 6-10.30, Sun 12-10; modern British; ££-£££).

One-O-One

Something (deliciously) fishy in Knightsbridge

Award-winning One-O-One (three AA rosettes) at the Sheraton Park Tower is one of London's best seafood restaurants and home to critically-acclaimed Breton chef Pascal Proyart. His repertoire is modern with a French accent – plus Asian and Mediterranean touches – with the emphasis on sustainability, so you're likely to find farmed tiger prawns and turbot on the menu, alongside wild Norwegian king crab and Manx queenies (scallops). The combination of fresh fish, excellent wines and the finest French cooking are a sure-fire winner.

Proyart also presents masterclasses in cooking fish/shellfish, game and festive food (see theparktowerknightsbridge.com/en/forms/masterclasses).

One-O-One, Sheraton Park Tower, 101 Knightsbridge, SW1X 7RN (020-7290 7101; oneoonerestaurant.com; Knightsbridge tube; Tue-Sat – see website for times; seafood; £££).

The Opera Tavern

A night at the opera never tasted so good

The Opera Tavern (formerly a pub) is a highly acclaimed (Bib Gourmand) bar and tapas restaurant in Covent Garden. The cosy ground floor bar is the best place to eat, with its leather bar stools, copper spotlights and open charcoal grill.

Specialising in Italian and Spanish influenced tapas, the Opera cooks up all manner of tasty treats, from chargrilled venison haunch with celeriac mash and walnut dressing to courgette flowers stuffed with goats' cheese and drizzled with honey. A well-chosen Spanish-Italian wine (and sherry) list adds to the authentic appeal.

The Opera Tavern, 23 Catherine St, WC2B 5JS (020-7836 3680; operatavern.co.uk; Temple tube; Mon-Fri 12-3, 5-11.30, Sat 12-11.30, Sun 12-5; tapas; ££-£££).

Orrery
Sanctuary for French food lovers

Escape the clamour of Marylebone High Street for the sanctuary of Michelin-starred Orrery, a superb French restaurant housed in a converted stable block, boasting an elegant dining room, cosy bar and lovely rooftop terrace – one of the city's hidden treasures. The menu is classic French enhanced by inventive touches from Ukranian chef Igor Tymchyshyn, complemented by an extensive award-winning wine list. The lunch _menu du jour_ is great value at £24.50 for two courses (£27.50 for three).

Orrery's also operates the Orrery Epicerie, where you can enjoy breakfast or a light lunch and stock up on gourmet food to go.

Orrery, 55 Marylebone High St, W1U 5RB (020-7616 8000, orrery-restaurant.co.uk, Regent's Pk tube; daily – see website for times; French; ££-£££).

Otto's Restaurant
Classic French food with heart and soul

Enjoy an outstanding meal at Otto's, a classic French restaurant in Bloomsbury with lovely '50s kitsch décor, splendid service and delectable nouvelle cuisine, such as beef fillet with seared foie gras and rich truffle sauce, or fig tart with almond ice cream, caramel and butter sauce. The restaurant's signature dish is the celebrated _canard de Rouen a la presse_ (pressed duck, for two, served in two courses) or, for seafood lovers, pressed lobster.

The fine French wines are an oenophile's delight (with some of the lowest mark-ups in town), while the lunch menu is a steal. _Superbe!_

Otto's Restaurant, 182 Gray's Inn Rd, WC1X 8EW (020-7713 0107; ottos-restaurant.com; Chancery Ln tube; Mon-Fri 12-1.45, 6-9.45, Sat 6-9.45; French; ££-£££).

Patio
Old world charm and vodka too

Tuck in to blinis, borscht, and dumplings at the Patio Polish restaurant in Shepherd's Bush. Established in 1991, the unpretentious Patio looks more like a retro middle-class drawing room than a restaurant. It's a lively, family-run (Eva and Kaz Michalik) venue, brimming with old world charm and service (and host to the occasional live piano recital).

The Patio is very much a labour of love, offering a masterclass in traditional Polish cuisine, such as *bigos* and *pierogi*, accompanied by shots of excellent vodka. It's expat comfort food at very sensible prices.

Patio Restaurant, 5 Goldhawk Rd, W12 8QQ (020-8743 5194; patiolondon.com; Shepherd's Bush tube; Mon-Fri 12-3, 6-11, Sat-Sun 6-11.30; Polish; ££).

Pitt Cue Co
Cowboy hog heaven

Beginning life as a street food vendor under Hungerford Bridge on the South Bank, Pitt Cue Co now has punters queuing round the block for their delicious American barbecue grub. Their Soho base consists of an austere basement dining room/bar, with low lighting and blues-rock soundtrack, seating just 30 punters, but it's nirvana to fans of pork/beef ribs, beef brisket, chicken wings and pulled pork, served with coleslaw, salads and pickles on enamel trays. Fun, hip, friendly, efficient, inexpensive and really tasty!

It's best to avoid peak times (and the queues), although the food is well worth the wait.

Pitt Cue Co, 1 Newburgh St, W1F 7RB (020-7287 5578; pittcue.co.uk; Piccadilly Circus tube; Mon-Sat 12-3, 5.30-11, Sun 12-4pm; American barbecue; £; no reservations).

Polpo Soho
A taste of Venice in Soho

Polpo (Italian for octopus) is an inspired restaurant in Soho modelled on a *bàcaro*: a humble Venetian restaurant serving simple food and young local wines. (Coincidentally, 41 Beak St was once home to the Venetian painter Canaletto.) It's the brainchild of co-owner Russell Norman, who toured Venice's back-street wine bars and *bàcari* in search of authentic flavours. The shabby-chic styling, however, is more New York Soho diner, with rough brick walls, tiled floors and scuffed plaster, brown-paper menus and glass tumblers.

Now part of a small chain, Polpo's award-winning, inventive take on Italian 'tapas' (*cicheti*) has spawned imitators across the capital. The great-value small plates include the likes of braised octopus (what else?) with Treviso lettuce and borlotti beans; spinach, parmesan and egg pizzette; sliced flank steak with rocket and parmesan; lamb and green peppercorn meatballs; and much more. Wines are served in carafes (three sizes) and start from £6 for 250ml. Dinner is first-come first-served, but you can book for lunch (or grab a free bar seat).

Polpo has a great atmosphere, heavenly food, friendly service and is brilliant value. And if you want to take the experience home with you, there's a lovely cookbook containing 140 recipes from the restaurant.

Polpo Soho, 41 Beak St, W1F 9SB (020-7734 4479; polpo.co.uk; Oxford/Piccadilly Circus tube; Mon-Sat 12-11, Sun 12-10; Italian; ££).

Provendor
A French classic in the 'burbs'

Agreat little café/brasserie in the unlikely setting of Wanstead in northeast London, Provendor serves classic French food in laid-back surroundings – think exposed brick walls and banquette seating. The owner's passion for French cuisine is evident from the extensive menu, which includes all the usual bistro favourites and more; from steak frites to charcuterie and rillettes, celeriac remoulade to cassoulet, escargots to duck confit. There's even a French take on a Sunday roast!

The classic all-French wine list is well worth exploring, as are the good-value prix fixe lunch/dinner menus and great weekend brunch.

Provendor, 17 High St, E11 2AA (020-8530 3050; provenderlondon.co.uk; Snaresbrook tube; Mon-Fri 12-10, Sat 9.30-10.30, Sun 9.30-9; French; ££).

The Providores & Tapa Room
The most innovative fusion food in town

One of London's most original restaurants, the Providores is run by Kiwis Peter Gordon and Michael McGrath, who create some of the most innovative fusion food in town. On the ground floor is the Tapa Room (the name comes from the Pacific tapa cloth on the wall), an all-day café/wine bar packed with locals enjoying great coffee, New Zealand wines and an all-day menu of small plates.

Upstairs is the more formal Providores restaurant, where you can indulge in inventive flavour combinations that shouldn't work but do – brilliantly! Don't miss the breakfast and weekend brunch.

The Providores & Tapa Room, 109 Marylebone High St, W1U 4RX (020-7935 6175; theprovidores. co.uk; Baker St/Bond St tube; open daily – see website for times; fusion; ££).

Rasoi by Vineet Bhatia

Indian haute cuisine

Vineet Bhatia needs no introduction for London foodies. Formerly head chef at Michelin-starred Zaika and the Cinnamon Club, in 2004 he opened his own restaurant, Rasoi (Hindi for 'kitchen'). It earned its own Michelin star in 2006 and is considered to be the haute cuisine of Indian cooking, on a par with the very best fine dining, while Bhatia (assisted by his wife Rashima) has been lauded as the Indian chefs' chef.

Rasoi is located in an elegant Chelsea townhouse (you ring the doorbell to gain entry) and has an intimate, homely atmosphere and vibrant décor. The finely-tuned menu is as far from a chicken tikka masala as you can get, and the best way to appreciate Bhatia's skills is to dive into the seven-course 'prestige' tasting menu (there's also a vegetarian option), accompanied by a bottle of wine from the impressive list. At nearly £90 it's expensive, but it could be the best Indian food in the world.

A more affordable option is the set lunch where two courses start from £24. Or buy a copy of Vineet Bhatia's widely-acclaimed cookbook, *Rasoi: New Indian Kitchen* (published in 2009) and try to conjure up some of his magic at your own stove.

Rasoi by Vineet Bhatia, 10 Lincoln St, SW3 2TS (020-7225 1881; rasoi-uk.com; Sloane Sq tube; Mon-Fri 12-2.30, 6-10.30, Sat 6-10.30, Sun 12-2.30, 6-9.45; Indian; ££-££££).

Roka
Rousing Roka is a revelation

Award-winning Roka in Charlotte Street (there are other outlets in Mayfair and Canary Wharf) specialises in contemporary Japanese *robatayaki* (fire-side) cuisine. The striking room is dominated by the central *robata* grill, with food prepared in full view of diners, while in warm weather the floor to ceiling windows are opened to create a semi-alfresco ambience.

The creative cuisine tastes as good as it looks, ranging from finely sliced yellowtail sashimi with truffle yuzu dressing to lamb cutlets with Korean spices, seared beef with black truffle dressing and rice hot pot with Japanese spices. Downstairs, the Shochu Lounge has some amazing cocktails and spirits.

Roka, 37 Charlotte St, W1T 1RR (020-7580 6464; rokarestaurant.com; Goodge St tube; open daily – see website for times; Japanese; £££).

The Rooftop Café
Hidden gem with views to di(n)e for

Perched on top of co-working enterprise The Exchange in the shadow of the mighty Shard, the Rooftop Café is worth seeking out for its stunning views, spectacular roof terrace, striking décor and – especially – delicious food.

The café serves hearty breakfasts, tasty lunches and delicious dinners (Thu-Sat). The inventive, ever-changing menu may include the likes of panzanella (Tuscan salad) and marinated anchovies; crab, samphire and chilli; pork belly, beans and asparagus; butterfly mackerel, gooseberry, pink fir apple potatoes and watercress; pistachio, lemon cake and crème fraiche; and much more. There's also an interesting wine list.

The Rooftop Café, The Exchange, 28 London Bridge St, SE1 9SG (020-3102 3770; theexchange. so/rooftop; London Br tube/rail; Mon-Tue 8-3, Wed-Fri 8-3, 6-10.30, Sat 10-4, 6-10.30; modern eclectic; £-££).

Royal China Club

Dim sum palace fit for an emperor

If you like dim sum then you'll love the Royal China Club, one of the best places in London to enjoy these moreish Chinese delicacies. Founded in 1996, this is the flagship restaurant of the prestigious award-winning Royal China chain and – for many – the best.

The striking gold and black interior and soothing piano music is smart enough for any occasion, while the dim sum is not only delicious but also affordable. Head chef Man Tin Cheung creates a wealth of tasty morsels such as crab and spinach steamed dumplings, prawn and chives in batter, and steamed lobster dumplings in rice wine. Divine.

Royal China, 24-26 Baker St, W1U 7AB (020-7487 4688; http://rcguk.co.uk/rcc.html; Baker St tube; Mon-Thu 12-11, Fri-Sat 12-11.30, Sun 11-10; Chinese; ££).

RSJ

RSJ is A-OK

RSJ – yes it really is named after a rolled steel joist used to prop up the 19th-century stables that house the restaurant – is one of London's longest running success stories, opened in 1981 and still going strong. The unprepossessing frontage belies a cosy interior, featuring wood, grey walls and crisp linen, and the tasty European cuisine is excellent value, particularly the all-day prix fixe menus. RSJ is famous for its award-winning 250-strong wine list, which concentrates almost exclusively on the Loire Valley.

RSJ also hosts wine tastings, themed evenings and cookery classes (see website).

RSJ, 33 Coin St, SE1 9NR (020-7928 4554; rsj. uk.com; Waterloo tube/rail; Mon-Fri 12-2.30, 5.15-11, Sat 5.15-11; modern European; ££).

St John Smithfield
Best of British from nose to tail

There's nowhere better to celebrate British food than at the Michelin-starred St John Bar and Restaurant in Smithfield. Housed in a former Georgian townhouse/smokehouse close to the market, Fergus Henderson's ground-breaking restaurant is a honeypot for carnivores.

St John's well-sourced, traditional cuisine has stood the test of time for over 20 years, and remains one of the City's most reliable and exciting places to eat. Our growing awareness of farming methods, passion for farmers' markets and seasonal ingredients all owe much to the team behind St John, who have long championed British food. There are few parts of the animal that don't find their way onto the table, from hearts to bone marrow to trotters – this is genuine nose-to-tail cooking.

The menu changes daily, but you could start with crispy pig's cheek and dandelion or roast bone marrow and parsley salad, followed by pigeon and Jerusalem artichokes or braised kid, fennel and aioli (there are also fishy options). Plus some great puds such as chocolate terrine and crème fraiche. It's pricey food but as a special treat for serious foodies, there are few places to beat it.

St John Smithfield, 26 St John St, EC1M 4AY (020-7251 0848; stjohngroup.uk.com/Smithfield; Barbican tube; Mon-Fri 12-3, 6-11, Sat 6-11, Sun 1-3; British; ££-£££).

Shayona
Vegetarian food of the gods

One of London's best vegetarian restaurants is in the grounds of the BAPS Swaminarayan Mandir – or Neasden Temple as it's more commonly known. Shayona offers a wide range of contemporary cuisine that's faithful to the best culinary traditions of the Indian subcontinent, from the thalis of Gujarat and rich curries of the Punjab, to the street chaats of Mumbai and delectable dosas of southern India. The Gujarati buffet on weekday afternoons is a real treat, and also excellent value.

Shayona has no alcohol license and you cannot 'BYO', but a jug of *lassi* (yogurt drink) goes brilliantly with Indian food.

Shayona, 54-62 Meadow Garth, NW10 8HD (020-8965 3365; shayonarestaurants.com; Neasden tube; Mon-Fri 11.30-10, Sat-Sun 11-10; vegetarian; £).

Sushi Tetsu
A shrine to sushi

Owned and run by Toru Takahashi – who worked for five years at Nobu – Sushi Tetsu is a tiny traditional Japanese sushi bar hidden away in Clerkenwell. Together with his wife Harumi, chef Toru creates classic, unpretentious, mouth-watering fresh sushi (nigiri and maki) and sashimi. There are no hot dishes, not even miso soup, just glorious sushi.

If you're a fan, order the *omakase* menu (in advance), a combination of sashimi and sushi chosen by the chef using the best fish and shellfish available on the day. To drink there's saké, beer or tea. Booking is essential as there are very few seats.

Sushi Tetsu, 12 Jerusalem Passage, EC1V 4JP (020-3217 0090; sushitetsu.co.uk; Farringdon tube; Tue-Fri 11.45-2, 5-9.30, Sat 5-9.30pm; Japanese; ££-£££).

Tayyabs
A legend in its own lunchtime

Founded as a small café in Whitechapel in 1972, family-owned Tayyabs gradually swallowed up its neighbours (including a pub) and developed into the thriving business you see today. It serves the finest Pakistani Punjabi cuisine, from its famous mixed grill and fiery grilled lamb chops to more traditional dahls and *masala channa* (spicy chickpeas). There are exquisitely spiced lamb curries, plus north Indian staples such as tikkas, kebabs, onion bhajis and delicious naan bread.

Tayyabs is one of London's most popular curry restaurants and there are long queues at peak times, so booking is essential. No alcohol is served but you can 'BYO' and they'll uncork it for free.

Tayyabs, 83-89 Fieldgate St, E1 1JU (020-7247 8521; tayyabs.co.uk; Aldgate East or Whitechapel tube; daily 12-11.30; Punjabi; £-££).

10 Greek Street
Treasure on the streets of Soho

The small, unprepossessing 10 Greek Street is a buzzy, cramped gem of a neighbourhood restaurant, serving inventive modern European cuisine. The short, daily-changing menu is chalked up on a blackboard and includes the likes of pork and pistachio ballotine; wood pigeon with cauliflower, pine nuts and raisins; Brecon lamb, olive oil mash, kale and salsa verde; plaice with mussels, clams, monk's beard and baby leeks; and rum and caramel pannacotta with prunes. It's all delicious, good value food.

The impressive wine list was voted Great Value Wine List of the Year 2014 by *Imbibe* magazine. Sadly there's a 'no reservations' policy for dinner, but you can book for lunch.

10 Greek Street, W1D 4DH (020-7734 4677; 10greekstreet.com; Tottenham Ct Rd tube; Mon-Sat, 12-11.30; modern European; ££).

Terroirs
Salt of the earth

This attractive, buzzy restaurant and wine bar has been reaping the plaudits (including a Michelin Bib Gourmand) since opening in 2008. Terroirs is spread over two floors, each with its own menu; the Parisian-inspired ground floor is a wine bar serving charcuterie, cheeses and tasty small plates for sharing, while the basement restaurant features more robust cuisine, including the likes of Cornish mussels, pork and pistachio terrine, smoked mackerel, Welsh lamb chops and Tuscan-style black leg chicken.

The award-winning wine list runs to around 200 bins and majors in 'natural' wines produced organically and/or biodynamically, dominated by France and Italy.

Terroirs, 5 William IV St, WC2N 4DW (020-7036 0660; terroirswinebar.com; Charing Cross tube/ rail; Mon-Sat 12-11; French; ££).

Texture
Champagne and fine dining – what's not to like?

Opened in 2007, Texture – the brainchild of Agnar Sverrisson and Xavier Rousset – is a modern European restaurant and champagne bar with Scandinavian influences. Awarded a Michelin star in 2010, Texture is both conventional and inventive, combining excellent British produce with ingredients from Sverrisson's native Iceland, such as Icelandic cod, lamb from Skagafjordur, and Icelandic herbs and *skyr* (yogurt). It has prices to match its prestige, but there's a good-value set lunch menu.

Sommelier Rousset is responsible for the eclectic wine list and the champagne bar – voted 'Champagne List of the Year 2014' by *Imbibe* magazine – and runs the partners' other venture, the 28°-50° Wine Workshop & Kitchen.

Texture Restaurant & Champagne Bar, 34 Portman St, W1H 7BY (020-7224 0028; texture-restaurant.co.uk; Marble Arch tube; Tue-Sat 12-2.30, 6.30-12pm; modern European; ££-£££).

Tinello

Little Italy in Pimlico – that's amore!

Opened in 2010, Tinello is a delightful Italian restaurant in Pimlico co-owned by the Sali brothers – Massimiliano (Max) is the wine guy, while Federico conjures up his magic in the kitchen – previously the sommelier and head chef respectively at Locanda Locatelli. The immediate impression is one of professionalism – these guys know what they're doing – with a warm and comfortable Italian welcome. The long (dark) room, with a bar at one end, is rustic-chic, with bare brick walls, dark wooden floors, stylish furniture, shiny black tiles and hanging copper lamps.

The creative menu includes all the usual suspects, plus a section labelled 'small eats' catering to the latest fashion for tapas (two of which are equal to an antipasti starter). You could start with char-grilled squid, chick peas and 'nduja, or white peach, oyster mushroom and almond salad, followed by pan-fried monkfish with roast peppers, cannellini beans and black olives, or char grilled jumbo quail, corn and girolle mushrooms. Pasta fans can tuck into homemade pumpkin ravioli or hare and liquorice risotto, and there are delicious *dolci*, such as chocolate tart and pistachio ice cream. The extensive Italian wine list is good value, with plenty available by the glass. *Perfetto!*

Tinello, 87 Pimlico Rd, SW1W 8PH (020-7730 3663; tinello.co.uk; Sloane Sq tube; Mon-Sat 12-2.30, 6.30-10.30; Italian; ££-£££).

Tonkotsu East
Noodle nirvana in East London

Tonkotsu East in Haggerston (there's another branch in Soho and a concession in Selfridges) is a temple to ramen, enjoyed throughout Japan. This national dish is a soup made from wheat noodles, meat and vegetables, all served in a meat or fish-based broth flavoured with soy sauce or miso. *Tonkotsu ramen* (from which the restaurant takes its name) consists of authentic homemade thin noodles in pork stock with tasty pork belly slices, fresh vegetable garnishes and a lovely runny egg.

There's also a selection of side dishes, and a bar offering a range of British and Japanese beers, saké, Japanese whisky and soft drinks.

Tonkotsu East, Arch 334, 1A Dunston St, E8 4EB (020-7254 2478; tonkotsu.co.uk; Haggerston rail; Mon-Fri 12-3, 5-11, Sat-Sun 12-11; Japanese noodles; £).

Trinity
A Sunday lunch to die for

Award-winning Trinity (three AA rosettes) opened in 2006 and quickly put Clapham on the foodie map. Chef Adam Byatt's creative, flavoursome and beautifully-presented cuisine is a delight, with changing seasonal menus including a tasting menu, set lunch (good value) and Sunday lunch. The latter is three courses of splendid indulgence, with options including crab bisque, samphire and brown crab toastie; 40-day aged Dexter beef, Yorkshire pudding, horseradish, bone marrow and cauliflower cheese; and passion fruit and chocolate Eton mess. Scrummy!

The wine list runs to some 350 bins and wine lovers can expand their knowledge by attending one of the regular masterclasses.

Trinity, 4 The Polygon, SW4 0JG (020-7622 1199; trinityrestaurant.co.uk; Clapham Common tube; Tue-Sat – see website for times; modern British; ££-£££).

Trishna
No ordinary Indian restaurant

Located in Marylebone Village, Michelin-starred Trishna specialises in the cuisine of southwest India. The chic décor – wooden floors, whitewashed brick walls, brass pendant lamps, antique mirrors and marble-topped tables, with doors opening onto the street – is a long way from the generic curry house décor, but then this is no ordinary Indian restaurant!

Trishna's creative, sophisticated cuisine puts the spotlight on British (sustainable) fish and seafood, spiced up with the flavours of Kerela – meat, poultry and game dishes also feature. Everything is perfectly cooked, subtly seasoned and beautifully presented. There's a wide choice of menus, including tasting menus with a vegetarian option, seasonal and speciality menus, e.g. game, lunch and à la carte.

The five-course Taste of Trishna menu (called Koliwada, after a colony of Kolis or fishermen) is an indulgent pleasure, consisting of shrimp with ginger and smoked chilli chutney, salmon tikka, duck kebab, lamb masala or Keralan tiger prawn curry, culminating with toothsome chocolate *chikki* (groundnut and jaggery) cake or cardamom *kheer* (rice pudding). The Lunch Bites menu is a great introduction to the restaurant and very reasonably priced.

Trishna has an impressive wine list – all dishes come with recommended paired wines – plus exotic cocktails and a 'library' of rare and elegant teas.

Trishna, 15-17 Blandford St, W1U 3DG (020-7935 5624; trishnalondon.com; Bond/Baker St tube; Mon-Fri 12-2.30, 6-10.30, Sat 12-2.30, 5.30-10.30, Sun 12-3, 6-9.30; Indian; ££-£££).

Trullo

The perfect neighbourhood trattoria

Named after the weird conical houses of Apulia, Trullo is a lovely Italian neighbourhood restaurant in Islington. Rustic and simply furnished, it has the air of a classic Italian trattoria: scuffed wooden floors, white walls, white linen tables and an open kitchen.

The brief seasonal menu includes a delicious handmade pasta dishes and mains such as lamb rump, mackerel and whole Dorset crab cooked on a charcoal grill. There's also an award-winning Italian wine list. Flavoursome food, friendly service, nice ambience and good value – well worth a trip to N1.

Trullo, 300-302 St Paul's Rd, N1 2LH (020-7226 2733; trullorestaurant.com; Highbury & Islington tube/rail; Mon-Sat 12.30-2.45, 6-10.15, Sun 12.30-3; Italian; ££).

Wild Honey

Nectar of the gods

The second restaurant of chef Anthony Demetre and Will Smith (the team behind Arbutus), Mayfair's Wild Honey opened in 2007 and was awarded the inevitable Michelin star in its first year of trading. The bright and stylish dining space features modern photographic artwork, red leather banquettes and wood-panelled walls, while the French-inspired, daily changing menu employs fresh seasonal ingredients to produce exciting dishes. There's an interesting wine list – some wines are available in 250ml carafes – and great cocktails too.

The working lunch/early supper menu is good value at £29.50 for three courses.

Wild Honey, 12 St George St, W1S 2FB (020-7758 9160; wildhoneyrestaurant.co.uk; Oxford Circus tube; Mon-Sat 12-2.30, 6-11; modern European; ££-£££).

Zoilo
More than just big, juicy steaks

Zoilo is proof that there's much more to Argentinian food than just beef. Chef Diego Jacquet's 'cocina Argentina' explores this vast country's regional cuisine, from Salta down to Patagonia and from the wine region of Mendoza to the Pampas. Zoilo's menus include fashionable 'small plates' – including delicious empanadas, sea bass ceviche, grilled scallops with pork belly, even veal sweetbreads – all designed to be shared. And for diehard carnivores, there are several prime steaks.

Housed in a lovely townhouse in Marylebone, the restaurant is split over two levels – downstairs you can sit at the bar and watch the chefs at work. Not surprisingly, the wine list is entirely Argentinean.

Zoilo, 9 Duke St, W1U 3EG (020-7486 9699; zoilo. co.uk; Bond St tube; Mon-Sat 12-3, 5.30-10.30; Argentinian; ££-£££).

Zucca
Viva Italia! Viva Zucca!

This understated and classy Bermondsey restaurant was one of the trailblazers for London's new wave of simple Italian eateries, offering delicious food at affordable prices. Zucca (pumpkin) is a shiny, modern Italian restaurant using first-class ingredients to create dishes with maximum flavour – cooked with passion and to perfection.

Delicious cocktails (try Bermondsey gin with rose-flavoured lemonade and a twist of orange skin), brilliant house bread, wonderful starters (carpaccio, salt cod and roasted tomato bruschetta, ox tongue, and pumpkin fritters), fantastic mains (veal and calves' liver like only Italians can make), superb silky pasta, great homemade gelato and a well-sourced Italian wine list. *Buon appetito!*

Zucca, 184 Bermondsey St, SE1 3TQ (020-7378 6809; zuccalondon.com; London Br tube; Tue-Fri 12-3, 6-10, Sat 12-3.30, 6-10, Sun 12-4; Italian; ££-£££).

Zuma

The epitome of glamorous Japanese dining

Appropriately located in fashionable Knightsbridge, trendsetting Zuma offers a sophisticated take on the traditional Japanese *izakaya* (pub) style of informal eating and drinking. It opened in 2002 but the striking postmodern design – a mixture of steel, glass, wood, stone and granite – is still achingly trendy.

With *izakaya* dining, food is usually ordered slowly over several courses rather than all at once, and many dishes are designed to be shared. The authentic menu is comprehensive and alluring – packed with bold, intense flavours and showcasing fashionable ingredients such as Wagyu beef, langoustines, black cod, scallops and king crab. You can sample mouth-watering sushi and sashimi at the sushi counter and watch the chefs preparing food on the *robata* grill. Even the desserts are fantastic;

try the yuzu lime pie with Ivoire white chocolate and peach yuzu sorbet.

The saké bar stocks more than 40 different kinds plus a wide range of tempting cocktails, including many made from fresh fruit juices combined with saké and Japanese spirits such as shōchū.

Reassuringly expensive – if you have to ask the price, you shouldn't be eating here – Zuma is somewhere that lovers of Japanese food should visit at least once in their lifetime.

Zuma, 5 Raphael St, SW7 1DL (020-7584 1010; zumarestaurant.com/zuma-landing/london/en/welcome; Knightsbridge tube; Mon-Fri 12-3, 6-11, Sat 12.30-3.30, 6-11, Sun 12.30-3.30, 6-10.30; Japanese; £££-££££).

Brick Lane Market

9.
Street Food

You can feast on London's streets for under a fiver, and the sheer theatre of watching your meal being prepared at the roadside is hard to beat.

The word on the street is – delicious!

Street food covers the almost limitless range of 'food-to-go' sold on the street, at markets and in other public places, often from a mobile stall or van (but not a café or restaurant), to be eaten with minimal ceremony, usually on the move.

> The best street food is carefully sourced and expertly prepared, delicious and inexpensive, usually healthy, often messy and – most of all – fun!

Street food – with aspirations higher than the late-night burger van parked in the High Street – is a relatively new concept in the UK, compared for example with the Americas, Asia and the Middle East, where locals having been enjoying it for centuries. These regions provide the inspiration for much of the food available on London's streets today, where street food is revolutionising the city's eating habits.

Thanks to its dynamic, multicultural population, London has a surprisingly large number of street food vendors. Many can be found at established markets such as Exmouth Market and Whitecross Street, general food markets like Berwick Street and Borough Market, and weekend events such as the Southbank's Real Food Market. They are also found at farmers' markets (see page 175), foodie festivals (e.g. realfoodfestival.co.uk) and pop-up street food markets such as Street Feast (streetfeastlondon.com).

The 'street' menu is almost inexhaustible and includes everything from burgers and hot dogs to sliders and po' boys, fish and chips to jerk chicken, burritos to dosas, pad Thai to jhal muri… Best of all is the price – you can get a filling meal for a fiver and have a blow-out for under £10. But it isn't simply about saving money: some of the best food in London is served not on fancy china in top-notch restaurants, but alfresco on plastic plates, in paper napkins or between slices of crusty bread.

Borough Market
Explore a world of flavours in SE1

In addition to being London's finest artisan food market (see page 172), Borough Market is also one of the city's best street-food destinations. This atmospheric market attracts many of the country's top producers and retailers and is at its most lively from Wednesday to Saturday when all the stalls are open (it's quieter Mon-Tue but you can still get lunch in the Green Market). Stallholders eagerly press free samples onto passers-by and after a few circuits someone on a tight budget could stave off hunger without spending a penny, although a tasty filling lunch will cost you no more than a fiver.

You can eat your way around the world at Borough Market: try a spicy Spanish chorizo and rocket roll from Brindisa; meaty stew wrapped in *injera* (spongy pancake bread) from Ethiopian Flavours; crispy pastry parcels (*boureka*) from Balkan Bites or artisan sausage rolls from Yorkshire butchers Ginger Pig. Vegetarians are also well-catered for with toasted cheese sandwiches (Kappacasein Dairy), organic salads (Total Organics) and veggie curries (Veggie Table). To drink there are freshly-squeezed juices, smoothies, craft beers and ciders, and excellent coffee. Try to leave space for a Thai coconut pudding (Khanom Krok).

The market also offers a huge choice of cafés, restaurants and bars.

Borough Market, 8 Southwark St, SE1 1TL (020-7407 1002; boroughmarket.org.uk/lunchtime; London Br rail/tube; Mon-Thu 10-5, Fri 10-6, Sat 8-5).

Brick Lane Markets
Eat the world in East London

Brick Lane in Tower Hamlets got its name in the 15th century when it was the home of brick and tile manufacturers, although it later became a centre for the brewing industry. Today, it's a chaotic, artistic, multicultural melting pot, and its weekend markets attract hordes of people in search of second-hand furniture, unusual clothes, arts and crafts, bric-a-brac and food… great food!

The food markets offer a world of irresistible tastes and smells. First stop is the celebrated Boiler House Food Hall (in the Old Truman Brewery), with its spectacular soaring ceilings and more than 30 stalls offering culinary delights from around the globe; from Asia to India, the Mediterranean to the Caribbean, plus tasty treats from Ethiopia, Korea, Malaysia, Poland and many other countries. There's also a bar with outdoor seating.

Also within the brewery complex, the Sunday Upmarket in Ely's Yard houses over 200 stalls, including a large indoor food area where you'll find everything from Moroccan couscous to Thai curries, Spanish tapas to Turkish sweets, and Ethiopian hand-roasted coffee to Indian masala chai. The list of flavours is endless – and so is the pleasure of sampling them.

Brick Lane Markets, The Old Truman Brewery, 152 Brick Ln, E1 6RU (020-7770 6028; boilerhouse-foodhall.co.uk, sundayupmarket. co.uk, visitbricklane.org; Aldgate E or Shoreditch High St tube; Sat 11-6, Sun 10-5).

Brixton Market
Soul food in south London

Brixton is widely acknowledged to be the symbolic soul of black Britain, and Brixton Market (see page 173) – actually a number of markets – has a unique character and cultural mix that distinguishes it from other London markets. In recent years it has become the destination for budget eating in south London and has one of the most vibrant restaurant scenes in the capital.

The market area is packed with creative street-food vendors, although the best choice of food is in the Food Corner (Mon-Fri lunchtimes) and the Friday Market (Fri 10-5), both located on the junction of Brixton Station Road and Pope's Road. Among the traders here are Pangea Street (rice, noodles, chilli, surf and turf, burgers and kebabs), Bunnychow (mini loaves with various fillings such as crispy pork with shallots, peppers and BBQ sauce), Bare Bones Cue (pulled pork served in sourdough), Woodbox Pizza (sourdough pizzas baked in a wood-fired oven), Route 66 (Mexican burritos and tacos) and many more.

If you're looking to eat in more style (and comfort), Brixton Village (in the Granville Arcade) is one of the best foodie destinations in London with a wealth of inexpensive cafés and restaurants, plus shops selling everything from charcuterie to coffee. There's also a Sunday farmers' market (10-2) offering more delicious street food.

Brixton Market, Electric Ave, Pope's Rd and Brixton Station Rd, SW9 (020-7926 2530; brixtonmarket.net; Brixton tube; see website for opening times).

Broadway & Netil Markets

Just the ticket for street food theatre

A magnet for East London fashionistas, Broadway and Netil Saturday Markets (see page 174) are also celebrated for their great street food. Broadway Market (between Regent's Canal and London Fields) is one of London's oldest chartered markets and has reinvented itself over the last ten years as a destination for foodies. It offers a cornucopia of tastes and cultures with its quaint shops, traditional pubs, eclectic restaurants and charming cafés. But the market is the star attraction.

Most of the food-based stalls are clustered around the Westgate Street end of the market, where there's a world of tasty grub, including delicious fish pies from Two Fishwives; spicy Ghanaian food from Spinach & Agushi; freshly-grilled burgers from Northfield Farm; Georgeta Decuseara's cheesecakes, tarts and éclairs (Ion Pâtisserie); mouth-watering mezze and Damascene falafel wraps from the Arabica Food & Spice Company; delicious Vietnamese coffee and tea from Ca Phe VN, and much, much more.

Just around the corner on Westgate Street is Netil Market, which is a bit less frenetic and home to more gorgeous food stalls and places to stock your larder.

Broadway Market, E8 (broadwaymarket.co.uk; London Fields rail; Sat 9-5) and Netil Market, 13-23 Westgate St, E8 3RL (netilmarket.tumblr.com; Sat 11-6).

Camden Lock Market

Arts, crafts...and a foodie melting pot

Created as an arts and crafts market in the '70s, Camden Market is one of the city's most popular destinations for trendy Londoners and visitors, who flock to buy art, bric-a-brac, clothes, jewellery, furniture and food – especially street food. The West Yard hosts the Global Kitchen, which wafts its heady aroma of spices across the canal-side terraces.

It's home to some of London's most exciting street food vendors, selling tasty international cuisine at affordable prices: from Ethiopian curry to kangaroo burgers, falafel wraps to Turkish flatbread pizza (*lahmacun*), gourmet mac and cheese to Brazilian barbecue. Irresistible!

Camden Lock Market, Chalk Farm Rd, NW1 8AF (020-7485 7963; camdenlockmarket.com; Chalk Farm/Camden Town tube; Mon-Sat 10-6).

Exmouth Market

Perfect spot for an alfresco lunch

This car-free shopping street lies at the heart of Clerkenwell, a once-seedy corner of the capital that has been gentrified beyond recognition: it's now a major destination for fashionistas, foodies and design junkies, and home to some of the city's best independent shops, cafés, restaurants and bars.

Exmouth hosts a small but vibrant weekday market offering an eclectic international mix of street lunch options including Mexican burritos, French galettes, Ghanaian stews, Thai noodles, New York-style salt beef sandwiches and Spanish chickpea and chorizo stew. If you prefer to eat sitting down there are also plenty of pavement cafés to choose from.

Exmouth Market, between Farringdon Rd and Rosoman St, EC1R 4QL (exmouth-market.com; Farringdon tube; Mon-Fri, food 11-2.30).

Greenwich Market

Take time to sample a world of flavours

Greenwich has hosted a market since the 14th century, but the present one dates from 1700 and is set in a courtyard of elegant Georgian buildings. It's considered by many to be London's best covered market, and sells delicious street food.

Choose a country at random and it's quite possible that its food will be represented here, from Thai noodles and Chinese dim sum to Punjabi lamb Rogan Josh; Israeli falafel to Japanese sushi; Dutch-style pancakes to Brazilian doughnuts; Argentinian empanadas to Spanish tapas. In addition there are cakes, juices, chocolates, and all manner of veggie/vegan, gluten- and dairy-free options. The non-food shopping options are tasty too.

Greenwich Market, SE10 9HZ (020-8269 5096; greenwichmarketlondon.com; Cutty Sark DLR; Tue-Sun 10-5.30).

Kerb

Leading the street food revolution

Kerb is an organisation at the vanguard of the street food revolution, and organises regular events throughout London, including lunches, weekend gatherings and special street food festivals; it also caters for private events, launches and parties. Kerb's strapline is 'Making cities taste better', working with over 50 of the city's best street food traders (see website for details), many of whom appear regularly at venues such as Granary Square, King's Cross, N1 (Tue-Fri 12-2 and selected Saturdays 11-6) and the Gherkin, St Mary Axe, EC2 (Thu 12-2).

If you yearn to hit the London streets with your own mobile food factory, Kerb holds workshops for would-be traders.

Kerb (kerbfood.com; various locations, days and times – see website).

Leather Lane Market
Lunch with the Cockney traders

One of London's oldest and most interesting markets, Leather Lane can trace its history back some 400 years. It's a real 'barrow-boy' market where the traders sell a bit of everything, from fruit and veg to fashion and phones, all at bargain prices. But it also serves up a wealth of great grub from a host of food stalls and cafés, including falafel wraps, hog roasts, jacket spuds and dishes of steaming curry. It isn't the fanciest street food but is great value, authentic and tasty.

If you fancy a coffee, Leather Lane is also home to Prufrock's flagship café (see page 72), one of the city's best coffee shops.

Leather Lane Market, Leather Ln, EC1N 7RJ (leatherlanestars.wordpress.com/the-market; Chancery Ln or Farringdon tube; Mon-Fri 10-2).

One New Change
Street food for City boys

One New Change is an upmarket City development close to St Paul's Cathedral, housing over 60 stores, restaurants and cafés, including the Madison, Gordon Ramsay's Bread Street Kitchen and Jamie Oliver's Barbecoa. It's also the unlikely home of an excellent artisan street food market on Fridays (9-3) and Saturdays (11.30-5), plus the first Wednesday (9-3) of each month.

Over 20 stalls offer a feast of local and international specialities such as Argentinean empanadas, Creole food, sweet and savoury pancakes, English pies, award-winning Moroccan soups, French patisserie, handmade cupcakes, chutneys, quiches and more. Once fed, pop up to the roof terrace and take in the stunning view.

1 New Change, EC4M 9AF (onenewchange.com/whats-on/food-markets2; St Paul's tube; Fri 9-3, Sat 11.30-5).

Portobello Road Market
A world of flavours in W10

One of London's best known markets, Portobello Road (see page 180) offers much more than antiques, art and cutting-edge fashion, and is a hotspot for foodies as well. Every day of the week (except Sundays) you'll find a United Nations of stalls serving some of the best street food in the capital, including falafel, kebabs, tagines, burgers, jerk chicken, paella, bratwurst, hog roast, curries, crepes and much more, while summertime sees cool drinks, ice-cream and frozen yoghurt added to the menu.

Many of the stalls are clustered around the Elgin Crescent area, while Golborne Road has great Afro-Caribbean food and an award-winning Moroccan soup stand.

Portobello Road Market, W10 (portobellomarket. org and shopportobello.co.uk; Ladbroke Rd or Notting Hill Gate tube; Mon-Wed 9-6, Thu 9-1, Fri-Sat 9-7).

St Katharine Docks Good Food Market
Street food with a view

Friday is a great day for foodies to visit picturesque St Katharine Docks, as it's the day the Good Food Market sets up shop on Marble Quay. Some 25 food stalls serve lunch at this lovely location outside the Dickens Inn, overlooking the marina. Traders here are noted for their healthy menus and for using ingredients that are, whenever possible, ethically and locally sourced.

There's a world of traditional cuisine from South America to the Far East, including Argentinian prime steak sandwiches, Burmese noodles, Jamaican curried goat, Spanish paella, Turkish mezze, and even British stew and dumplings.

Good Food Market, St Katharine Docks, Marble Quay, E1W 1UH (www.skdocks.co.uk/what's-on/ good-food-market; Tower Hill tube; Fri 11-3).

Whitecross Street Market
Global gourmet grub for less than a fiver

Whitecross Street Market began trading in the 17th century, making it among the City's oldest markets. Today it's one of London's coolest shopping destinations, home to a general market on weekdays, although it's the superb lunchtime street food – the best choice is on Thursdays and Fridays between 1 and 2pm – that draws the crowds and has been instrumental in revitalising the area. Like most market streets, it has an eclectic, independent vibe that's missing from many of the capital's high streets.

Whitecross offers something for everyone whatever your tastes, be it Brazilian, Caribbean, Chinese, French, German, Indian, Italian, Mexican, Portuguese, Thai, Turkish...or even British cuisine. You can choose from fresh salads, homemade pork pies, pie and mash, hog-roast or salt-beef sandwiches, wild game and more, plus mouth-watering cakes, pastries and cookies from the likes of Comptoir Gourmand patisserie. And pretty much everything costs less than £5.

There are also stalls offering great coffee, freshly-squeezed juices, homemade cakes, proper cheeses, authentic Italian charcuterie, plump olives and real bread. You can buy everything you need for a picnic, and eat it on the Barbican Centre's lakeside terrace.

Whitecross Street also hosts street entertainment, food festivals, an open-air art gallery and the famous Whitecross Street Party (wxstreetparty.co.uk) in July.

Whitecross Street Market, Whitecross St, EC1 (Barbican tube; general market Mon-Fri 10-5, food market Thu-Fri 11-4).

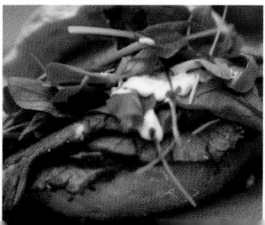

10.
Wine, Beer
& Spirits

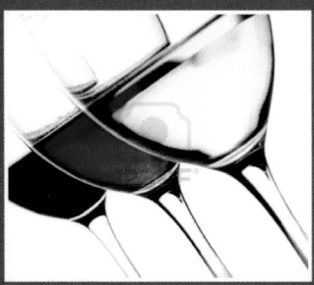

'Accept what life offers you and try to drink from every cup. All wines should be tasted; some should only be sipped, but with others, drink the whole bottle.'

(Paulo Coelho, *Brida*)

Master the art of imbibing...

The appreciation of fine wine, craft beer and skilfully mixed cocktails is greatly enhanced by an understanding of their history and production and how best to enjoy them. Just as watching cricket is more pleasurable when you understand the rules, so it is with wine (although it's easier to become a Master of Wine than it is to understand the finer points of cricket...).

London has an ever-increasing number of courses and 'experiences' for wine, beer and spirit lovers, ranging from meeting the brewers of craft beer to learning the art of cocktail mixology, although the majority focus on wine. Many are fun classes aimed at beginners, although there are more serious studies for those planning a career in the drinks industry.

No one loves a wine (or beer) bore, but being able to distinguish wine by more than its colour is a useful skill. It saves you feeling confused when faced with a wall of supermarket plonk or being intimidated by a chalkboard of bizarrely-named brews in a real ale aficionados' pub. It can also save you money.

Learning about alcohol is fun and a great way to make friends with like-minded people.

Whether your favourite tipple is wine, beer, whisky or gin, you can swoosh and spit, swirl and sup somewhere in London. From Berry Bros & Rudd – founded in 1698 – to new kids on the block such as Thirty Fifty; from long-established traditional brewery Fullers to craft beer

microbreweries such as Meantime; and from the bar tenders at Harvey Nicks to Gerry's emporium of rare and unusual spirits, there's a wealth of experts waiting to educate your palate.

This chapter isn't just about gaining knowledge, but also offers suggestions on where to buy your chosen tipple. We've included some of London's best merchants, including those dealing in rare wines, world beers or oddball spirits. Most also host tasting events or classes, offer expert advice and have informative websites. All you need to do is fill your glass and say cheers!

69 Colebrooke Row Cocktail Masterclasses
Cocktail alchemy

Known by its address (and dubbed 'The Bar with No Name'), 69 Colebrook Row in Islington is one of London's most innovative cocktail bars. Tucked away behind an anonymous exterior, this intimate venue blends '50s Italian café-style with a film noir feel. It was opened in 2009 by award-winning bartender Tony Conigliaro, who uses molecular mixology to create his legendary bespoke cocktails in the lab upstairs. The menu changes with the seasons but may include the Rhubarb Clover Club or the Smoked Old Fashioned, along with Tony's re-invention of the Prairie Oyster.

Twice a month, 69 offers punters the opportunity to learn the stories behind some of the world's classic drinks – such as the Daiquiri, Martini, Margarita, Tom Collins, Manhattan and the classic Champagne Cocktail – not forgetting lessons from a master bartender in how to create them. Classes are inspirational and hands-on, and you get to try what you create, so don't plan on driving home afterwards!

Classes cost £40 and last for two hours (usually 2-4pm on a Saturday), and follow themes such as rum-, gin- or champagne-based cocktails. The *Mad Men* masterclass – a nod to the TV series – is especially popular and explores the '60s' fascination for cocktails.

Cocktail Masterclasses, 69 Colebrooke Row, N1 8AA (07540-528593; 69colebrookerow.com; drinks@69colebrookerow.com; Angel tube).

Berry Bros & Rudd
Where the royals buy their wine

The oldest wine and spirit merchant in Britain (and probably the world), Berry Bros & Rudd has traded from the same premises since 1698. Berry Bros first supplied wine to the Royal Family during the reign of George III and continues to do so today: it currently holds two royal warrants. The shop resembles a time capsule, having changed little in over 300 years, while its vast cellars – running under the courtyard as far as Pall Mall – contain over 200,000 bottles.

Not only is Berry Bros London's premier wine dealer, it's also a leading provider of wine masterclasses and was proclaimed 'Wine Educator of the Year' at the 2012 International Wine Challenge. Its events – usually held in the wine cellar beneath the shop – include day, lunchtime and evening classes on a wide range of subjects, for both novices and wine connoisseurs, including tastings, 'lunch and learn' and wine school. The shop's wealth of experience and expertise – the staff include no fewer than five Masters of Wine – means you're in very good hands.

So, whether you wish to buy wine for pleasure or investment, expand your wine know-how or become an expert, Berry Bros is your one-stop shop.

Berry Bros & Rudd, 3 St James's St, SW1A 1EG (0800-280 2440; bbr.com/wine-events; Green Pk tube).

Bottle Apostle
Champion of the wine gods

Bottle Apostle is a new kid on the block, with just three outlets, in Hackney, Clapham and Crouch End. The first shop (Hackney) opened only in 2009 but Bottle Apostle has quickly gained an enviable reputation for its wines and expertise and also for its approachability, and was judged Britain's Best Small Wine Shop in 2011 by *The Daily Telegraph*.

All stores have Enomatic sampling machines, which allow you to try before you buy, and host regular informal wine-tasting events. They also stock ciders and craft beers from London's top artisan breweries.

Bottle Apostle, 95 Lauriston Rd, E9 7HJ (020-8985 1549; bottleapostle.com; Cambridge Heath/ London Fields rail; Mon-Fri 12-9, Sat 10-8, Sun 10-6).

DR.iNK of Fulham
Beer lovers' paradise

DR.iNK of Fulham is a dedicated specialist beer boutique (and deli), offering an exceptional range of beers from around the world; some 600 examples of British, Belgian, German, American, Antipodean and other world beers are stocked. Opened only in 2010, DR.iNK champions craft beers from throughout the UK and tracks down offerings from far-flung corners of the globe, constantly adding to its stock.

There are monthly Supper Club evenings (see website for dates) when beer aficionados can enjoy a range of beers and dishes in a unique food and beer pairing.

DR.iNK of Fulham, 349 Fulham Palace Rd, SW6 6TB (020-7610 6795; drinkoffulham.com; Parsons Grn tube; Tue-Fri 2-8, Sat 11.30-8, Sun 12-4).

Fuller's Brewery
Tour the home of London Pride

Fuller's historic Griffin Brewery in Chiswick has brewed beer since the Civil War over 350 years ago, and is one of the few remaining breweries in London. The Fuller family's involvement in the business began in 1829 and descendants of the first partners are still involved in the business today. Over the years Fuller's has established a reputation for running great pubs (they now have around 400) and brewing outstanding beers, including London Pride, ESB and 1845, all of which have won numerous awards. In fact, three Fuller's beers – London Pride, ESB and Chiswick Bitter – have been chosen as Champion Beer of Britain, a feat unmatched by any other brewery.

Fuller's offers brewery tours that provide a fascinating look behind the scenes of a working brewery, from the arrival of the raw materials via the production process through to the packaging of the beer on the cask racking line – with the option of a tasting session at the end. Visitors can also have lunch at the in-house pub, The Mawson Arms (020-8994 2936), and there's a shop selling Fuller's beers, plus a selection of wines, spirits and champagnes.

Fuller, Smith & Turner, The Griffin Brewery, Chiswick Ln South, W4 2QB (020-8996 2000; fullers.co.uk; Turnham Grn tube).

Gerry's Wines & Spirits
A Mecca for mixologists

This 'alcohol emporium' (as Gerry's styles itself) claims to stock the UK's largest range of spirits and liqueurs, and is an old curiosity shop dedicated to drinkers. First opened in 1984, this Soho store is an Aladdin's cave of rare, weird and wonderful examples of the distiller's art – from Croatian pear liqueur to Lebanese arak. Crammed to bursting with hand-labelled bottles, its décor stuck in a time warp, Gerry's is more like a spirits museum (where you can buy the exhibits!) than a shop.

There are usually a number of bottles open for informal tastings, so you can try before you buy.

Gerry's Wines & Spirits, 74 Old Compton St, W1D 4UW (020-7734 2053; gerrys.uk.com; Piccadilly Circus tube; Mon-Thu, Sat 9-6.30, Fri 9-7.30, Sun 12-6).

Harvey Nichols Cocktail Masterclasses
Get your cocktail kicks at Harvey Nicks

Learn the art of mixology at a Cocktail Masterclass in the exclusive environs of Harvey Nichols' Champagne Bar in Knightsbridge. Bartenders introduce you to cocktail bar alchemy, classic combinations and their top tips before you're let loose to practise and perfect your technique. Much more than simply a lesson in drinks mixing, each session begins with a light breakfast and ends with a two-course lunch. You also receive a signed certificate attesting to your cocktail-shaking skills.

The masterclasses run at weekends (Fri, Sat and Sun), with themes taking in five well-known cocktail countries including France, Cuba and the US.

Harvey Nichols, Fifth Floor, 109-125 Knightsbridge, SW1X 7RJ (020-7201 8786; harveynichols.com>stores>knightsbridge> what'son>cocktail masterclasses; Knightsbridge tube).

The London Wine Academy
The A-Z of wine education

Established in 1997 by wine expert Leta Bester, the London Wine Academy aims to provide friendly and accessible courses to wine lovers of all levels. It offers a variety of courses and workshops lasting from two hours to five weeks and covering a wide range of topics, including tasting, matching wines to foods and understanding individual grape varieties. The academy's tutors have accumulated over 100 years' of wine knowledge between them and include Masters of Wine, wine buyers and sommeliers, so you know you'll be in experienced hands.

The LWA's introductory one-day tasting workshops are held at weekends throughout the year and are an excellent way to gain a comprehensive overview of the world of wine. They are designed to provide a good knowledge of the main grape varieties and benchmark styles from around the world, and to teach you how to taste wine and understand its structure and nuances. There are also more specialised workshops, e.g. Italian Wine with Food or exploring the complexities of Old World Wines.

Professional tasting glasses and course notes are provided for all workshops, and a two- or three-course lunch is included, with wine pairing a key theme.

London Wine Academy, 60 Cannon St, EC4N 6NP (0800-690 6115/0845-555 1100; londonwineacademy.com; Mansion House tube).

Meantime Brewing Co.
Microbrewery magic

The Meantime Brewing Company in Greenwich was founded in 1999 and quickly earned a cult following for its craft beers. It's the only British brewer to win medals at the World Beer Cup (worldbeercup.org), and the British Guild of Beer Writers named its founder and brewmaster Alastair Hook its Brewer of the Year in 2008.

Meantime offers guided tours of its state-of-the-art brewery, and a popular Saturday evening ticket is the Pie & Pint Night: a brewery tour and tasting of a selection of beers followed by a pint with a homemade (beef or veggie) pie and mash.

Meantime Brewing Company, Lawrence Trading Estate, Blackwall Ln, SE10 0AR (020-8293 1111; meantimebrewing.com; N Greenwich tube).

Michael Schuster
Taste wine with the experts' expert

Michael Schuster is an internationally recognised wine expert with some 30 years' experience. He studied wine tasting in Bordeaux, where he gained the University Tasting Diploma, and in the early '80s created an award-winning retail wine business.

Since 1986, Michael has worked independently as a writer and lecturer, and runs his own wine school in London where he offers three categories of wine tasting: there are two evening courses of one evening a week for six weeks, one for beginners and one focused on fine wines, plus one-off evening tasting events and blind tasting weekends to prepare would-be Masters of Wine for their exams.

Michael Schuster, 10 Hatton Gdn, EC1N 8AH (020-7254 9734; michaelschusterwine.com; Chancery Ln/Farringdon tube).

Mixology Events
Mixing up a storm

A specialist cocktail company, Mixology Events offers a range of cocktail-based services including mobile bar hire, masterclasses and an online shop. The two-hour cocktail-making workshops are held in a custom-built lounge and cocktail venue in Shoreditch, where small groups of five or six students share a cocktail bar station.

As well as learning the basics, you get to mix four cocktails and pit your skills against other bar teams. Even teetotallers are welcome, as each cocktail has a 'mocktail' (non-alcoholic) equivalent. Mixology Events can also design and create bespoke cocktails and cocktail menus.

Mixology Studios, 3 Ravey St, EC2A 4QP (020-3131 3219; mixologyevents.co.uk; Old St tube/rail or Shoreditch High St rail).

Philglas & Swiggot
An oasis for oenophiles

Founded in 1991 in Clapham, Philglas & Swiggot (get it?) is one of London's most exciting wine merchants (London Wine Merchant of the Year 2002-06). The owner is an Aussie, therefore it's no surprise that it majors in Antipodean wines, but it also stocks one of the city's best selections of Italian, regional French, Californian and Spanish wines. And it's a great place to seek out less well-known wines from Austria, Hungary, Portugal and further afield.

Now with three outlets (Clapham, Marylebone and Richmond), its mission is to bring the world's more interesting and innovative wines to its customers – which it does in spades.

Philglas & Swiggot, 21 Northcote Rd, SW11 1NG (020-7924 4494; www.philglas-swiggot.com; Clapham Jct tube/rail; Mon-Fri 11-7, Sat 10-6, Sun 12-5).

Real Ale
A real ale emporium

Since opening its doors in 2005, Real Ale has become a honeypot for beer aficionados from London and around the UK; it was voted National Independent Beer Retailer of the Year in 2013 and 2014 (Drinks Retailing Awards). A veritable beer emporium, it stocks a vast range of beers from Britain and abroad, including craft beers from microbreweries in Belgium, Germany, Japan, Sweden, the US and many other countries, plus ciders, perries and wine.

Real Ale hosts monthly 'meet-the-brewer' events, where you can taste, compare and match beers to food.

Real Ale, 371 Richmond Rd, TW1 2EF (020-8892 3710; realale.com; Richmond tube/rail or St Margarets rail; Mon-Thu 12-8, Fri 12-9, Sat 10-9, Sun 11-6).

Roberson Wine
An Aladdin's cave of fine wines

Established in 1991, Roberson Wine is one of London's most dynamic and exclusive independent wine merchants, with an Aladdin's cave of quality wines including many old, rare and fine vintages. The beautifully designed Kensington store is fully air-conditioned, with an extensive fine wine section upstairs, while regular tastings are held in the downstairs cellar. Although its stock spans the world, Roberson specialises in fine French wines, with Bordeaux and Burgundy accounting for well over a third of its stock and Champagne much in evidence, plus smaller offerings from the Loire and the Rhône.

Roberson also has an acclaimed wine club (see website).

Roberson Wine, 348 Kensington High St, W14 8NS (020-7371 2121; robersonwine.com; Kensington Olympia/High St Kensington tube; Mon-Sat 10-8, Sun 12-6).

The Sampler
Try a sip of something special

The Sampler is an independent wine merchant with two stores (Kensington – featured here – and Islington), stocking over 1,500 classic, unusual and interesting wines from around the world. The Sampler's unique selling point is that 80 of its wines – the selection changes every few weeks – are available to sample at any one time from its ten sampling machines. Prices start from as little as 30p and tasting notes are provided.

The sampling machines, which use nitrogen to preserve the wines' freshness, allow you to try some of the world's most expensive and exclusive wines, such as Chateau Lafite, without winning the lottery.

The Sampler, 35 Thurloe Pl, SW7 2HP (020-7225 5091; thesampler.co.uk; S Kensington tube; Mon-Sat 11.30-10, Sun 11.30-7).

ThirtyFifty
Wine with latitude!

ThirtyFifty – named after the latitudes (between 30 and 50 degrees) where most of the world's wine grapes are grown – was established in 2002 by Chris and Jane Scott. They began by organising wine tastings in clients' homes and expanded to offer wine courses pitched at enthusiastic amateurs, including evening, one-day and weekend courses. The popular Saturday tasting course runs from 10.30am to 4.30pm and includes 18 wines and a delicious three-course lunch.

ThirtyFifty run courses throughout Britain and were winners of the International Wine Challenge Wine Educator of the Year award in 2008. They also organise corporate events and have an online wine shop.

ThirtyFifty (020-8288 0314; thirtyfifty.co.uk).

Vinopolis

A metropolis for wine enthusiasts

Situated within the dramatic Victorian railway arches of London Bridge, Vinopolis boasts five bars and restaurants, and is the venue for one of London's premier 'wine experiences'. You can choose from three different wine-tasting packages, which allow you to sample up to 16 wines, with a total of over 100 wines, spirits and champagnes to explore. Wines are accessed via tokens pre-loaded onto a card and dispensed from Enomatic wine-dispensing machines which keep wine in optimum condition.

It's a self-guided tour that you take at your own pace, but there are experts on hand to teach you tasting techniques – how to sniff, swirl and slurp like a pro – which will enhance your experience. You can also use the interactive technology provided to develop your taste profile.

Vinopolis offers a wide range of packages and events, and a combination of wine-tasting experiences and dining options – perfect if you're looking for something quirky to impress a date. There are also several masterclasses that cover wine, whisky, cocktails, and how to match wine with cheese or chocolate. If you want to take your wine knowledge a step further you can train for an internationally-recognised qualification from the Wine & Spirit Education Trust (see page 272).

Vinopolis, 1 Bank End, SE1 9BU (020-7940 8300; vinopolis.co.uk; London Br tube; Wed 6-9.30, Thu-Fri 2-10, Sat 12-9.30, Sun 12-6).

The West London Wine School

Go west, young man (or woman)...

This Fulham-based wine school was voted Educator of the Year 2012 by the Wine & Spirit Education Trust (WSET – see page 272) and is an excellent place to expand your knowledge of wine. There's a wide range of tastings and courses catering to everyone from complete novices to enthusiasts wishing to gain oenological qualifications. The school's events include evening tastings (some focus on fine wines), one-day introductory courses (Saturdays) and four- or eight-week courses for those seeking more in-depth knowledge. There are also WSET level 2 and 3 courses for professionals.

The eight-week course (one evening a week) is an exceptional introduction to the world of wine, and the school's learn-by-taste principals means you get to experience a lot of wines: some 60 are included, including French, European and New World wines. The course also covers wine and food matching, spotting wine faults, storing and serving wine, and where to obtain the best value-for-money wines. It's great value too, at just £115 for eight sessions.

The West London Wine School also offers tutored tastings of beer, sherry (with tapas) and whisky.

West London Wine School, The Wine Cellars at Big Yellow Storage, 71 Townmead Rd, SW6 2ST (020-8144 2444; westlondonwineschool.com; Imperial Wharf rail/Fulham Broadway tube).

The Whisky Exchange
Make mine a double

Originally an online shop, the Whisky Exchange now has a retail outlet at Vinopolis (near Borough Market) where it stocks around 1,000 whiskies and some 800 other types of spirit. You can visit for expert advice, sample the goods – there are regular tastings – or fill your own bottle from a selection of casks.

The Whisky Exchange deals in rare, old and exclusive single malt Scotch whiskies, but also stocks American, Canadian, Irish and Japanese whiskies, and even examples from Holland, India and Wales.

The Whisky Exchange, Vinopolis, 1 Bank End, SE1 9BU (020-7403 8688; thewhiskyexchange. com; London Br tube; Mon-Thu 11-7, Fri 11-9, Sat 10.30-8, Sun 12-6).

The Wine & Food Academy
Cooking and quaffing with Harry

As its name suggests, the grand-sounding Wine & Food Academy puts as much emphasis on matching wine to food as it does on cooking the food in the first place. In the words of founder Kenneth Harry Putt, 'the aim of the academy is to demonstrate the pleasures of harmonising wines and food'.

There are two five-week courses, including Harry's Wine & Supper Club, which matches wine to different cuisines, such as Indian or Italian, and Know Your Wine. One-day courses include Connoisseur wine days and the aptly named Cooking & Quaffing (Saturdays). Courses take place at various south London venues.

The Wine & Food Academy, 93 Hazelbourne Rd, SW12 9NT (020-8675 6172; winefoodacademy. com; Clapham S tube).

The Wine & Spirit Education Trust

The Oxbridge of wine schools

'creating the trade professional'

WSET® Level 4 Diploma in Wines and Spirits

www.wsetglobal.com

The Wine & Spirit Education Trust (WSET) was founded in 1969 to provide high-quality education and training in wines and spirits, and is the foremost international body in this field. However, WSET isn't just for professionals or those in the drinks trade; it offers an increasing number of courses for 'consumers' who simply wish to enhance their knowledge of the ever-increasing variety of wines and spirits.

WSET operates through a network of approved programme-providers around the world – including many in London – and also has its own school near London Bridge, offering courses at every level for both professionals and amateurs.

Whether you're interested in wine or spirits, qualifications or tastings, masterclasses or food-and-wine pairing events, WSET's London Wine & Spirit School offers something for you. The classroom courses and Saturday school lead to certificates, from level 1 (beginners) up to level 4 (diploma), and some can be taken online.

In addition, there are a number of tasting events for those wishing to learn more about a particular topic without worrying about qualifications. They're designed to be both fun and educational, and cover a huge range of topics, from prosecco to gin.

WSET London Wine & Spirit School, 39-45 Bermondsey St, SE1 3XF (020-7089 3841; wsetschool.com; London Br rail/tube).

The Wine Education Service

Educate your palate from grape to grain

The Wine Education Service (WES) was the first school in the UK to offer a comprehensive range of impartial wine tastings, wine courses and events designed primarily to appeal to amateur wine drinkers rather than aspiring members of the wine trade. It holds an unparalleled range of courses, and with over 25 years' experience, you're in good hands – all tutors are qualified to WSET diploma level and are members of the UK Association of Wine Educators.

Most courses are geared towards beginners or those with intermediate knowledge, although there are specialist classes which delve into high-quality wines from specific regions, such as Bordeaux or Burgundy. In addition to weekly wine tastings, the WES offers more than 30 introductory courses a year in London (plus other UK cities), over 20 intermediate and advanced courses and, for those with hectic weekday schedules, wine tasting workshops on Saturdays, with lunch an integral part of the day.

Courses are held in various venues across London (see website) and there are even wine tasting holidays offered through Wine Voyages Limited, a sister company of WES.

If wine isn't your thing, there are whisky-tasting courses too.

The Wine Education Service Limited, Vanguard Business Centre, Alperton Ln, Western Ave, UB6 8AA (020-8991 8212/3; wine-education-service. co.uk, Hanger Ln tube).

INDEX OF ENTRIES BY AREA

Central

City of London

East

North

West

Southwest

Southeast

INDEX

London Sketchbook

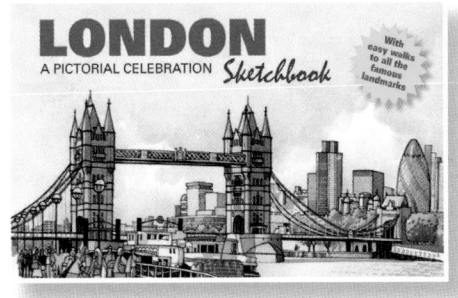

ISBN: 978-1-907339-37-0
Jim Watson

A celebration of one of the world's great cities, London Sketchbook is packed with over 200 evocative watercolour illustrations of the author's favourite landmarks and sights. The illustrations are accompanied by historical footnotes, maps, walks, quirky facts and a gazetteer.

Also in this series:

Cornwall Sketchbook (ISBN: 9781907339417, £10.95)
Cotswold Sketchbook (ISBN: 9781907339108, £9.95)
Devon Sketchbook (ISBN: 9781909282704, £10.95)
Lake District Sketchbook (ISBN: 9781907339097, £9.95)

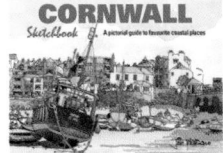

LONDON'S HIDDEN SECRETS

ISBN: 978-1-907339-40-0
£10.95, 320 pages
Graeme Chesters

A guide to London's hidden and lesser-known sights that aren't found in standard guidebooks. Step beyond the chaos, clichés and queues of London's tourist-clogged attractions to its quirkier side.

Discover its loveliest ancient buildings, secret gardens, strangest museums, most atmospheric pubs, cutting-edge art and design, and much more: some 140 destinations in all corners of the city.

LONDON'S HIDDEN SECRET'S VOL 2

ISBN: 978-1-907339-79-0
£10.95, 320 pages
Graeme Chesters & David Hampshire

Hot on the heels of London's Hidden Secrets comes another volume of the city's largely undiscovered sights, many of which we were unable to include in the original book. In fact, the more research we did the more treasures we found, until eventually a second volume was inevitable.

Written by two experienced London writers, LHS 2 is for both those who already know the metropolis and newcomers wishing to learn more about its hidden and unusual charms.

LONDON'S SECRET PLACES

ISBN: 978-1-907339-92-9
£10.95, 320 pages
Graeme Chesters & David Hampshire

London is one of the world's leading tourist destinations with a wealth of world-class attractions. These are covered in numerous excellent tourist guides and online, and need no introduction here. Not so well known are London's numerous smaller attractions, most of which are neglected by the throngs who descend upon the tourist-clogged major sights. What London's Secret Places does is seek out the city's lesser-known, but no less worthy, 'hidden' attractions.

LONDON'S SECRET WALKS

ISBN: 978-1-907339-51-6
£11.95, 320 pages
Graeme Chesters

London is a great city for walking – whether for pleasure, exercise or simply to get from A to B. Despite the city's extensive public transport system, walking is often the quickest and most enjoyable way to get around – at least in the centre – and it's also free and healthy!

Many attractions are off the beaten track, away from the major thoroughfares and public transport hubs. This favours walking as the best way to explore them, as does the fact that London is a visually interesting city with a wealth of stimulating sights in every 'nook and cranny'.

LONDON'S SECRETS:
BIZARRE & CURIOUS
ISBN: 978-1-909282-58-2
£11.95, 320 pages
Graeme Chesters

London is a city with 2,000 years of history, during which it has accumulated a wealth of odd and strange sights. This book seeks out the city's most bizarre and curious attractions and tells the often fascinating story behind them, from the Highgate vampire to the arrest of a dead man, a legal brothel and a former Texas embassy to Roman bikini bottoms and poetic manhole covers, from London's hanging gardens to a restaurant where you dine in the dark. *Bizarre & Curious* is sure to keep you amused and fascinated for hours.

LONDON'S SECRETS:
MUSEUMS & GALLERIES
ISBN: 978-1-907339-96-7
£10.95, 320 pages
Robbi Atilgan & David Hampshire

London is a treasure trove for museum fans and art lovers and one of the world's great art and cultural centres. The art scene is a lot like the city itself – diverse, vast, vibrant and in a constant state of flux – a cornucopia of traditional and cutting-edge, majestic and mundane, world-class and run-of-the-mill, bizarre and brilliant.

So, whether you're an art lover, culture vulture, history buff or just looking for something to entertain the family during the school holidays, you're bound to find inspiration in London.

LONDON'S SECRETS:
PARKS & GARDENS
ISBN: 978-1-907339-95-0
£10.95, 320 pages
Robbi Atilgan & David Hampshire

London is one the world's greenest capital cities, with a wealth of places where you can relax and recharge your batteries. Britain is renowned for its parks and gardens, and nowhere has such beautiful and varied green spaces as London: magnificent royal parks, historic garden cemeteries, majestic ancient forests and woodlands, breathtaking formal country parks, expansive commons, charming small gardens, beautiful garden squares and enchanting 'secret' gardens.

LONDON'S SECRETS:
PUBS & BARS
ISBN: 978-1-907339-93-6
£10.95, 320 pages
Graeme Chesters

British pubs and bars are world famous for their bonhomie, great atmosphere, good food and fine ales. Nowhere is this more so than in London, which has a plethora of watering holes of all shapes and sizes: classic historic boozers and trendy style bars; traditional riverside inns and luxurious cocktail bars; enticing wine bars and brew pubs; mouth-watering gastro pubs and brasseries; welcoming gay bars and raucous music venues. This book highlights over 250 of the best.

A YEAR IN LONDON
Two Things to Do Every Day of the Year

David Hampshire

ISBN: 978-1-908282-68-1, £11.95, 256 pages

London offers a wealth of things to do, from exuberant festivals and exciting sports events to a plethora of fascinating museums and stunning galleries, from luxury and oddball shops to first-class restaurants and historic pubs, beautiful parks and gardens to pulsating nightlife and clubs. Whatever your interests and tastes, you'll find an abundance of things to enjoy. With a copy of this book you'll never be at a loss for something to do in one of the world's greatest cities.

LONDON'S SECRETS:
Peaceful Places

David Hampshire

ISBN: 978-1-907339-45-5, £11.95, 256 pages, hardback

London is one of the world's most exciting cities, but it's also one of the noisiest; a bustling, chaotic, frenetic, over-crowded, manic metropolis of over 8 million people, where it can be difficult to find somewhere to grab a little peace and quiet. Nevertheless, if you know where to look London has a wealth of peaceful places: places to relax, chill out, contemplate, meditate, sit, reflect, browse, read, chat, nap, walk, think, study or even work (if you must).

Peaceful Places contains over 200 of the author's favourite sactuaries, from restful gardens and serene churches to silent libraries and inspiring galleries – and much, much more. So whether you're seeking a place to recharge your batteries, rest your head, revive your spirits, restock your larder or refuel your body; somewhere to inspire, soothe or uplift your mood; or you just wish to discover a part of London that's a few steps further off the beaten track, *Peaceful Places* will steer you in the right direction.